# Welcome into The Soul Clinic of The Lord

## Christians, Demons and Deliverance

## Gina Osei

**Kingdom
Publishers**

Welcome into the Soul Clinic of the Lord
Copyright© Rev Gina Osei



All Scripture Quotations have been taken from the New International Version and the
King James Version of the Bible.

ISBN: 978-1-913247-55-3
1st Edition by Kingdom Publishers
Kingdom Publishers
London, UK.

You can purchase copies of this book from any leading bookstore

or email **contact@kingdompublishers.co.uk**

# Dedication

I dedicate this book to my God, my Lord Jesus Christ and the Precious Holy Spirit without whom it would have been impossible to have written and concluded this book.

My special thanks go to Rev. Christina Obeng for her undying support and encouragement. Her relentless push for this project has been from day one. God bless you Woman of God.

Miss Barbara Yeboah, you have been a pillar through and through, your patience and longsuffering is greatly appreciated and know that eternity will reward you for consistent and fervent support. You are a rare Gem and I greatly appreciate you.

A big God bless you to Miss Jayne Kumi who helped me in editing this book. Thank you, Jayne, for all the time spent in spite of your busy schedule to help me conclude this project.

Thank you to my biggest supporter Mr. Stephen Clandfield, you have been one special person in it all and I greatly appreciate you.

My heartfelt gratitude goes to Reverend Isaac Collins. Man of God, God Almighty bless you abundantly. I often ask myself, what did you see in me for you to take me under your wings and nurtured me the way you did seeing I met a lot of young ones like me at the time. Then I answer myself, but he is a Prophet of God! I am eternally grateful to the Almighty God for leading me to you. I bless that fateful day you led me to Christ. Eternity will reward you for the seed you sowed in me. Thank You.

God bless everyone who supported me one way or the other.

# Contents

# Introduction

The church of Jesus Christ has been divided on the subject of deliverance for a very long time now and this can be attributed to the fact that Satan does not want this truth to be known and accepted by the modern-day church. This is to continue to weaken the church through ignorance. However, the Lord wants the church to wake up and recognise what the enemy is doing to keep us in bondage and oppression. I have come to realise that everything that attracts so much controversy ought to be considered carefully and critically; this is because the enemy confuses and obstructs this  ideology in order to promote his Kingdom here on earth.

Jesus Himself had to face the enemy who was working through the Pharisees, the Sadducees and the Scribes bent on holding on to their old ways. They opposed the Lord in every way, calling Him the devil and leading themselves further and further from the truth.

*"Then answered the Jews, and said unto Him, say we not well that you are a Samaritan, and have a devil? [48]Jesus answered, I have not a devil; but I honor my father, and you dishonor me. [52]Then said the Jews unto Him, now we know that you have a devil."* John 8:48...

Such controversies have been present before time itself, with the devil fighting the Deliverer and His message of redemption. Our Lord Jesus Himself attracted a torrent of controversy in His day and still does today. The question is why? This is because anything or anybody that challenges the status quo becomes an object of interest and controversy. The devil will use people to resist and fight anything that expose him, even to the extent that some will tell you there is no devil and there is nothing like deliverance, in the Kingdom of God.

Yes, Ministers are publicly speaking out against other Ministers who are operating differently from them. Sad to say, the enemy is using God's people to turn the truth into controversy. It is time for the church to wake up from this deception to embrace the true and full gospel of Jesus Christ. Jesus cast out devils and so did His disciples.

Apostle Paul, who wrote a third of the New Testament, also cast out devils in Acts 16. He had not personally been with Jesus, as he was probably very young when Jesus conducted His ministry; but he knew supernaturally how to conduct the ministry of the Lord Jesus the moment he had that encounter with Jesus on his way to persecute the Christians in Damascus.

Psalm 2 says *"Why do the heathen rage, and why do the people imagine a vain thing? The kings of the earth set themselves, and the rulers take counsel together against the LORD, and against his anointed."* The devil has set nations, governments, governors, heads of state and members of the judiciary in the governments of the nations of the world. These prominent people are set against the Kingdom of our God, His Christ and His government. . Is it not amazing that there are so many religions, sects and cults but not one of these attracts the hostility that Christianity receives all over the world?

Even in democratic and so-called free nations Christianity is under fierce attack. It has been covered up in a deceptive language of political correctness. They set traps for Christians who dare to live their faith openly and refuse to compromise, in order to persecute them. Why would homosexuals go to a bed and breakfast that is run by Christians who have made their faith and values known on their websites but will not go to Muslim run facilities? After all, both believe in similar values!

They know that Judges will not handle such cases as it will be incited as an infringement on their beliefs as Muslims, and no one wants to be labeled as Islam phobic. So what about the Christians? Brethren let us wake up and see what is happening and resist the enemy and stop him cold in his tracks. We are busily fighting one another over doctrine whilst the devil is breaking down the hedge that keeps us protected as people of the Light.

My prayer is for the fathers in the Kingdom to speak out and restore sanity in the body of Christ in order to equip and prepare a people for His coming. Have you ever heard of a Muslim or a Hindu or a Buddhist being arrested, beaten and tortured (in some cases killed) for their belief or faith? No, but Christians are being arrested, beaten, tortured and killed all over the world for making their choice of faith and belief. And yet this is a free world and everybody has the right to exercise his or her democratic right.

Satan has orchestrated all this hostility and violence against Christianity from the beginning until now. Look at how Herod reacted to the news that the King of the Jews had been born; in Matthew. 2:1 *"Now when Jesus was born in Bethlehem of Judaea in the days of Herod the king, behold there came wise men from the east to Jerusalem. Saying, where is he that is born King of the Jews? For we have seen his star in the east and are come to worship him...* (Now look at the reaction that this great news generated)...*³Now when Herod had heard these things, he was troubled, and all Jerusalem with him."*

Here we see the fulfillment of Psalm 2; not only was King Herod troubled, but all Jerusalem with him. This is a prophetic Psalm. The Pharisees and the Sadducees took over all of Israel and resisted Jesus until they crucified Him, and now this has spread to the uttermost part of the world where the name of Jesus is a dread and an offense to many. The above had been prophesied thousands of years before Jesus was actually born. Not only did Herod and all Jerusalem become troubled about this King, but also this trouble has continued even until today and will continue until Jesus comes to get us or we go and meet Him. This is the spirit of the anti-Christ, which Jesus warned us about. I believe the picture is more evident than ever.

Even though we are seeing these manifestations all over the world, my main concern is not about those outside, but about those of us in the Kingdom of our God, that is, Christians. We have allowed the devil to bring this hostility to the Body of Christ to cause confusion, distraction and strife, which in effect is weakening the Body of Christ. Jesus said a kingdom divided against itself will not stand. Satan knows this truth and has made this very issue of deliverance a contentious topic and doctrine in the Body of Christ.

Deliverance has been the most controversial topic of our time throughout Christendom yet deliverance originates from the time of the Exodus. What did God say in Exodus. 3:7, *"And the LORD said, I have surely seen the affliction of my people which are in Egypt, (a place of bondage) and have heard their cry by reason of their taskmasters; for I know their sorrows…. [8]. And I am come down to deliver them out of the hands of the Egyptians, and to bring them up out of that land unto a good land, and a large, unto a land flowing with milk and honey. [9]Now therefore, the cry of the children of Israel has come unto me: and behold I have also seen the oppression wherewith the Egyptians oppress them. [10]Come now therefore, and I will send you unto Pharaoh that you may bring forth my people the children of Israel out of Egypt."*

God spoke to Moses about oppression and deliverance in the above statement so why will a man of God state boldly on a national Television that there is no such word as deliverance in the Bible?. It is either we believe the whole Bible or we do not.

We cannot pick and choose simply because a particular subject does not fit our theology. The Word was there before man was created so we should not attempt to tamper with it. Right now, we are not in physical bondage like in the days of old as described in the Bible, but spiritually, many of us are.

The Bible clearly states that the old is the shadow of the new.

Ecclesiastes 3:15 says, *"That which has been is now; and that which is to be has already been; and God requires that which is past."* The same Preacher said there is nothing new under the sun. So, you see, God's people have been in bondage before and we are not any different from them; as it was then so it is now and so shall it be until the end.

Is it pleasant to preach or teach this? The answer, honestly, is no. However, we have to in order to liberate God's people as in the times of old. Did the children of Israel cry out to the Lord God? Are we still crying out to Him today concerning our afflictions? If yes, then know that the same God, who delivered Israel, will deliver us today in Jesus name.

Now, I would like us to look at today's Israel as a nation. From the exodus until now, there has always been an enemy on their tail. In fact, Israel is surrounded by formidable foes both around their country and also from those around the world. Nevertheless, God has never forsaken them; and any time they are in trouble, He comes down to deliver them. An example is the six-day Arab Israeli war. God miraculously defeated the enemies and gave Israel the victory.

What about the Entebbe raid? This was an awesome demonstration of the power of God to deliver His people. There are many more such examples of God's intervention as far as Israel is concerned that serve to fulfill Eccles. 3:15.

The fact that the children of Israel were once delivered did not stop further oppression from their enemies. The fact that we are born again does not stop the oppression by the devil. As a matter of fact, we are hated and this calls for more afflictions; but thanks be to our God who causes us to triumph at all times. Victory will only come when we cry out to Him for help, and He will surely come and save us.

The enemy of our soul would not want us to know anything about the existence of his kingdom, (the kingdom of darkness) how it operates and how we should deal with it. Satan knows that the moment there is knowledge and a deeper understanding of how he and his demons oppress humans and destroy their lives, he will be exposed and deposed. He surely knows that if we know how he and his cohorts operate, there will be liberation for the believer and they (devil and his cohorts) will be in trouble.

For this reason, Satan has sown confusion in some Christian circles as far as deliverance is concerned. We as Christians know that the Holy Spirit is not the author of confusion and the Bible also tells us that, where there is strife every evil works abounds. The moment there is a strong debate and strife about any interpretation of the Word, you know the devil is at work. Why do we believe certain parts of the Bible without argument, while other parts are put up for debate? And so, if some unbelievers contend that there is contradiction in the Bible, how would we respond if we ourselves are divided? The Bible says in 2 Corinthians 10:5, *"that we should cast down imaginations and every high thing that exalt itself above the knowledge of God."* This means everything that generates any argument based on our own fleshly imaginations, and anything that is not in accordance with the Word of God and the personality of God, must be discarded.

This leads me to believe that we cannot work the Word of God based on our human preferences and theology. It is the Word of God all the way and nothing else! We cannot pick and choose which doctrine we think is applicable to us and declare the rest as false. The work of the Holy Spirit must be left for Him alone to do in the Kingdom of our God and not for man. Who knows the things of God save His Spirit? Let God be true and every man a liar the Bible says. We need the Holy Spirit to guide us into the Word of God with proper interpretation in order not to overthrow the faith of others with false doctrine as the Bible teaches in 2Tim. 2:17-18 *"Their word will eat like as doth a canker: of whom Hymenaeus and Philetus; who concerning the truth have erred..."*

It is believed by some that all this deliverance and demonology is a mindset, meaning it is all in our mind and that there are no  such things as demons. 2 Corinthians 10:5 was, I believe, erroneously quoted to back this up, so I ask, is Ephesians 6:12 a *mind thing*?

When Jesus was casting demons out of people, was He dealing with mindsets or actual satanic oppression? He tried in vain to argue His case but then I decided to leave him and pray for the listeners. 2Tim. 2:23-25, *"But foolish and unlearned questions avoid, knowing that they do gender strives. And the servant of the Lord must not strive; but be gentle unto all men, apt to teach, patient. In meekness instructing those that oppose themselves; if peradventure God will give them repentance to the acknowledging of the truth. [26]And that they may recover themselves out of the snare of the devil, who are taken captive at his will."*

Was Paul the Apostle in Acts 16:16-18, dealing with a mindset or real case of demonisation? The spirit by which this woman was operating was a real demonic power called divination. This is one of the ways in which Satan operates through human vessels to deceive people. This spirit has no boundaries. It goes after Christians and non-Christians alike. Do you know it took the gift of discerning of spirits (one of the gifts of the Holy Spirit) for Paul to detect this? Anointed as the Apostles were, it took several days for Paul, even Paul to detect and cast it out.

Acts 16:16-18 *"And it came to pass, as we went to prayer, a certain damsel possessed with a spirit of divination met us, which brought her masters much gain by sooth saying: the same followed Paul and us, and cried, saying, these are the servants of The Most High God, which show us the way of salvation. And this she did many days. But Paul, being grieved, turned and said to the spirit, I command you in the name of Jesus Christ to come out of her. And he came out the same hour."*

Is this a mindset or a real situation of dealing with a real devil? A real spirit was addressed here, he turned to the spirit and spoke to the spirit by ordering it to come out of the woman.

Look at the reaction of the masters or the employers of this woman in verse 19-23: *"And when her masters saw that the hope of their gains was gone, they caught Paul and Silas, and drew them into the market place unto the rulers, and brought them to the magistrates, saying these men being Jews, do exceedingly trouble our city. And teach customs which are not lawful for us to receive, neither to observe, being Romans."*

These were lies; they were falsely accused and put in prison after being publicly flogged. The demon spirit used by these men through the woman was cast out. With the evil spirit gone, so was their financial gain. She could not operate anymore under that influence but became delivered from the demon spirit of divination.

The question then remains that, if this is a mindset, what came out the woman? Why did the people react the way they did? Why were the Apostles, Paul and Silas, cast into prison?

Please people of God, I am begging us all to rise up and curb this deception that has been propagated by the devil, and let us minister deliverance to the people of God. The Church needs to know whom *The Deliverer* is, and who the *Oppressor* is. It is very important to teach both, otherwise we have failed in delivering the full Gospel of Jesus Christ. Let us bear in mind that a delivered people means a delivered church and a delivered church produces a clean and healthy church. A healthy church creates a habitation where the Lord is pleased to dwell and such a church will be fruitful in every way; and the glory of the Lord will be there to perform the goodwill of the Father in Jesus name.

The Bible says Jesus Christ is the same yesterday, today and forever. As it was in the beginning, so shall it be until the end. Nothing will change. Believe this? I believe! Amazingly, there are some Christians who do not even know the devil exists let alone his messengers nor his evil deeds and operations. Oh yes, there are lots of them. How can we know when our Pastors do not believe there is a demonic orchestration against the church of Jesus Christ and against the individual?

We will continue to shout it from the rooftop until Satan is fully and properly exposed in Christendom. Many are they who have jumped on the bandwagon and are writing books about what they know not. The little insight they have is what they share, confusing their readers the more, all because fundamental questions are not answered and information given is not enough to keep the believer in the know.

Let us allow the Holy Spirit who is the author of the Scriptures, to guide us in this and every other area of the truth. The Proverbs 3:5-6 says, *"Trust in the Lord with all your heart, and lean not unto your own understanding. In all your ways acknowledge Him and He shall direct your paths."* Let us not use our limited knowledge and understanding to deal with issues that pertain to the Kingdom of our God. I pray that the Holy Spirit himself will breathe upon this book to help somebody understand what He wants us to know and understand.

We become born again when we accept Jesus as our personal Lord and Saviour.

The Bible declares in Romans 10:9-10, *"if you shall confess with your mouth the Lord Jesus, and shall believe with your heart that God has raised Him from the dead, you shall be saved. For with the heart man believes unto righteousness, and with the mouth confession is made unto salvation."*

This means, believing in your heart and confessing with your mouth that Jesus Christ is the Son of God, and that He came to earth as a human- being lived and died on the Cross to save humanity from hell and destruction; and that He ascended to Heaven after His resurrection, and is coming back to judge the quick and the dead. In short, Jesus Christ is the sacrificial Lamb of God, who gave Himself as a ransom to set us free from the bondage of sin and to reconcile us unto God. His precious blood qualifies us to be called sons and daughters of God the moment we accept Him as our Lord. This is what we as believers call *Salvation* according to the Bible. It is our spirit that is regenerated.

The Holy Spirit does this and it is instantaneous but our soul is not born again. The reason for this is that, it is the soul that controls the human being. Our will, our intellect and emotions are all embedded in the soul and because of that, we will need to choose to surrender our soul unto the Lord, and as we do that, the body has no choice but to follow.

In effect, the moment we become born again, our spirit man is instantly regenerated and it becomes one with the Spirit of the Lord. By this I mean our spirit, which is originally the breath of God, is surrendered back to God and we are able to communicate with Him as it was before the fall of man in the Garden of Eden.

Even though we are now born again, we have the soul to deal with and everything in the soul now is a matter of choice and total surrender. The reason for this is, unlike the devil that imposes his wills on us, God does not force His will on us and has given us the free will to make choices. In the soul realm, demons still can operate in the believer even though they are born again. The Bible plainly states this in Hebrews 4:12: *"For the Word of God is quick, and powerful, and sharper than any two-edged sword, piercing even to the dividing asunder of soul and spirit, and of the joints and marrow, and is a discerner of the thoughts and the intents of the heart."*

The Bible is saying it takes the Word of God to bring every soul into submission and to comply with the will, plans and purposes of God, as the soul can easily be influenced by demons that can operate in our sub-consciousness. The Lord told me that there is a very fine line separating the spirit and the soul and within this line demons can operate. He said to me this is why, when believers pray "soulish" prayers and something awful happens to a person, they instantly believe God has answered their prayers. But he said He is not the one who answered that prayer but demons that operate between the spirit and the soul, pick up the words and quickly act on them. The result is there for all to see.

Please do not get me wrong; God can act in similar ways to deal with our adversaries; but there has to be a balance in everything we do including our prayers. First of all, praying that people will come to repentance and to the saving grace of our Lord Jesus whose will for all, is to be saved and not perish in our sins. I will explain more about the soul in other chapters as we go along.

There are three dimensions to salvation. I call it the "three Ds". Salvation is a broad canopy and under it, are the spiritual and the physical.

**Spirit** - Born-Again – because it was dead to sin

**Soul** - Deliverance – our souls in bondage and doing only what Satan required

**Body** - Healing – whatever affects the soul has a weight on the body and sickness came into the world as a result of sin

## Everything was perfect in the Garden of Eden.

In the Garden of Eden, God used to come down to communicate with man face to face. This is because man was like God, a lesser god, of course. God Almighty's breath was in man and man knew no sin, as such it was indeed a Father and son relationship. Adam was as pure as God. He was as *holy* as God and this created a free flow communication with God, the Creator. God took relaxed strolls in the Garden of Eden and enjoyed Himself just chatting with Adam.

This is seen in Genesis 3:8, *"And they heard the voice of the Lord God walking in the Garden in the cool of the day: and Adam and his wife hid themselves from the presence of the Lord God amongst the trees of the garden."*

God had an intimate relationship with man, to the extent that He would visit man just to have a chat on daily basis. This was until the serpent, possessed by the devil, deceived man to sin, causing the direct line of face-to-face communication to be cut off. It was cut off because God is holy and cannot behold sin.

This is exactly what took place in the Garden of Eden; Satan who was the first creature to rebel against his maker and was excommunicated from heaven, brought that spirit into the Garden and seduced man to do the same against God. The devil knew that God will not tolerate this act and man will also be barred from the presence of the Lord. When this happened, man became alienated from the presence of God Almighty. Satan quickly established his own line of communication with man and made man as rebellious as he is. This caused a spiritual death in man, as there was no more life flowing from the Creator to the creature. Sin became a way of living because the Holy Communion with God had been taken over by the devil that from then on perverted everything that man knew from God.

The devil did all this to have rule over the earth realm and all that is in it, including man and all that God has placed under man's rule in the earth realm. I believe there was nothing in the earth for the devil to rule over or even lay hold on, so he waited patiently for God to finish everything and put man in charge, before launching his attack. God had another plan and that was to take back from the devil that which he had illegally obtained through man and restore it back to man. This is the Salvation plan of God; sending down His Royal Seed to come and buy back what the devil had obtained through deception.

The currency for this transaction was His precious blood. Ooh, what a price He paid for us to be reconciled back unto God our Creator! *"For this purpose, was the Son of God made manifested, that He might destroy the works of the devil."* 1 John 3:8. God never intended for the devil to rule over His creation at all and, why should He?

Lucifer had everything going for him in heaven; as an archangel, he had rule over a division of one-third of the angels of God but he chose to rebel against the One who created him and had honoured him as an archangel. This is because he (Lucifer) wanted to be like the Most High. Isaiah 14:13: *"For you have said in your heart, I will ascend into heaven, I will exalt my throne above the stars of God: I will sit also upon the mount of the congregation, in the sides of the north: I will ascend above the heights of the clouds; I will be like the Most High."*

This was the heart of Lucifer against God Almighty. Why then should Lucifer be rewarded by God to have dominion over any of His creations? Especially not over the Man into whom God had put His breath. For this reason, Jesus, the second Adam, had to come to take back and restore man to his original position. He had to, first of all, come in a human form to be able to live as a man in a satanic dominated realm. He felt the pain of man's oppression, imprisonment and slavery in order to be able to rescue mankind from the claws of Satan. He did this by offering Himself as the sacrificial Lamb of God whose blood is the only currency accepted eternally as the sin offering to save mankind from the taskmaster, the devil.

This was done so that man, by accepting this Truth, will be saved from his sins that keep him bound by the devil. This is what we call being *born again*. Someone may ask, what is born again? It is being born back into restored fellowship with God so we can commune with God as it was in the beginning. It means we take on the nature of God, as it was when He knew Adam with no sin until the serpent possessed by the devil appeared. It means accepting Christ for the work of the Cross, and acknowledging Him as our Deliverer and Saviour.

Born again from spiritual death means that once upon a time we were dead as a result of our sin. We were separated from God, our Creator. The breath of God was squeezed out of man and the lifeline to God was cut off. In short, the penalty for sin is our spiritual death. The Bible says In Romans 6:23 that *"the wages of sin is death but the gift of God is eternal life through Christ Jesus our Lord."*

On conversion, our once dead spirit receives life that is the breath of God; the precious Holy Spirit. At this point, the soul is not so much affected in the area of reconciliation to God. The Bible says the soul that sins shall die. In other words, even after conversion, it is possible to sin. In fact, it is only by working on the soul by the application of the Word of God in our daily walk that we can stay out of sin.

Still it depends on our definition of sin, because there are diverse kinds of sins. We tend to look at what we call the cardinal sins, and declare ourselves "sinless" like the Pharisee who justified himself by making comparison with others and with the publican that stood next to him in prayer. In Luke 18:10-12, it states, *"Two men went up into the temple to pray; the one a Pharisee and the one a Publican. The Pharisee stood and prayed thus with himself, God, I thank you, that I am not as other men are, extortionists, unjust, adulterers, or even as this Publican. I fast twice a week and I give tithes of all I possess."*

This Pharisee was walking in self-righteousness, which was a result of his works and not according to the grace bestowed upon us through Christ Jesus. The Bible is clear about this; that it is by grace we are saved and not of works lest any of us should boast. It is grace and nothing else but grace. But, in some of us, and in most of us, we need healing in our once rebellious and sick soul and this is what we call *deliverance*.

This is where it all gets mixed—up. The Body of Christ is divided on this subject. Many frown upon it. It has been looked upon as a form of stigma and for this reason many believers are suffering in ignorance with the devil and his demon spirits free to propagate this controversy. A senior church elder once made this sad statement; that there is nothing in the Bible to suggest Deliverance as a ministry. In other words, there is nothing like deliverance! Let us define Ministry then.

## What is Ministry?

"It is the vocation or the profession of a religious Minister or the office of the priest". If we believe when the Bible says that we are Royal Priesthood, then it is one of our duties to set the captives free, which is deliverance. This makes it a ministry within Ministry, which everyone in the fivefold Ministry should administer to God's people whenever needed or the case presents itself.

Some will argue that it is not included in the fivefold Ministry. My answer to that is: what are the duties or the assignments of the different ministries? When the various Prophets introduced Jesus in the Old Testament, the word *deliverance* was not used to describe His purpose of coming.

My question to people like the elder is, what was Jesus doing casting out devils from people who were possessed? If the Master did it, why shouldn't we? After all, He said we would do even greater works than he works that He did. He even named the things we should be doing in Mark 16:16-18.

Are we believers in the Lord Jesus Christ? If yes, then I do not think we should be debating about what is and what is not to be done, because the Bible is clear about it. Mark 16:15…is when Jesus gave us what is called the Great Commission. *"[15]And He said unto them, Go ye into all the world, and preach to every creature. [16]He that believes and is baptised shall be saved, but he that believes not shall be damned. [17]And these signs shall follow them that believe, in my name they shall cast out devils; they shall speak with new tongues; They shall take up serpent; and if they drink any deadly thing it shall not hurt them; They shall lay hands on the sick and they shall recover." (underlining mine)*

Are we preaching the Word to all nations and kindred? Is the message of Salvation winning souls for the Lord? Is it not the greatest miracle of all; that all persons including Satanists, respond to the salvation message and convert from their evil ways? Are we laying hands on the sick to witness supernatural healing? How then has the casting out of devils become a topic of debate? Is it not included in the command of the Great Commission?

Wake up people of God and let us drive out demons from the church to have the church become as God intended it to be.

We all agree that the answer to all these questions is, yes! If the answer is yes, then demons will have to respond to the anointing upon the Word from which we draw the power to heal and do all that the Word says. I have been in services where demons manifested in response to the release of the power of God that was present during the worship; and when the demon was told to be quiet, they indeed obeyed!

Was the demon cast out because it was ordered to be silent? No, the demon now silent and humiliated will now go on the offensive to torment this person more than before because it has been exposed but not cast out. We therefore should not only allow the anointing to expose them but do as Jesus did, and commanded us to do. He cast them out and we are supposed to do the same. Cast those demons out and let the captives be set free, in the name of Jesus!

Throughout His ministry, wherever and whenever He showed up there was a reaction from demons and He dealt with them differently. Some He asked questions, others He commanded to hold their peace and come out. All these He did to teach us how to deal with demons in any occasion they show up.

Ministers who minister deliverance to the demonised are debating these methods. Some say we should not interview demons; just cast them out. Others believe you should interview them. I believe such debates are irrelevant if the Spirit of the Lord is leading you.

He will lead you and guide you as to what to do in different situations and occasions, as no two situations are the same.

The Pharisees were operating by the demon spirit of ignorance and blindness; this made them religious without power as stated in 2 Timothy:5. *"Having a form of godliness but denying the power thereof: from such turn away."* This also blinded them from knowing and accepting Jesus as the Son of God. Paul says in 2 Corinthians 4:3-4: *"But if our gospel be hid, it is hid to them that are lost: In whom the god of this world has blinded the minds of them which believe not, lest the light of the glorious gospel of Christ, who is the image of God, should shine unto them."* Jesus dealt with these religious demons by confronting them with the power and authority of His person, letting them see themselves for who they really were.

This I call the power of the Word, which is able to heal and deliver without any human command for the spirit to come out of the person or persons in question. The other way Jesus dealt with demons, was to cast them out by commanding them to leave the person. This resulted in violent manifestations and a clear demonstration of the very real realm of satanic infestation in us human beings.

An example is found in Mark 5:2-5: *"And when He was come out of the ship, immediately there met Him out of the tombs a man with an unclean spirit, who had his dwelling among the tombs; and no man could bind him, no, not with chains: Because he had been bound with fetters and chains, and the chains had been plucked asunder by him, and the fetters broken in pieces; neither could any man tame him. And always, night and day, he was in the mountains, and in the tombs, crying, and cutting himself with stones."*

Does this sound familiar? Have you ever seen or heard anything like this in your life? As a believer, what is your take on it? This happened in the days of Jesus and it is still happening now. Are people not cutting themselves with knives and other sharp objects as this man was doing? Yes, they are and it is the demons that are making them to do it.

What do we do if they are in your church and you find out? I believe we have to do what Jesus did and what He would want us to do: cast the spirit out of the person and set the captives free. Let us look at the reaction of this man when he saw Jesus. Verse 6 says, *"But when he saw Jesus afar off, he ran and worshipped Him, and cried with a loud voice, and said, what have I to do with you Jesus, You Son of the Most High God? I adjure you by God, that you torment me not, for He said unto him, come out of the man, you unclean spirit."* This is real folks, this is real.

The devil is tormenting many of God's people and we need to set them free by the Truth. What would Jesus do? We should always ask ourselves this question when we are confronted by some bizarre and weird manifestation in our meetings and even in some unplanned moments when we encounter demons. We should do what He did on such occasions.

It is my prayer that this book, inspired by the Holy Spirit, will help many to know and understand the concept of deliverance, embrace it and be freed to enjoy the full pack of Salvation. It is my prayer also, that the devil will lose this battle of deception, which has divided us as a people of God.

May the Good Lord breathe upon you as you read this book and embark on discovering the truth about deliverance. It is about being delivered from the lies and deception of the devil, it is about deliverance from demonic influences, oppression and possession. It is also about learning how demons can enter into our mind and soul. It is about how to close doorways that can let in demons to harass us.

May the Holy Spirit grant you the grace to discern the truth and clear every shadow of doubt in your mind, in Jesus name. The Spirit of Truth will bear witness to the truth in this book, which is Bible-based. Sit tight and let the Spirit of the Lord journey with you through this book and I know you will be greatly blessed and empowered by the truth.

God bless you.

# CHAPTER ONE

# Salvation

This is the rebirth or regeneration. In Isaiah 53, the prophecy spoken by the Prophet was about the coming Messiah; who would bring salvation to His people, the Jews first, then the gentiles. In all, He came to die to save all humanity.

The Oxford dictionary explains salvation as: "saving from disaster, esp. from consequences of sin." That is exactly what Jesus came to do for mankind. He came to set us free from eternal damnation, and to reconcile us with our God, the Creator.

The prophesy given by Isaiah reads: "*⁶He was wounded for our transgressions; He was bruised for our iniquities: the chastisement of our peace was upon Him; and with His stripes we are healed. All we like sheep have gone astray; we have turned everyone to his own way; and the Lord hath laid on Him the iniquity of us all. ⁷He was oppressed and afflicted, yet He opened not his mouth.*"

This is the message of salvation. In this context, we are right to assume that deliverance is included in the pact of Salvation. Remember He was oppressed and afflicted.

In light of this, let us then look at the entire picture of Salvation, as prophesied by the Prophet Isaiah in chapter 53.

## He was wounded for our transgressions
## What are Transgressions?

A transgression is to go beyond the bounds or limits as set by a commandment, law, etc.; violates; infringes. This means when the human race fell through of Adam and Eve, sin entered the world. Man became automatically sinful because the knowledge of good and evil had been unveiled unto him.

Man began to live a life contrary to God's divine rule of law and order. Mankind went against the very nature of God including Holiness and Righteousness, and became rebellious against God and His ordinances. This broke the fellowship between God and man.

By declaring that man was created in the image and likeness of God, the Bible makes us one with what God is. This was the case before the fall of man. Then, after the fall, we took on the adornment of sin and man became sinful in nature. We took on the nature of the devil instead of the nature of God. Throughout the Scriptures, we see how God's heart broke when man turned away from the purpose for which he had been created and put on this earth. Many are still in rebellion as long as they are not surrendered to the Lord.

**He was bruised for our iniquities
What is Iniquity?**

1. Wickedness; unrighteousness. 2. Gross injustice

This shows how the fall of man brought chaos into the earth. Lawlessness, wickedness and unrighteous lifestyles remain the order of the day. These are all against the rule of God, the commandment of God and His purposes for us. Iniquity is living continuously in sin and showing no sign of repentance.

Some people are literally dead to their conscience; they commit sin without any sense of guilt let alone repentance. They are simply iniquitous. It is sad to say that today sin is as rife in the church as it is outside the church. This is the truth and Ministers are often afraid to address it for fear of losing members

In some instances, it is the Ministers themselves who are iniquitous. Do not get me wrong, I am not judging anyone as the Lord Jesus Christ is the only judge who has the power to bring judgment, but it is no secret that we need repentance in the church, from the pulpits to the pews. We, the church however, need to understand that it is the devil who wants the church to be weakened by causing us to sin against God thus displeasing Him. We need to confront the demonic activities in the church. It is these demonic infestations that cause even Ministers to sin and to become iniquitous.

What will the flock do if their ministers become victims of demonization? Psalm 11:3 *"If the foundation be destroyed, what can the righteous do?"* Who will deliver the flock under him if the shepherd is continuously fighting the demons of his past? This is real folks; this is very real and is why the church is in the state it is now.

Brothers and sisters, I cannot emphasise it any more than this! Prayers ought to be consistently offered for our Pastors and Prophets, especially, as they are our first port of call and, if they fall, we all fall.

The church needs cleansing and this is nothing to be ashamed of as the only person to be put to shame here, is the devil. Let us put a smile on Jesus' face and a frown on Satan's. We need to do what Jesus commanded us to do; cast out devil, heal the sick and preach the gospel. Let us do all of these with nothing left out, and that is the full Gospel of Jesus Christ.

## The chastisement of our peace was upon Him

I believe that, as believers, we can agree that anything outside the will of God, even if it brings us "happiness" is only for a brief moment. Why would some very rich people in society commit suicide? Why would people who appear to be very successful lose their minds? Why would people who appear to have great marriages, children and everything that should make them happy, battle with depression?

The answer is, anything that does not include God's plan of salvation for us, is false. The peace we often declare we have, is false peace. Real and true peace of mind comes only from God. Real peace or true peace comes from the author of peace Himself, Jesus Christ. That is why Jesus made a bold statement about peace. He said, *"My peace I give to you" John 14:27.* He called it my peace, why? It is simply because He paid for it with His own blood. If you pay for something it is yours, isn't it? That is why it is only the blood of Jesus that can give you the peace of God that surpasses all understanding.

Someone may say, but I have peace even though I have not been through deliverance. That is fair enough and I am not going to say it is not possible, but what I want to get you to understand is that, as believers, we have been taught not to confess anything negative and not to believe anything negative.

This is Biblical, and it is good and it is also true, but I have seen something in Christianity now, which makes the application of the above, very flawed. You see, we have to be taught the difference between truth and fact.

If I were to say to a sister or brother that I have a headache, I am simply stating a fact. This is because the headache is real; I am feeling it at this particular moment and denying it does not make it go away.

On the other hand, this fact has to be balanced by the truth which is, 'by His stripes, I am healed'. Denying you do not have a headache is walking in denial and that is not faith. You acknowledge the fact but confess the truth and that truth cancels the fact because faith is activated when we confess the Word of Truth to counteract any adverse situation.

In John 11, there is a story of a man named Lazarus. A message was first sent from his sisters, Mary and Martha, to Jesus. *"[3]Therefore, his sisters sent unto him, (Jesus) saying, Lord, behold, he whom you love is sick."* The sisters were stating the fact, Lazarus was indeed sick unto death. It was true, they were not lying and they were not denying the fact. Lazarus was sick. The response from Jesus is: *"[4]When Jesus heard that, He said, this sickness is not unto death, but for the glory of God, that the Son of God might be glorified thereby."*

Do you see what I am talking about here? Even Jesus did not say "don't say Lazarus is sick, for that is a faithless talk." Jesus acknowledged the fact that Lazarus is sick and went on to declare the word of Truth; this sickness is not unto death, but for the glory of God! Simple! So you see, when we deny that there is something wrong and go about your life as usual, you are actually walking in false peace and hope as, not confronting it does not make it disappear.

Where is the peace if you know within your sub- conscious mind the problem exists? Peace that is from God, is stating the fact and cancelling fact with the Truth. Hallelujah! The devil is a liar; we will apply the Truth the way it is supposed to be applied so it will work for us. Praise God!

## And by His stripes, we are healed.

Supernatural healing comes only through the blood of Jesus. Some may have a problem believing this, but it does not change the fact that Jesus heals even today. The Bible says *"Jesus Christ is the same yesterday, today and forever," Hebrews 13:8*. So why do we believe He healed yesterday but He cannot or does not heal today or tomorrow? And, if we believe that He is still healing the sick today, why do we shun deliverance or the casting out of devils?

Whatever He did then, He is still doing it today. The only difference is He did it in person then but now He is doing it through His anointed servants, by the power of His Precious Holy Spirit. The devil is a liar. We believe in the full Gospel of Jesus Christ. Although we see the manifested healing in the physical, I can boldly say it can also be evident in every area of our lives including our emotions. The Bible declares in 3 John 2: *"Beloved, I wish above all things that thou may prosper and be in health, even as thy soul prospers."* God in His infinite wisdom knew before time that after the fall, man would need healing in his soul, and this is what deliverance is all about. It is healing to the sick soul.

The Scripture says *"All, like sheep, have gone astray…"* We have strayed from God's designated path and for this reason; we need to be steered back on track. This means restoring the broken fellowship between God and man.

When man fell, it would take the blood of animals to atone for his sins. Genesis 3: 21 *"And unto Adam also and to his wife did the Lord make coats of skins and clothed them."* The blood of animals was used to cover their sins and nakedness. Following that, anytime the children of Israel sinned, animals had to be slaughtered for atonement.

God decided to make a onetime sin sacrifice of atonement for all mankind. This is the purpose of Christ's coming into the world. Jesus Christ, the perfect sacrifice, who was to pay the ultimate price, was given unto us. Isaiah 9:6 *"Unto us a child is born, unto us a son is given."*

Jesus came to die on the cross to reconcile us unto our Creator, the only true Living God. Before He died, He taught, He preached, He healed, He performed miracles and He also cast out devils. This is evidenced in various books of the Bible especially in the four Gospels. An example is in the book of Matthew 4:23-24, *"And Jesus went about all Galilee, teaching in their synagogues, and preaching the gospel of the Kingdom, and healing all manner of sickness and all manner of diseases among the people. And His fame went throughout all Syria: and they brought to Him all sick people that were taken with diverse diseases and torments and those who were possessed with devils, and those which were lunatic, and those that had palsy; and He healed them."*

Jesus came to preach the Kingdom and all that pertains to it. That is the full Gospel! Salvation means being born again by the Holy Spirit. This means our spirit man is delivered from his/her spiritual death and alienation from God. Salvation is a whole package. In it is healing for our physical bodies and also healing for our souls.

At this point, would it be wrong to say that as believers we need deliverance at some point in our lives? Some of us in the Kingdom of God do not believe healing is for today's generation. They believe it stopped when Jesus was crucified. This is very wrong, and unscriptural. Some believe in healing but not deliverance. This is equally ridiculous and unscriptural. If we believe Jesus came, taught, preached, healed, delivered, performed miracles, was crucified, died and resurrected, then we cannot take anything out of this package.

The Gospel of Jesus Christ ceases to be complete if any aspect of it is taken away. How then can we embrace healing and the working of miracles and, at the same time, reject the very essence of salvation? The greatest miracle of all is the transformation of a life and that includes being delivered from the darkness unto the marvelous light of God.

The church is suffering as a result of this truth: not recognizing the need for, what I call the missing link of the Gospel. I call it the missing link because the enemy has all but successfully taken it out of the church of Jesus Christ by propagating lies and twisting the truth about deliverance as he did in the Garden of Eden.

In the Garden, he twisted the Truth and the woman was deceived. The devil will always twist the truth to deceive us if it is possible. This is because, if he invents his own theory, the believer will be quick to reject it as an unacceptable piece of information, because there would be no biblical backing or proof. For this reason, the devil always and forever will use the truth to produce and create his counterfeit. He even used the Word of God in Matthew 4 to tempt Jesus.

Another reason is that Satan is a created being and cannot create anything. There is only one Creator in the entire Universe and that is Jehovah God.

There will be inventions, yes, but inventions are made out of already made, created items. There can be no counterfeit without the original. There is fake gold because there is real gold. There are real diamonds and fake diamonds, real currency and fake currency. It takes a criminal to produce fake substances. Why is that? This is because it is against the law of every land to produce fake items especially fake currency. It is simply a criminal act in violation of the law of the land.

In the case of the supernatural, there is also a spiritual criminal in the person of Satan, the fallen archangel. He violated the laws of Heaven attempting a coup against Almighty God who had created him. Since then this spiritual criminal has been on the rampage producing and reproducing counterfeits. His main aim of doing this is to deceive, distract and destroy mankind. Remember what Jesus said in John 10:10, *"The thief cometh not, but for to steal, to kill, and to destroy:"* This is the primary reason why the devil is twisting the Truth: to pollute the mind of God's people. Do not forget that when he went to Jesus in the wilderness, after Jesus had fasted forty days. He did not tempt Him with his own satanic theory but with the very Word of God.

The same happened in the Garden of Eden. This shows just how far the devil will go. He is no respecter of persons. He has no shame or pride. Definitely, he must have known that he would be defeated by the Lord Jesus, yet he went anyway. Nobody is immune to the devil's deception, distractions and lies, all these, when one succumbs, will lead to bondage and sin. Please note that this happens as a result of the twisted truth?

As believers and followers of Jesus Christ, we must be careful what we propagate, because this can cause a precious soul to stumble and fall, or to suffer needlessly. I say needlessly, because if the teachers of the truth are deceived, what will become of the *"Lambs and the Sheep?"* They will become spiritual casualties and prey to the teeth of the enemy.

The Bible says, *"If the foundation be destroyed, what will the righteous do?" Psalm 11:3.* If the very truth is destroyed or twisted by the devil and is ignorantly propagated in the church of Christ, what will be the outcome? The answer is simple. They will be destroyed for lack of knowledge. They will become needless casualties of war as we battle among ourselves as to who is right and who is wrong, instead of letting the Word of God speak for itself.

Let God be true and every man a liar.

# CHAPTER 2

# Sound Doctrine

Every doctrine in the church of Jesus Christ must be sound, pure, and unadulterated. It must be based wholly on the Word of God, and not on human ideology or theology. 1 Timothy 1:3, *"As I besought thee to abide still at Ephesus, when I went into Macedonia that thou might charge some that they teach no other doctrine. Neither give heed to fables and endless genealogies, which minister questions, rather than godly edifying which is in faith: so, do… desiring to be teachers of the law; understanding neither what they say, or wherewith they affirm."*

Jesus made it clear in Mark 16:16, *"And He said unto them, Go ye into all the world, and preach the gospel to every creature. He that believeth and is baptised shall be saved; but he that believeth not shall be damned. And these signs shall follow them that believe: in my name, <u>they shall cast out devils, they shall speak with new tongues; they shall take up serpents,</u> and if they drink any deadly thing, it shall not hurt them: they shall lay hands on the sick and they shall recover." (Underlining mine)*

Which of the above Scripture is not being fulfilled in our days? Are we praying for the sick in the name of Jesus? Are the sick recovering from their infirmities? The answer is yes! Are we speaking with new tongues? Again, the answer is yes!

Taking up serpents, does not literally mean going into the bush to look for serpents to pick up; it is figurative speech. It means we will be able to confront and defeat demonic powers like those that He did. Are we doing that now? The answer is a resounding, yes, in Jesus Name!

I was listening to a testimony of a converted Muslim and part of his story was what he had suffered from his own father who gathered people to kill him. When that failed, they concocted some deadly drink to poison him. This, they forced down his throat and left to him die. From his account, an angel of the Lord woke him up in the night and led him out of the village. A couple of years later, he went back to the village to visit and pray the sinner's prayer with his dying father. The father recovered from his sickness and instructed the entire family to accept the Lord Jesus. This was the plan of God for the family and it came to pass.

In my personal life, I have seen my own son poisoned by an acquaintance who put rat poison into his food and the Lord allowed him to live to tell the tale. This is another classic example of the power of God and His faithfulness. This does not mean we should tempt God as some cults do. You will die if you do that.

Some cults literally pick up live serpents and dance in "church" with these snakes quoting the above Scriptures. Some were bitten to death including the "Pastor". The Word of God works, folks; it works! God is faithful to His covenant with His people. God wants to set His people free and that is why He put it in the covenant.

We always have to allow the Spirit of the Lord to show us exactly what He means in a particular Scripture. If we keep on saying once one is born again, one does not need deliverance, then we are becoming like Hymenaeus and Philetus who, as the Bible says, *"have erred concerning the truth."* 1 Timothy 2:17-18, *"... and their word will eat as doth a canker: of whom is Hymanaeus and Philetus; who concerning the truth erred, saying the resurrection is past already; and overthrow the faith of some."*

This is very sad when you think about the fact that the faith of many was overthrown because of their error. We still have the likes of these men in the Kingdom today. They might not be saying the resurrection is past but they are saying different things which are equally dangerous because it is also overthrowing the faith of many in our times.

It is very important for us to walk worthy of our vocation. Ephesians 4:1, *"I, therefore, the prisoner of the Lord, beseech you that ye walk worthy of the vocation wherewith ye are called. With all lowliness and meekness, with longsuffering, forbearing one another in love; endeavouring to keep the unity of the Spirit in the bond of peace."*

In other words, let us walk in our own calling. If you are called as a carpenter, be just that. If you are called to be a doctor, be a doctor. As a doctor, if you try to do the work of the carpenter, there would be imperfect outcomes and you would suffer loss and people would suffer. The book of Joel talks about not breaking ranks.

Joel 2:7-8 *"They shall run like mighty men; they shall climb the wall like men of war; and they shall march everyone on his ways, and they shall not break their ranks: neither shall one thrust another; they shall walk everyone in his path."*

The Bible says in Ephesians 4:1, *"And he gave some, apostles and some, prophets; and some, evangelists; and some, pastors, and some, teachers for the perfecting of the saints, for the work of the ministry, for the edifying of the body of Christ."*

All these ministries have been set up by the Most High in His infinite wisdom to supply the needs of His Kingdom. The ministry of the apostle is different from the ministry of the prophet and so on and, unless you are given the opportunity by God Himself to operate in another ministry at any given time, you are actually breaking ranks if you make any presumptuous moves. There will be no anointing to operate effectively in such a ministry.

God anoints us when He sends us on any form of assignment and in the ministry into which, He Himself has called us. I was listening to a prophet whose prophetic utterances I have come to find accurate. My spirit bore great witness to the truths from him as a prophet of God but during one of his programs, I felt a sudden sense of deflation when he unexpectedly launched an attack on preachers who preach on generational curses. These were his words "Some have preached about visiting the iniquities of the fathers upon the third and the fourth generations, this is not true, why should you pay for the sins that you know nothing about? Plus, when you become born again that was it…"

The man of God was really watering down the concept of deliverance. All I could say to myself was that here is a beautiful and anointed prophet. If you have not been given to the knowledge of demonology and deliverance, please do not mess up the minds of the people of God, because it is part of the gospel of Jesus Christ. The point is, irrespective of what individuals believe: the Truth is the Truth. Lamentation 5:7 *"Our fathers have sinned and are not and we have borne their iniquities."*

The Bible speaks for itself and in *Jeremiah 31:29-30 it states, "In those days they shall say no more, the fathers have eaten a sour grape and the children's teeth are set on edge. [30]but every one shall die for his own iniquity: every one that eats a sour grape, his teeth shall be set on edge."* This will be after the new covenant is made by the blood of Jesus and according His teachings.

In the New covenant, there is salvation, healing deliverance peace and everything that comes with it. If we disagree with some doctrines that are biblically true, then we have a problem and there is nothing we can do about it. 2 Timothy 2:13-14, *"if we believe not, yet He abides faithful: He cannot deny Himself. Of these things, put them in remembrance, charging them before the Lord that they strive not about words to no profit, but to the subverting of the hearers."*

The Apostle Paul was first a Pharisee who persecuted the church for preaching the Gospel of Jesus Christ. A true Jew, he describes himself as, and a Pharisee of the Pharisees, a very proud one for that matter, a very learned man and a Bible scholar. He believed his theology was the correct one and anyone that preached Jesus was a target for persecution and, in some cases, death.

However, when he had an encounter with the King of Glory, his theology changed. He encountered the "Christ" of the Gospel and in Acts 16, he was the one who identified and cast out the spirit of divination that was operating in the woman. I ask; what about those who were actually with Jesus and witnessed Him casting devils out of people? The answer is simple. If they have done the same, it may have been said that they were copying Jesus; yet the one who did not see Jesus physically but supernaturally, did it as an example for us to know that it is part of the Great Commission. I believe God chose Paul to show us that it is the will and plan of God to cast out devils from human beings especially those that are born again.

In fact, Paul spoke of the spirits (demonic spirits) and warfare more than any of the Apostles who were with the Lord did. From the book of Corinthians through to Timothy, Paul warns about the spirits of the devil and their operations. Paul warns the churches not to be ignorant of the devices of Satan, his lies and deception. In short, Paul exposed more of the kingdom of darkness than all the Apostles did; how it can affect us if we lose sight of this reality.

Beloved, the spiritual realm is very real; heaven is real and hell is also real, so we must not allow the devil to deceive us. In 2 Corinthians 11, Paul speaks in depth about deception and expresses his concern about it. *"[3]But I fear, lest by any means, as the serpent beguiled Eve through his subtlety, so your minds should be corrupted from the simplicity that is in Christ. For if he that comes preaches another Jesus whom we have not preached, or if you receive another spirit which you have not received, or another gospel, which you have not accepted, you might well bear with him... [vs. 13-15] for such are false apostles, deceitful workers, transforming themselves into apostles of Christ. And no marvel; for Satan himself is transformed himself as an angel of light, therefore it is no great thing if his ministers also be transformed as the ministers of righteousness; whose end shall be according to their works."*

Is it a surprise then that the enemy of our soul is deceiving us into believing that there is nothing like demonic invasion in this day and age? In fact, the opposite is true. There is advancement in the demonic realm and the church of Jesus Christ is wallowing in ignorance.

Look at what is happening in the world now and tell me there is nothing wrong. The Scripture is being fulfilled right before our eyes and we think it is normal? Isaiah 60:2a *"For, behold, the darkness shall cover the earth and gross darkness the people."* What was prophesied a long time ago is now unfolding before our eyes. He said, *"The Darkness and gross darkness"* "The" is the pronoun qualifying darkness which means *darkness* is personified and, I believe, that is the devil. "...and *darkness the people",* is without any qualifier so it is talking about the demons from the kingdom of darkness.

I will put it in this context. Behold the devil shall take over the earth and his demons shall propagate his evil plans all over the world. This is to cause men to walk in disobedience and rebellion against the ordinances of God. As God uses Christians to manifest the glory that is in heaven in the earth so the devil uses demons to manifest the advancement of the plans of the kingdom of darkness. Demons are as real today as they were in the days when Jesus walked on the earth. Spirits do not die so those medieval spirits have now advanced themselves and are using human beings to do their bidding.

# CHAPTER 3

# We Need House Cleaning

In my early years as a believer, when the name of Jesus was mentioned there was an immediate reaction of demonic manifestation, but now, they are all undercover in the churches without fear. This is because the church is weakened by the lies of the enemy with ministers not dealing with the issues that are dear to the Lord, the liberation of souls of men through the preaching of the true and full gospel of Jesus Christ. I pray we will visit the ancient landmarks once again before the coming of that great and dreadful day. There is a day of reckoning as to what we did to the flock, what we did with, and what did for them. May the Good Lord Himself help us as we embark on the journey to visit the ancient landmarks.

## Back To Basics.

The truth has to be preached unapologetically. We have to love the sinner and hate the sin, addressing sin and dealing with it with all urgency before it festers and affect the soul of the church. As long as ministers refrain from speaking the truth and not confronting sin in the church, the enemy will continue to weave his web of deceit and lies. Let us go back to preaching holiness, righteousness and the fear of the Lord. Satan hates such preaching and teachings and will do anything to suppress it, yet we have a charge to keep and a God to glorify, and we cannot back down and allow the devil and his demons to hijack the reins of any church of Jesus Christ.

Let the intercessors arise and take their position and never leave their post until discharged, and the devil will flee from the church that does just that. We are supposed to be in the Light, so let us reflect Him to expose darkness any time it shows up. Demons are not supposed to co-habit with us in the church. No, it is not supposed to be so. Nor are we to permit it. If we do not cast out demons from the people who are manifesting demonic oppression and infestation, the church will soon be infested and taken over by demons. Eccles. 10:1 *"Dead flies cause the oil of the perfumer to putrefy and send forth a vile odor; so, does a little folly in him who is valued for wisdom outweigh wisdom and honour." (Amp)*

The anointing, when contaminated by demons, sends a vile odour. It is polluted with dead flies, demons and unaddressed ongoing sin. That means the power of the anointing of the Holy Spirit diminishes and it is only a matter of time before it will be totally absent from the infested church.

Jesus said in Matthew 12:43-45 *"When an unclean spirit is gone out of a man, he walks through dry places, seeking rest, and he finds none. [44]Then he says, I will return into my house from where I came out; and when he is come, he finds it empty, swept and garnished. [45]Then he goes and takes with himself seven other spirits more wicked than himself and they enter in and dwell there:*

*and the last state of that man is worse than the first. Even so shall it be also unto this wicked generation."*

Jesus, in this Scripture, teaches us that demons can live in human and do things through them. He also makes us aware that even when the demons are expelled, we have to keep our house clean and filled with godly things and living a godly life. It is only then can we keep the demons out completely. If we fail to keep a "clean house", the demons can return and when they do, they come back with vengeance.

Praying deliverance for church folks is a form of spring cleaning our house and our body, which is the temple of God. This should be a perfectly normal thing to do in the church of Jesus Christ but instead it has been stigmatized and declared a no-no.

Take, for instance, a car. Every good and responsible driver takes his car for an annual servicing before it can go for an M.O.T. Some old plugs have to be replaced, the dirty oil has to be drained, and the engine cleaned. New oil is then put in to affect the smooth running of the engine. This also prolongs the longevity of the vehicle.

Our body, as Christians, is the vehicle of God and has to be kept clean for effective spiritual operations or journeys, which the Lord has assigned. We need to clean it periodically and maintain it in good condition.

It is very important to either pray self-deliverance for ourselves or, in the extreme cases, ask an anointed Minister to pray a prayer of deliverance over you. If this were not necessary, the Lord Jesus Himself would not have taught it. The devil is real, demons are real and deliverance is necessary.

Paul taught us about the nature of our warfare (New struggles) and the weapons with which we need to arm ourselves. Ephesians 6:11-18 *"Put on the whole armor of God that you may be able to stand against the wiles of the devil. For we wrestle not against flesh and blood, but against principalities, against powers, against the rulers of the darkness of this world, against spiritual wickedness in high places. Wherefore put on the whole armor of God that you may be able to withstand in the day of evil."* The Apostle Paul taught us how to handle the demonic powers and live a victorious life in Christ Jesus.

The Bible makes us to understand that as individuals, we do not have it all, and we do not know it all. The day we get to know it all, He ceases to be God. Paul was a man with great spiritual insight and abundance of revelations, but he tells in plain language that whatever we claim to know, we only know in parts.

Even with prophecies, we only prophesy in parts. So, you can see that we cannot boast in knowing it all. Many prophets may be in a meeting but God reveals different things to them individually. This is the reason why God, in His infinite wisdom, has given us the power to judge prophecies.

Based on these Scriptures, I believe we should walk in the calling to which we have been called and not tread on areas that we are not called or anointed to, or have not received the mandate to tread.

Some Christians criticize the so-called healing ministries, saying healing ceased when Jesus died. Others believe that healing is still the believer's portion, even to unbelievers; God chooses to heal even atheists to glorify His name. The fact that there is division on these subjects does not change the awesome truth about the healing power of Jesus.

Simon Peter was a disciple of Jesus but things were happening, and the Lord knew that even though this was his disciple, there was an area of his life that allowed the enemy to operate around him. Hence that statement in Luke 22:31 *"And the Lord said, Simon, Simon, behold, Satan hath desired to have you, that he may sift you as wheat: but I have prayed for you, that your faith fails not: and when you are converted, strengthen your brothers."*

What picture do we see here? You can be a disciple and still need deliverance. What was the prayer the Lord prayed for Simon Peter? It was a prayer for deliverance, to deliver him from the behaviour that opened the door that gave the enemy free access into Peter's life. It was not the only time that the Lord Jesus addressed Peter that way. Jesus had referred to Satan's operations when he dealt with Peter, in Matthew 16:23 *"but He turned and said unto Peter, get thee behind me Satan, thou art an offence unto me for thou savor not the things that be of God, but those that be of men."*

Who is perfect save the Lord Jesus! Peter was a disciple but had issues that were demonically infused. Jesus always dealt with it and carried on loving him. Jesus or the rest of the disciples did not shun him. It is not a shameful thing to be delivered, rather it a shameful thing not to be delivered. The devil will ridicule your belief in the Lord by occasionally exposing cracks that can cause demons to manifest themselves through you. You may be a Pastor, or a Deacon or an Elder, do not be afraid to confront the demons in you or around you. They can easily cause you to make serious mistakes or commit a sin that will shock everyone else including yourself.

The devil is not playing games at all but we, the Christians, are. It is about time that we expose and deal with him and clean our houses. Deal with the issues now or the issues will deal with you in the latter years of ministry. No one is above deliverance. Paul cried out, so why not you or I.

Let us cry out for God to deliver us.

# CHAPTER 4

# Healing is a Form of Deliverance

Now let us check what the Bible says about deliverance. Many a times in Jesus' earthly ministry, He cast out demons and, in most cases; this took place before He healed. An example is recorded in Mark's gospel, chapter 9:17 where the Bible talks about an epileptic boy who was brought to Jesus for healing *"And one of the multitude answered and said, Master, I have brought unto thee my son, which hath a dumb spirit; And where so ever he takes him he (That is the spirit) tears him: and he foamed, and gnashes with his teeth, and pines away: and I spoke with thy disciples that they should cast him out; and they could not... [20]and they brought him unto Him: and when he saw him, straightway the spirit tare him; and he fell on the ground, and wallowed, foaming... [25]when Jesus saw that the people came running together, He rebuked the foul spirit, saying unto him, thou deaf and dumb spirit, I charge thee, come out of him, and enter no more into him."*

This is a clear case of an epileptic condition. It is a medical condition in our modern terms, so why did Jesus not administer healing straight away but instead had to deal with the spirit of that infirmity first? This does not mean that every sickness or disease is demonic, no, that is not what I am saying, but there are some that even modern medical technology cannot heal, but the supernatural power of God can. I have personally seen an AIDS patient healed at a Morris Cerullo conference in Birmingham, England. This man and his wife who were both suffering and afflicted with this horrible disease, were instantly filled with the Holy Ghost and began to speak in tongues. They were Muslims who knew nothing about the Bible and had been invited by a friend to the conference. They came all the way from Sweden. I know this much because my friend and I befriended them and chatted during break times. They even told us how they did not have the money to come but God miraculously provided for them to make the journey.

Beloved, there is power in the Name and the Blood of Jesus to both deliver and heal even to raise the dead. Medically speaking, it might seem impossible. But Jesus heals all manner of diseases, demonic or non-demonic. Surely, no believer can forget Mark 16:17, "*And these signs shall follow them that believe; in my name shall they cast out devils they shall speak with new tongues…. They shall lay hands on the sick, and they shall recover.*"

Deliverance can never be taken out of the Gospel of Jesus Christ. On conversion, our spirit man is born again but not the soul. Bear in mind that we do not sin with our spirit, but with our soul. Oh yes, we sin with our soul. Where is the mind? Where is the heart? It is all in the soul. Ezekiel 18:4 says *the soul that sins shall die.*

All sins start from the mind. Jesus said if you look at a woman lustfully, you have already committed adultery with her. You see, the mind is a very powerful faculty in the body. It controls the entire operational system of the human body. Basically, Jesus is saying the moment the mind focuses on an image; it is difficult to shake it off. Nevertheless, it can be done if we mortify our flesh and not allow the flesh to dictate what we should do but rather allow ourselves to be led, and directed by the Holy Spirit.

It takes the grace of God not to follow the mind. If an image is locked up in the mind, it is easy for the heart to follow, and as the heart follows, the seed, whether good or bad, is allowed to germinate. The seed is then nurtured in the incubator of your heart. At this moment, it is difficult for the seed to be aborted. The end product has to be brought forth.

James 1:14-15, *"But every man is tempted, when he is drawn away of his own lust, and enticed. Then when lust has conceived, it brings forth sin: and sin, when it is finished, it brings forth death."*

It is now time for the soul to receive healing. This is the reason why, even in the medical field, there are psychiatrists. They do not deal with visible conditions or any seen or visible ailments but the mental and emotional aspect of life that may be causing some unexplainable behaviour. The psychiatrist cannot perform surgery on the human body but can administer oral therapy for the mentally unstable. This is called counseling. In Christendom, we administer this kind of therapy too. This is what deliverance is all about.

You teach about the condition to make the person understand what is actually happening. Many people do not understand what is happening; neither do they know why they are going through what they are going through.

A few years ago, I was on holiday with two friends and we spent time in prayer and fasting at a local Prayer Center. On the first night, as we were praying, the spirit of the Lord led me to pray for one of them. The Lord told me that the same spirit that had attacked her mother and caused her premature death is the same spirit that was now attacking her. I prayed and spoke with her, and she confirmed the things the Lord was saying to me. On the second night I was led to administer deliverance to her. Praise God she was delivered.

The following week she invited me to her residence for a weekend of prayer. The three of us met again to fast and pray. During the third night the other woman was led by the spirit and requested that we pray for the host's daughter. As we began to pray, this woman who is also an intercessor began to command the spirits to come out of the girl. There was no response and, as she was dealing with it a little aggressively, I felt the need to take over from her.

The first thing I did was to minister to the girl as to what we were doing and why. When she understood what we were doing and praying for, she started to cooperate and was more relaxed. As soon as I was through with counseling and had begun to command the devils to come out, there was a serious demonic manifestation with spirit after spirit emerging from this girl.

Weeks after my return, I received their feedback and testimonies of visible changes that the Lord had brought into their lives both as a family and also as individuals. I proceeded to walk them through how to maintain their deliverance. She has now moved on to become a lecturer in the University where her husband is also a Dean. She owns companies, her husband who was an alcoholic has been delivered, and the changes in their lives are incredible. To God be the glory! In my friend's own words, she said, "the Lord made you buy your own ticket to come and bring deliverance to my whole household." Praise the Lord for His mercies flow! The tremendous transformation is there for all to see. Deliverance is real and is needed in our world as it stands today.

In the natural, when you buy a house or move into an apartment, you clean it up and re-arrange things for your comfortable habitation. That is how God wants His temples to be; well cleaned up for His habitation. The Scripture is very clear about deliverance. Christ did it to show us that it is a reality and not a fantasy. If it were not so, He would not have taught His disciples different levels and methods in casting out devils. Remember, He said to the disciples: "... *nevertheless, this kind goes not forth but by fasting and praying."* Are we applying these teachings of Jesus today as ministers and as Christians? If yes, are we applying all or just some? Do we have to pick and choose which ones to apply and which ones to reject? It is very, very, sad to see the Body of Christ divided over this and other issues. We simply have to foll ow the teachings of the Lord and watch Him bring the results.

Several times Jesus would first rebuke and cast out the spirit of infirmity before He would administer healing. The Lord was teaching us that some sicknesses and diseases are perpetuated by demons. We now know how to pray for the sick effectively.

Deliverance is a form of healing to the soul.

# CHAPTER 5

# Walking Worthy of Your Vocation

The Bible says in Ephesians 4:1 *"I therefore, the prisoner of the Lord, beseech you that you walk worthy of the vocation wherewith you are called, with all lowliness and meekness, with longsuffering, forbearing one another in love; Endeavoring to keep the unity of    the Spirit in the bond of peace. There is one body, and one Spirit,   even as you are called in one hope of your calling; One God and  Father of all, who is above all, and through all and in you all. But unto every one of us is given grace according to the measure of the gift of Christ... He that descended is the same also that ascended up far above all heavens, that he might fill all things. And he gave some apostles; and some, prophets; and some evangelists; and some pastors and teachers. [12]For the perfecting of the saints, for the work of the ministry, for the edifying of the body of Christ: until we all come to the unity of the faith, and of the knowledge of the Son of God..."*

As I said earlier, it is very important to stay focused on our calling and not to meddle in areas in which we are not yet called. I use the word *yet* because I sincerely believe there are ministers who operate in all five-fold ministerial gifts and there are others who operate in two or three. However, our God is able to use us in areas in which we are not yet endowed to operate, if we humbly wait upon Him.

A friend in the US told me of a situation that demonstrates this point. People were being drawn to the church she attended with her host because the Pastor was also a seer. This meant that people from other churches 'changed lanes." This is when people in one congregation leave their church to join another church. She said prior to their going to this prophetic church, they were attending a different one where the Pastor did not move in the prophetic. One day, they went back to their former church just because they were late for their new church. To their amazement, this man of God, after preaching told the congregation, he was now entering into the prophetic ministration and began to prophesy to the congregation. This surprised my friend as she could tell the man was trying hard to keep the members from leaving so he had become a prophet overnight. She felt it was a farce and phony.

Having a personal knowledge of this Minister and his calling, I know that he is definitely not a prophet by calling. He is not the only one. There are several others who have stepped out of their "lane" and are messing up the children of the Kingdom of Christ.

This actually causes confusion in the body of Christ. My prayer is that we let God be God in His church. It is His church and we are His employees and we are supposed to do as we are told and not what we want to do. In every organisation, we find different departments and different operations and each works in their area of expertise and responsibility. Unless the boss authorizes you to do something different, you stay where you have been posted. We should walk in our own calling and not interfere in areas where God has not given us insight or anointing. We need to leave it to those who have been assigned to that particular ministry, and concentrate on our calling or ministry. This can bring about harmony in the Kingdom of our Father.

Do you know, we can be in the same music ministry and yet we operate differently? We can be in the choir and yet not sing the same keynotes? God loves diversity. That is why he incorporated diversity in all that He created. Look at the family of monkeys; there are many different species. Look at the birds of the air, again there are diverse species. When you watch nature documentaries, you will see diverse kinds of fish in the seas and the oceans.

Let us look at mankind; even though we are created as one there is great diversity. Among the so-called *black* race there are multiple and diverse groups, families, nations and more. The same is true of the other races. And yet God is the creator of all. 1 Corinthians 12:4 *"Now there are diversities of gifts, but the same Spirit. And there are differences of administration, but the same Lord. And there are diversities of operation, but it is the same God which works all in all."*

If we can get this into our hearts, we will be at peace with each other's ministry, and pray for one another so that every joint will work to enrich the Kingdom of our dear Lord Jesus. No one is greater than the other. There needs to be an anointing from God to minister under the direction of the Holy Spirit. One may sing with a tenor voice and another in a baritone yet they are equally important. Both will receive their rewards from the Lord as long as they are singing to the glory of God.

The fact that someone sings a different key from you does not make them wrong. Like everything else, even in the prophetic ministry, each prophet has their unique message and the way God uses them. No two prophets are the same. Everyone has their individual way of operation. We are each very unique. God made it to be so.

Good old Ezekiel had to act out his prophecies. He was instructed to bake a cake mixed with human dung and eat it. It was only when he protested that the Lord changed it into cow dung. (Ezek. 4:12-15) *"And thou shalt eat it as barley cakes, and thou shalt bake it with dung that comes out of man in their sight... [15]Then He said unto me, Lo, I have given thee cow's dung for human dung, and thou shall prepare thy bread therewith."*

Now can somebody tell me which of the prophets was given such an unusual task through prophecy? Let us bring it to today's light and examine this particular act of God. Can He do the same thing again through a man or woman of God today? The answer is, YES. Will the critics accept it in the Kingdom? No. There will be name-calling, labels and tags applied to such a person. Does it change the fact that God can demand such an act? NO.

So, let us release one another to do the Father's business in the way He had purposed for us to do as individuals from the foundations of the world. Let God alone be glorified. The Bible says in Romans 8:29: *For whom He did foreknow, He also did predestine... moreover, whom he did predestine, them He also called, them he also justified: and whom He justified, He also glorified."*

It is God who calls. It is God who chooses and it is He who also anoints and uses us as He, God, wills and chooses. If this is the case, then why are we taking it upon ourselves to judge others because they are operating differently? Again, I say, let us release each other to complete the work to which we have been assigned as individuals and as a body. Let us support one another, help one another, encourage one another and fight our common enemy together. The Lord will cause His church to triumph in every situation.

As in the natural, the body is divided into various parts and each operates differently. So too is the spiritual body. Can you imagine the heart telling the kidney, "oh, see, how you operate, it is weird how you function. Ooh, this is how I function so if you don't function like me that means you are abnormal." The question is, has the heart the right or been given charge to oversee the operations of other organs?

The answer in my opinion is, No. When the Creator of the human body formed man, we were not present, but we can see how the body operates in harmony with every part functioning both independently and interdependently. In fact, I believe we can learn something from the way our physical body functions. There is harmony in our body. The interesting thing is if one part of the body aches, the rest of body reacts in respond to that attack. The body's defense mechanism quickly builds up a defense to counteract an attack on any part of the body.

It is amazing just how God Almighty has created the human body in His infinite wisdom. I believe Jesus had this in mind when He described His Church as *His Body*. Let us work in harmony and stop criticising one another, knowing that we are of one body unless otherwise discerned.

I believe the Church needs to understand what it means to be part of the Body of Christ. We may not fully know or understand how certain parts operate and, quite frankly, it is none of our business unless the church begins to preach heresies or propagate another gospel or the Lord reveals things to you.

We should not be busy-bodies. *"By their fruits, you shall know them."* God has a way of exposing the false prophets and ministers. He certainly will if they continue to destroy His people. It is the work of the devil to make us busy-bodies, to bring distraction and confusion to the Body of Christ. It is a strategy Satan has deployed to distract us from identifying the enemy and confronting him. Instead, we are criticising one another. It is time to wake up Church and know that we have one, and only one, adversary and that is Satan. I think some of us believe that it is only to us that God reveals things; we are the privileged few. This is deception and it takes me back to a story in the book of 1 Kings 22. A very interesting story showing how one Prophet slapped another Prophet simply because he deceived himself that he was the "Master Prophet" and God will not bypass him to speak through any other person.

*"²⁴But Zedekiah the son of Chenaanah went near and smote Micaiah on the cheek and said, which way went the Spirit of the*

This is how some Ministers feel today. They think they have it all. God speaks to them and them alone. This is a form of pride. Let us release one another to be who God Almighty has called us to be. Know that when God was giving you your commission or your assignment, I was not there and for this simple reason, I cannot say what you are doing is wrong if it is Bible based.

Yes, it is given to us to discern and identify the false among us, and that is the work of the Holy Spirit. Jesus said you shall know them by the fruits they produce. God has given us the Spirit to discern that which is of Him and that which is not. It is only the enemy who can bring about such a dissention in the Body of Christ over a crucial subject such as deliverance or what the Bible terms as casting out devils or demons.

What must we say then? Is the Bible to be believed totally or only when it fits our theology? Let God be true and every man a liar. If the concept of salvation remains unchanged, healing remains unchanged, then, I believe with all my heart that deliverance is and should be ongoing until Jesus comes to take us home. If the devil is allowed to win on this issue and I know he will not win, then many believers will die not experiencing the more abundant life.

Jesus promised us in John 10:10, *"The thief comes not, but for to steal, and to kill, and to destroy: I am come that they might have life, and that they might have it more abundantly."*

Think carefully about this statement that Christ made. You see, it is given unto us as spirit-filled Christians to rightly divine the word of truth. This is done by the Holy Spirit working though us, giving us the fervor to be able to rightly discern the truth, and to receive the true revelation of everything we read or study in the Word of God.

Let us surrender to Him and He will teach us.

# CHAPTER 6

# Deliverance

The Oxford dictionary's definition of deliverance is: 1. *An act or an instance of rescuing, the process of being rescued. 2. A rescue.*

From this, we can say our salvation could also be termed as deliverance. Not only can salvation be called deliverance, but it is itself also a form of deliverance. We were dead in our sins and hell-bound, but Jesus came to rescue us from eternal damnation. Our spirit man became saved - born again, saved by the blood of the Lamb. The fact that we are born again does not make everything right in and with us.

As man is a tripartite being, consisting of the spirit, soul and body, all three components must benefit from the pack of salvation. The spirit is delivered, the soul also must be delivered, and the body as well. Deliverance is, therefore, by my own definition, healing to the soul. So, in salvation, we have healing to the spirit that was "dead", a soul that was sick, and a body that may sometimes be sick as well. Deliverance is salvation extended to the soul as well as the body.

Now back to the Scripture in John 10:10 *"...but I am come that they might have it more abundantly."* Now on conversion, as we receive The Lord Jesus as our personal Saviour, we also receive life.

Remember, He is the Way, the Truth, and the Life. So as born-again Christians, we have life and, if we are able to stand and maintain our walk with the Lord, we will definitely make it to heaven. This is because we have received the "life" that is in Jesus the Christ.

The sad thing is that we do not question how to receive a "more abundant life" or how we should lay hold of it. The Master said, "That they might have". In other words, this is a matter of choice, as in all our dealings with the things of the Lord. Sometimes we think of the "more abundant life" as financial and material prosperity. To a degree, yes, but do you know we can have everything we need and yet lack peace in our lives, relationships, and marriages, and even find ourselves in bondages which seem unshakeable?

In this particular area of your life, nothing seems to shift. To the outside world, you are seen as successful, but only you alone know that you are fighting an unseen battle. You have fasted and prayed but nothing seems to move or change. This is where help is needed in the area of a higher anointing, to stand in the gap for you spiritually and also act to administer deliverance for you. Remember, Jesus came to set the captives free, to give hope to the hopeless, and to set loose the bound. It is not all about generational curses, even though they also play a part in some cases.

There is power in the Word of God. The Word that comes from anointed lips can deliver one. I watched a video of the late Dr. Morris Cerullo, during one of his World Evangelism Conferences. When the man of God spoke the Word of God; a lady with a demonic spirit was delivered instantly. In my own ministry, I have seen how effective the Word of God is in deliverance. I was ministering in an evening service when, in the middle of my message, there was a sudden violent demonic manifestation from a lady in the congregation. She began to literally mop the floor with her hair. That is the best way I can describe it. In another instance, there were two ladies who responded violently as well. One of them had her four-year-old daughter on her lap and, as I spoke the Word, she flung the child on the floor and reached for me. I rebuked the spirit in the name of Jesus and, you know, greater is He that is in me than the devil in her, so the devil had to bow to the Word.

The Word of God is very powerful. Hebrews 4:12, *"For the Word of God is quick, and powerful, and sharper than any two-edged sword, piercing even to the dividing asunder of the soul and spirit, and of the joints and marrow, and is a discerner of the thoughts and intents of the heart."* There is life in the Word!

Deliverance means to be set free from an entanglement or oppression. Deliverance means liberation from bondage. It also means to be released from a stronghold or from a wicked regime of slavery. The Bible talks about how a man called Sisera who mightily oppressed the children of Israel. He had nine hundred chariots of iron, which the children of Israel did not have to oppose this man or his mighty army. The Bible says he mightily oppressed the children of Israel and they were also intimidated by his arsenal. Sisera took advantage of the situation and, for twenty years, he oppressed them until Deborah spoke prophetically about God's promised deliverance.

Deborah pushed forward the agenda of heaven to bring *deliverance* to her people and it was then that God indeed delivered the children of Israel from this wicked regime. Judges 4:6 *"And she (Deborah) sent and called Barak the son of Abinoam out of Kedeshnaphtali, and said unto him, has not the Lord God of Israel commanded, saying, go and draw toward mount Tabor, and take with you ten thousand men of the children of Naphtali and the children of Zebulon? [7]And I will draw unto you to the river Kishon, Sisera, the captain of Jabin's army with his chariots and his multitude; and I will deliver him unto your hand."*

God brought deliverance to the children of Israel because they cried out to Him. If Deborah had not sought the Lord as a Prophetess and organized the whole thing, as led by the Lord, they would have remained in bondage and serious oppression by this wicked man, Sisera.

Beloved, God cares about every area of our life and desire for us to walk in the liberty He has given us through Christ Jesus.

Moses was sent to deliver the children of Israel from their oppressors, the Egyptians. Deliverance is as relevant today as it was then and as it was when Jesus walked the earth. If anything, we need it more today than ever because of the plagues of evil that have infested the earth. I believe there are more demons in the earth now with the advancement in technology, suppression of any dissenting voices and political correctness. These pave the way for demons to have their way. This is where the Apostle Paul warned us that, *"we wrestle not against flesh and blood but against principalities and powers..."* Ephesians 6:12.

We witness abominations taking place in the world today, propagated by people in positions of authority. Nobody dare express their opinion for fear of dire consequences if they do. Did God not give man his free will to make his own choices in life? We say democracy incorporates the freedom of speech, but why then, are we forced to accept those ideas, ideologies and lifestyles that we believe to be morally wrong and biblically unacceptable?

There are demonic forces working behind the scenes, through men, to push Satan's agenda in the world today. That is to oppress man and force us to conform or else be damned by the world. These are the powers and the rulers of darkness the Bible talks about in the book of Ephesians.

I have heard people say, "there is a voice in my heard telling me to go and kill myself." Some of us may not believe this but this is a tormenting voice of the demonic. If he or she does not get help, the demons will eventually cause this terrible outcome. I am not talking about non-believers; I am talking about people in church.

The subject needs to be taught extensively. Deliverance is needed and necessary for the church today. This generation is living a more stressful life than our predecessors did. Things do not just happen; there is always a connection in the spirit realm to what happens in the earth be it national or personal. Why do some people have premonitions and they manifest in real life? God warns us of the evil plan of the devil but some of us do not pay heed until it happens. Folks, there are unseen realms in the world and the world is controlled by the rulers of these realms.

If you check previous episodes of the Simpsons, you will see many postulated scenarios that actually came to pass years after they were featured in this cartoon. Let me tell you about a few of them; the death of the artist, Prince, the outbreak of Ebola (screened in 1997 and actually happened in 2014) The Simpsons correctly foresaw the Presidency of Donald Trump, and actually predicted the 911 attacks in 1997, four years before it happened in 2001.

How were these events so correctly predicted? The writers are either hearing from the ruling forces of darkness that are behind the occurrences or are Christian prophets who have received these revelations from God. There are powers operating from the unseen realm, controlling evil occurrences around the earth. I know some may find it difficult to believe but the Bible is clear on this. We need Jesus like the earth needs the rain.

Awake people of God and let us pray for heaven's agenda and the will of God to come on earth, *"Thy Kingdom come and thy will be done on earth as it is in heaven."* Believers, we need to pray this prayer more often than ever before as it appears that the forces of hell are advancing their agenda. Moreover, the church is growing weak in advancing the agenda of heaven. I pray that we will embrace the concept of deliverance and restore power to the universal church.

The church will not be able to demonstrate or manifest the glory of God if the majority of believers are spiritually unhealthy, oppressed and depressed by demons. Jesus *cleansed* the temple before going to the cross. He did this to prepare the temple for the outpouring of the Holy Spirit, which was to take place after His resurrection. He said, *"It is written, my house shall be called a house of prayer (fire, power) and you have made it a den of thieves (demonic infestation)" Matthew 21:13. (AMP) In verse 14 it says, "And the blind and the lame came to Him in the temple; and He healed them."*

We need the glory of God to be manifest in these last days as the end is drawing nearer and nearer. We cannot have this unless and until the temple is cleared and cleaned.

We need deliverance!

# CHAPTER 7

# Lack of Knowledge

The Bible says in Hosea 4:6 *"My people are destroyed for lack of knowledge…"*

Knowledge is very important, but it is the understanding of the knowledge and truth and its ultimate application that produces power for living a victorious life in Christ. We need to have understanding of the Word of God and know how it pertains to a particular area of your life. If we are to understand how our lives in the Lord have been arranged, how everything has been set in place for the believer from the foundation of the world, we would co-operate with the Lord in every area of our lives. The Bible says in 2 Timothy 2:19, *"Nevertheless, the foundation of God stands sure, having this seal, The Lord knows those who are His."*

He knows everything about us and He has made provision for us in every area of our lives. All we need to do is, to live with knowledge and understanding, in order to be equipped by His Word. First of all, we need to fully grasp that it is His will that we are saved, healed, delivered, restored and empowered. All these come by having knowledge of the truth and having an understanding of how to operate within this truth lest we be deceived and destroyed. The Body of Christ has been plagued with what I term, "Spiritual Illiteracy." This is interesting but very serious.

Believers today, especially from my own country, are very, very lazy in acquiring knowledge. Most believers will not take time in the Word of God, to know what is in it for them. Knowledge they may miss out on include the tricks of the devil, who the Lord is to them and much more pertaining to our lives and godliness.

Believers of today want instant gratification. They are easily deceived because they do not know the Word. This is dangerous as it makes one vulnerable and gullible and also an easy target to be preyed on by false prophets, teachers and pastors.

Do you know that half-truths are as bad as lies? A half-truth is a whole lie. It is diluted, and anything diluted loses its purity in quality. In fact, it is very dangerous. In the Garden of Eden, Eve was armed with a half-truth and that is why the serpent was able to deceive her. The Bible says in Genesis 2:9b, *"the tree of life also in the <u>midst</u> of the garden, and the tree of knowledge of good and evil." Skip to verse 16-17, "And the Lord God commanded the man, saying, of every tree of the garden thou may freely eat: <u>But the tree of the knowledge of good and evil, thou shalt not eat of it:</u> for in the day that thou eat thereof thou shalt surely die."*

Now let us look carefully at what was said by the serpent and the response from Eve. In chapter 3:1, *"...and he said to the woman, yeah hath God said, <u>ye shall not eat</u> of every tree of the garden?"* The underlined is a twisted truth. God was specific about what they should eat and what they should not eat and they were to eat the fruits of every tree except from the tree of the knowledge of good and evil.

*"And the woman said unto the serpent, we may eat of the fruits of the trees of the garden: <u>but of the fruit of the tree which is in the midst of the garden"</u> The* serpent got Eve right there because there were two trees in the midst of the Garden. The tree of Life and the tree of the knowledge of good and evil and it was only one of the two that God forbade them to eat thereof. *"God has said, ye shall not eat of it, neither shall you touch it, lest ye die".*

Do you see how the serpent twisted the information given by God and when he realised also that Eve was not well informed; he swiftly moved to sow the seed of confusion, rebellion and sin in her mind? She only mentioned one tree in the midst of the garden instead of two. Have you ever considered what if Eve had eaten the fruit from the tree of Life, which was also in the midst of the garden?

The devil does not care if you have knowledge, he will push to see if you truly understand the knowledge you have. I have asked myself many times why did not the devil go to Adam instead. And I believe he knew that Adam was well-armed with the truth. Remember the instruction was given to him before Eve was created. I also believe that Adam, on passing on the information to Eve was not detailed enough or omitted vital information about the tree of life also being in the midst of the garden.

The other thing I have also considered is, probably Eve did not pay attention to the details of the instructions. The Bible talks about taking heed to what we hear. It could be that Eve did not take heed to what she heard. I strongly believe the former is true. This is why we need to search for revelation, instruction and godly counsel in the Word for our self.

I was privileged to sit under the ministry of T.L. and Daisy Osborne during one of their programs in London, England. On this particular night, it was Daisy who ministered. I was so struck by the awesome anointing and sheer power under which the woman standing in front of me was ministering that I prayed there and then that God should make me like her. She said something during her ministration that challenged me to seek God for myself. She said in the early years of their marriage with a young child and a baby, they went to India to conduct a crusade and were fasting at the time. One afternoon, as she was attending to her child, her husband came out from the prayer room and his face was as bright as bright could be. The glory of the Lord was all over him and she asked him about it and he answered and said, "Honey, the Lord Jesus came to the room and spoke with me." Upon hearing this, her countenance dropped.

T.L. asked her, "why are you not happy for me?"

She replied, "No, I want to see Him for myself too." And lo and behold, that same afternoon, as she went in to pray after settling their child, the Lord Jesus appeared to her as well.

You can look at this with mixed feelings but that story really taught me to seek God for myself and not to base my knowledge of God on what others tell me about Him. I recommend the same for anyone who wants to know Him.

The Bible talks about a group of people called the Bereans in the book of Acts17:10-11. These were a group of Jews who, having heard the Word would conduct further research to establish for themselves if what they had received was the whole Truth or not. *"And the brethren immediately sent away Paul and Silas by night to Berea: who coming there went to the synagogue of the Jews. These were more noble than those in Thessalonica, in that they received all the word in readiness of mind, and search the Scriptures daily whether those things were so."*

Here, we see a comparison of two different sets of believers, one considered to be more noble than the other, why? Because the Bereans took time to study and to find out the truth for themselves, even after they had been preached to. The Lord, Himself, knows that knowledge is very important and the lack of it can be catastrophic to the believer. That is why He warns us in Hosea 4:6, *"My people are destroyed for lack of knowledge"* If we do not acquire knowledge, we can easily be led astray into the paths of destruction.

The book of Proverb 4:7 says, *"Wisdom is the principal thing; therefore, get wisdom: and with all thy getting get understanding."* This means the knowledge of God and to walk in the fear of God is our first and foremost priority. After that, you have to understand the whole concept of the Kingdom of our God and its principles.

Having accepted that Christ is good, and knowing His ways, comes by understanding the knowledge that we have learned about Him, and walking in His ways. The moment we come into the Kingdom of

God, as a result of an experience, of an encounter or because somebody took their time to tell us about Jesus, we come to the realisation of our need for Christ and the urgent need to know Him for ourselves. At this point, we have come to the knowledge of Christ but we do not have understanding yet of whom He really is, or what is expected of us as newborns in the Lord.

We can only know Him more intimately as we spend time with Him in prayer, fasting and in the Word. As we get to know Him more, we can understand His ways better. With our human mind, we cannot understand Him completely. We need to develop an intimacy with Him to know Him well enough to understand Him at all.

James. 2:19, *"you believe that there is one God; you do well: the devils also believe and they tremble."* Believing alone, like knowing, is not enough, but gaining insight and understanding your beliefs is the most important. Our walk with the Lord should go beyond just knowing Him as our God. Understanding of His ways that lead into the path of righteousness is vitally important.

Psalm 103:7, *"He made known His ways unto Moses, His acts unto the children of Israel."* God makes His ways known to mature believers, but unto the *babes* He demonstrates his acts, like the miracles he performed for the children of Israel, to show them He was who He said He was. He expects us to grow beyond the miracles, knowing that the miracles are our inheritance but we must grow in grace in order to be able to handle the issues of life without falling.

In the case of the children of Israel, the miracles did not change them because they lacked an understanding of the knowledge of the ways of their God that Moses re-introduced to them.

"Oh, Moses you said "The I am" says you should bring us out of bondage? OK. Let's go." (This was after much persuasion.) Then, when they saw Pharaoh's army pursuing them, they began to rain insults on Moses, saying, "are there no graves in Egypt, and you've brought us here to be swallowed by this vast sea?" This was because they did not have any understanding of the God they had been re-introduced to. He is a miracle working God, but, most importantly, He is our rescuer. Lack of knowledge makes the believer vulnerable.

This is a very dangerous situation for anybody to be in. We live in an era where people want *microwave* results and answers to their problems and needs. Many Christians today have the principle all upside down. The instruction is: *"seek ye first the Kingdom of God and his righteousness; and all other things shall be added unto you."* This is God's order. But human beings say, "give us the all the other things, then we will seek the Kingdom." Who is the boss here? Who can dictate to his or her boss the terms and conditions of employment? Would you even stand the chance of staying employed? Yet we want to dictate to The Creator as to how to handle affairs concerning us.

For this reason, we find it difficult to even embrace simple truth. The modern-day believer finds it hard to get to know God for himself or herself. You call for Bible studies and you can count on one hand, the number of people who turn up. Call for a prophetic meeting and the whole place is filled up. You ask yourself why? The answer is simple. This generation is not interested in seeking the knowledge of the Truth.

This is a hard saying but very, very true; highly sensational, loud in applause, but empty inside. There is so much hype in some meetings to the extent that you can feel the roof coming down instead of the demonic strongholds. Such people are just loud with no roots, they applaud what they do not understand and so, when they walk out of a meeting, all they can say, if you ask them how the meeting went, is that the anointing was strong or the man or woman of God was very powerful and that is it; no personal encounter with the Lord, nothing. The Bible describes them as clouds without rain.

The hype, oh the hype, is what is killing the Body of Christ today. It is all right to have an exuberant crowd and why not? Our God is an awesome God who is worthy of our praise. The Bible says to shout unto the Lord with a voice of triumph, so it is good to raise our voices in praising our God. Nevertheless, there is a time and a place. Many a minister will love the applause of the audience and why not? If the message is setting them free from their ignorance and lack of knowledge.

On the other hand, some ministers tend to feed on that applause and will load their preaching with Scriptures that will cause unnecessary shouting and screaming. An example would be if the congregation were to be asked what they had learnt from the message, they would be found wanting. I have come to recognize, rising through the ranks and in ministry, those Scriptures quoted specifically to arouse the crowds. These, when quoted, are mere words, which the Bible refers to as the letter.

An example of such is: "The wealth of the wicked is coming to you as children of God!" The response is "y-e-a-h!!!!!!!!!!!!!" accompanied by much jumping, shouting and dancing about. Some even take to running around the auditorium like crazy animals, thinking the moment it is quoted, that is it! They have the *wealth of the wicked*. The question they should ask themselves is, HOW?

Yes, how is that going to happen? Things do not just happen. It takes more than a mere quotation to bring results. If you are a believer, and you are not walking according to the principles of the Kingdom, not sowing any form of seed, not living right for the Lord, then the fear of God is not in you. So how do you then become a recipient of the wealth of the wicked? According to the Bible, you are wicked yourself, and have no right to quote His Word let alone believe it will work for you. You say, oh! That is harsh! Yes, it is, but that is the truth. Truth is always harsh to the flesh but I did not say it. Psalm. 50:14-20, *"Offer unto God thanksgiving; and pay thy vows unto the Most High, and call upon me in the day of trouble: I will deliver thee and thou shall glorify me... [16]But unto the wicked God said, what has thou to do to declare my statutes or that thou should take my covenant in thy mouth? Seeing you hate instruction, and cast my word behind thee... Thou give thy mouth to evil and thy tongue frames deceit... slanders thy own mother's son."*

This is the Word of God, and it is worth reading the whole of Psalm

50 to get the full picture. Literally, God is saying, as long as you hear His Word, time after time, and you constantly disobey it, you are wicked, and you have no right to expect any divine intervention from Him except you approach Him with true repentance. It does not matter how anointed the message is, it does not matter how much noise we make, it does not matter how much applause we give to the preaching, we will still come back empty because of our disobedience.

I believe an atmosphere that creates the presence of the Lord is what we need and not the hype. We need to take our time to expound Scriptures to the people of God, in order to equip them because lack of knowledge is killing the body of Christ. Jesus taught on deliverance and we have to follow the teachings of Christ, apply it, and demonstrate it as He has given us this charge "In my name you will cast out devils."

# CHAPTER 8

# Understanding Rulership

There is a need to understand the way the Kingdom of God operates in terms of rulership. From the beginning, man was given the authority to rule (have dominion) over everything in the earth realm. This God given authority was lost to the devil when man fell. The devil cunningly stole it from man. Now, in order for us to regain this authority and dominion, Christ came to dispossess the enemy of the stolen right to rule the earth. Christ gave back to man the legitimate right to rule the earth realm again. Praise God forevermore!

Now we have to bear in mind that Satan has had dominion over the earth and its inhabitants for a very long time and for this reason, he has infiltrated the minds of "his subjects." He has corrupted almost all of them, destroyed some of them, and lured others to worship him as their lord. As a matter of fact, before the Messiah came on the scene, we were all subjects of sin, and, for that matter, slaves to Satan. A slave, according to the Oxford dictionary, is a *person who is the legal property of another, and is bound to absolute obedience. 2. A helpless victim of some dominating influence.* There are other definitions but these two will suffice for our study right now.

From these definitions, we can better understand the state of man, before Jesus came to earth to set us free; we were *helpless victims* of a satanic dominating influence. In short, we were slaves of the devil until Jesus paid the price for our liberation and bought us back. Nevertheless, we have to realise that the psychological wounds suffered by living according to the dictate of this evil dictator's regime haunt some of us still. These wounds, if not dealt with, become a doorway for the evil one to come in to attack us. How does this attack happen?

This is not a physical attack but a spiritual one with a physical manifestation. What happens is that demons are assigned to isolate you from the things that might draw you closer to the Lord Jesus and His people. The devil's next move is to make you believe that his ways are the only way out for his victims, that is to say, there is no other way out but to stay bound to him. Sometimes he promises friendship, success, wealth and fame. If this is accepted, then Satan has regained his rule over your life again.

Satan then moves into the next phase of his attack; to oppress, suppress and possess his victims. At this point, he is in full control of the person's mind. He is now the ruler of this individual. He calls the shots; he dictates their life pattern.

One might think I am not talking about believers here: Oh yes I am. I have seen people come to church and become fully committed because of a need they are trusting the Lord for. I have seen the same get blessed by God and gradually fade away. When you call them to check on them, they come up with excuses to a point where they no longer answer your call. It's goodbye to church.

What has happened is, they have been distracted and deceived. The devil tells them, "now that you have received what you needed you no longer need God, you can make it all by yourself", and they believe him.

We have to keep it in mind that the devil still has a great deal of power on earth. As long as the whole earth is not *born again*, there are still devil-worshippers, there is disobedience in the house of the Lord, there is rebellion in the Body of Christ, as long as righteousness is fading fast from the lives of believers and as long as we continue to wallow in ignorance of the need for deliverance for the people of God today, the devil is happily regaining those territories he once lost.

Do not forget that Satan is the one questioning the Word of God, twisting it and causing controversy in order to create and spread a false doctrine through some people of faith to achieve his evil desires in the world today. Let us see what the Master said in Matthew 12:43, *"when the unclean spirit is gone out of a man, he walks through dry places, seeking rest, and finds none. Then he says, I will return into my house from whence I came out; and when he is come finds it empty, swept and garnished... and the last state of that man is worse than the first."*

Every preacher, who professes that a believer cannot be demonised, should think again. Ponder over these very words that the Lord Himself spoke. Even if the fact that a believer can be possessed is disputed, what do you make of the fact that, after one is born again, they can revert to a lifestyle of sin, the same lifestyle from which they had been redeemed? Will Satan flee from you or will he be laughing his way back inside of you by assigning several more wicked spirits to make sure you never escape from his grip again.?

This is exactly what Jesus is saying here. Can we then say: once saved, forever saved? Jesus taught us that is not the case. He did not leave us ignorant but has warned us. If the Lord, Himself, has spoken on this very topic of demon possession and deliverance, then who are we to discredit it?

Jesus came to set the captives free. He also taught us that the same captives, having been set free, could be "recaptured" if they do not abide by the rules of the Master who paid the price for their freedom. Like prisoner released after serving their sentence only to re-offend and be imprisoned again. This is because they could not conform to the law or the terms of their liberation. This is the best way In which to bring home the phenomenon of a Christian being demon possessed.

In order to reign with Him, we must maintain and guard the territory that has been restored to us by our Lord Jesus Christ and even gain more grounds. That is to say we need to grow in the things of God, we have to live right or else we shall fall back into the "snare of the fowler", the devil. The devil hates defeat and will not waste any time in fighting to recapture anyone who once was delivered from his shackles, has decided to walk in the righteous ways of God.

Remember, the Bible says he is the accuser of the brethren. Satan goes before God to accuse us. Why would he go to this length to humiliate himself before the host of Heaven? It is because he knows that God is a principled God and will not violate his own principles, but will punish sin. In other words, Satan knows that if he goes to put our sins before the Lord, he can then petition for our souls. Do not forget, Satan lived with God; he was an anointed cherub who covered God with worship, so he knows exactly what his rights are concerning a sinful or an iniquitous believer.

He devil goes to God to test the waters to see if he, Satan, gets an opportunity to make accusations against you and, in so doing, gain access to your life and soul. This he will do just to get you to utter words that will give him the chance to get you to sin and more so, he can once more take control over your life. In Job 1:6-7, Satan was present when the Angels of God assembled before God. *"[7]And the LORD said unto Satan, "whence cometh thou?" Then Satan answered the LORD, and said, "from going to and fro in the earth and from walking up and down in it." [8]And the Lord said to Satan, "hast thou considered my servant Job, that there is none like him on the earth, a perfect and an upright man, one that fears God and eschews (shuns) evil?" [9]Then Satan answered the Lord, and said, "does Job fear God for nothing? Hast not thou made a hedge about him, and about his house and about all that he has on every side? Thou have blessed the work of his hands, and his substance is increased in the land." [12]And the Lord said unto Satan, "behold all that he has is in thine power, only upon himself put not forth thine hand." So, Satan went forth from the presence of the Lord."*

Do you know why Satan went to this length concerning Job? He had located a doorway in Job's life. With all his uprightness, Job had fear in him and was constantly offering sacrifices for fear of losing it all. This is found in Job 3:25, *"For the thing which I greatly feared is come upon me and that which I was afraid of is come unto me. I was not in safety, neither had I rest, neither was I quiet; yet trouble came."* This tells me Job was constantly in fear of losing everything including his children. Look at the phrase he used "I greatly feared." This gave Satan the legal doorway to petition to attack Job.

I am not saying Job had sinned by being afraid. The Bible encourages us not to fear as fear has torment, and yet Job was consistently afraid of the tormentor. This paints a picture for the devil that Job did not have faith that God will preserve him and all that belongs to him; hence the challenge. Bear in mind that Satan is always looking for opportunities to attack and if possible, regain dominance over us. We need to understand that being delivered, and staying that way, is a vital biblical principle, program and promise for all believers.

# CHAPTER 9

# Get Understanding

The book of Proverbs says in chapter 4 from verse 5, *"Get wisdom, get understanding... ⁷wisdom is the principal thing; therefore, get wisdom: and with all thy getting get understanding."*

You know the Bible says it is only a fool who has said in his heart, there is no God. The opposite of fool is wise. It can go this way; the wise has acknowledged in his heart that there is God. In other words, wisdom is the knowledge of God, and the author of Proverbs is saying, first and foremost for us to get to know God and upon that get understanding.

I ask, understanding of what? It is the understanding of the knowledge of the Truth. Some of us know about God; we confess and believe and are born again, but it has to go deeper than that. We have to know Him intimately for ourselves.

The children of Israel knew only of the acts of God. He was their God but having been under oppression for a long time they forgot this God each time they faced a challenging situation. Even when God was re-introduced to them, it was really difficult for them to embrace and trust in Him, all because they lacked any understanding of the knowledge of who God actually is. They knew God only as the God of their fathers. They knew God based on what their fathers said about God. And because of that, they could not get to know who God actually is to them as a generation.

Even though they witnessed miracle after miracle, each time they faced a new challenge, they froze and attacked Moses. Had they known God intimately, they would have understood His ways and that every challenge was clearing the way and moving them closer to their promised land.

Any husband knows that, at a particular time of the month, his wife goes through changes that affect the way she conducts herself. A husband may know this but still takes it casually and say hurtful comments, which only add to an already bad situation. In such a case, there is a lack of understanding.

Another husband will have the same knowledge but will research what is actually going on in his wife body. This husband will now be sympathetic and supportive because he understands what is happening. Both husbands have the knowledge but the second husband went further to get understanding and so could deal with the issue properly. We, too, have peace when we know and understand what is happening around us.

The children of Israel moaned, complained, and murmured against Moses all through their journey in the wilderness because they did not have understanding in the things of God. Lack of knowledge is dangerous but lack of understanding is much deadlier. If you do not have understanding of the truth that you profess to know, the devil will come with his twisted truth as in the Garden of Eden. He will deceive you into sinning against God and will re-arrest you into his snare.

We know that Satan is our adversary but we have to also understand how he operates in order to resist him. As the Bible says in James 4:7b, *"Resist the devil and he will flee from you, and walk blameless before God."* What shall we say to these sayings of the Lord Jesus Christ in Mark 16:17-18, *"And these signs shall follow them that believe; In my name, they shall cast out devils; they shall speak with new tongues; they shall take up serpents; and if they drink any deadly thing, it shall not hurt them; they shall lay hands on the sick, and they shall recover."*

Are we seeing this Scripture being fulfilled? Yes! Do we see divine healing? The answer is, yes. Do we see demonic manifestations in some of the brethren in our churches? Again, the answer is, yes. The dead are being raised and many, many more notable miracles are happening around the world just as Jesus said it would be. Why then are we watering down the ministration of deliverance? It is about time the Body of Christ woke up from this deception and error, and embrace the FULL GOSPEL of Jesus Christ. One may then ask, what is the full gospel of Jesus? It is Salvation, Deliverance and Healing.

Once I listened to a man of God preaching on a Christian TV channel, He was seriously condemning the concept of generational curses and deliverance. He emphatically said there is no such thing as deliverance in the Bible. Basically, he said the word, Deliverance, is not in the Bible, period! He was so angry that it was clear he had not even taken his time to look up the word in the Bible. In 2 Kings 5:1 the Bible says Naaman was used by God to bring deliverance to

Syria.

*"Now Naaman, captain of the host of the king of Syria, was a great man, and honorable, because by him the Lord had given deliverance unto Syria: he was also a mighty man in valor."* What does deliverance mean? It means to rescue. The Lord used Naaman to rescue a people at a particular time.

In Genesis 45:7, *"And God sent me before you to preserve your posterity in the earth, and to save your lives by a great deliverance."* We know by the Scriptures that to ultimately bring deliverance to the people of Israel, God orchestrated Joseph's betrayal. There are many other Scriptures concerning deliverance.

Let me take you to Exodus 3:7-8. *"And the Lord said, I have surely seen the affliction of my people which are in Egypt, and have heard their cry by reason of their taskmasters; for I know their sorrows; And I am come down to deliver them out of the hand of the Egyptians..."* The book of Exodus is a book of deliverance.

Based on these Scriptures, and many others, the subject is clearly not for debates, rather it is established in the Word of God. Does the Bible not say Jesus came to set the captive free? Is that not deliverance? Was Jesus not casting out demons from people? Was that not deliverance?

Did Jesus not give instructions to His disciples after He commissioned them to go and preach the gospel that they should also cast out devils? Mark 16:17 *"And these signs shall follow them that believe; In my name, they shall cast out devils."* This command was not limited to the disciples, but to everyone that believes. Even demons asked Jesus, "have you come to torment us before our time?" They begged Him not to send them to the deep.

A fellow trusted Minister friend of mine once asked me a question: where did all the demons that Jesus cast out go? My immediate response was, do you know I have never thought about that, but now you are asking me, my answer is nowhere, they are still on the earth, as demons don't die. It is clear from this question and answer that, as they possessed human beings then, so are they doing today. As a matter of fact, demonic forces have increased in number and grown more sophisticated and wicked now. We need understanding into the ways people behave and deal with these demonic entities, but if we are left debating the subject, then we are giving the devil a hiding place from which he can freely afflict the people of God and destroy the church. If people are demonised, the devil can easily use them to bring chaos to the church.

When the Pharisees tried to debate with Jesus over the subject of not washing their hands as their tradition demands, He gave them a good lecture about what they should rather do. In *Matthew 15:15,* *"Then answered Peter and said to Him, declare to us this parable, in other words, explain this that you have said and the Lord said, are you also yet without <u>understanding?"</u>*

# CHAPTER 10

# WHY DELIVERANCE?

Jesus saw the need for deliverance and recommends it as part of His salvation plan. *Luke 4:17-18, "And there was delivered to Him the book (the Torah) of the Prophet Isaiah , and when He had opened the book, He found the place where it was written, [18]The Spirit of the Lord is upon Me, because He has anointed Me to preach the gospel to the poor; He has sent me to heal the brokenhearted. To preach <u>deliverance</u> to the captives, and recovering of sight to the blind, to set at liberty them that are bruised. [19]To preach the acceptable year of the Lord... [21]And He began to say to them, this day is this Scripture fulfilled in your ears."*

After this Jesus began His Ministry, as described above. He did everything by the book because He was anointed to do just that. *Matthew 10:1, "And when He had called to Him His twelve disciples, He gave them power against the unclean spirits, to cast them out, and to heal all manner of sickness and all manner of disease... [7]and as you go, preach, saying, the Kingdom of heaven is at hand. [8]Heal the sick cleanse the lepers, raise the dead, cast out devils."*

As in the case of the children of Israel, there ought to be a case of oppression, affliction or bondage before we can talk about deliverance. The Bible says, *"All have sinned and have come short of the glory of God."* Sin becomes a reproach and brings about a spiritual and emotional death. This all as a result of satanic influence and control, making us slaves to sin. "Slaves to sin", means the devil is the slave master who will stop at nothing to oppress and suppress his subjects. We, however, serve a God who cares about our total well-being; spiritually, emotionally, physically and financially.

3 John 2 says, *"Beloved, I wish above all things that thou may prosper and be in health even as thy soul prospers."* God cares about every area of our lives. This is the reason Jesus Christ came down to earth. It is an awesome reality that, as God the Father saw the affliction of His people and came down to deliver them from Egypt, in the New Testament, God the Son saw the affliction of His people and came down to deliver us. God went further to send down God the Holy Spirit to help us maintain our deliverance.

One may well ask if confessing Jesus as our Lord and Saviour is not good enough to set us free. The answer is both yes and no. The Exodus of the children of Israel clearly shows the Lord God Almighty bringing salvation to all, by the hand of Moses. You may say this is so confusing, but, no, it is not. Definitely not!

The devil will make us think this because he does not want God's people to understand what deliverance is, nor why we need it. It is a straightforward matter, just like everything in the Bible. God's Word is not complicated, as some would have us believe.

Salvation is a broad subject depending on the angle from which you approach it. We have salvation in the spirit; being born again. Salvation in the soul is deliverance, and physical salvation is healing. These are the three dimensions of Salvation, which can be used interchangeably.

What do you do with someone who dabbled in witchcraft and the occult and later gave their life to Christ? Do you, as a minister, lead them through the sinner's prayer and leave it at that? By accepting Jesus as their personal saviour, does the story end there? The answer is, no. Such a person once served a master, Satan. Satan has demonic forces that do his bidding on earth. In a similar manner, Jesus has believers to do His biddings; but before the Lord uses a believer, He first empowers him or her. This is done through the power of the Holy Spirit.

The Bible tells us that, the gifts of God are irrevocable. This is why Satan brought down his God-given powers, which were contaminated and perverted because iniquity was found in him. This is what he has been using rebelliously against God. Similarly, before the devil uses anyone, he will have to empower that person by his evil spirits or demonic forces of darkness.

So, the big question is, does the mere confession of Jesus Christ automatically expel those demonic spirits who had once empowered this Satanist who has become born again? The answer is, No! The spirit of the person is born again, but the soul needs cleansing to expel the demons living in the person. The Holy Spirit indwell in us the moment we receive Christ as our Lord and personal saviour. In the same way, when someone consults or willingly joins any form of occult or is initiated into any form of satanic work or activity, demons are released to carry out their master, Satan's biddings.

In our example, the devils ought to be cast before he or she can be totally free to serve a new master, Jesus. This does not simply apply to only those who dabbled in idolatry or satanic worship, but everybody. There are levels but we were all under the influence of the devil, committing one sin or another. This is what the Bible describes as, our sinful nature or the "Old Man."

The Apostle Paul was converted and yet in Romans 7, he spoke about his struggle to do the things that are good and expected of a believer. In verse 15 he says, *"For that which I do I allow not: for what I would, that do I not; but what I hate that do I. [16]If then I do that which I would not ... Now then it is no more I that do it but sin that dwells in me. [18]For I know that in me (that is, in my flesh,) dwells no good thing: for no will is present with me; but how to perform that which is good I find it not. [19]For the good that I would, I do not: but the evil which I would not, that I do. [20]Now if I do that which I would not, it is no more I that do it but sin that dwells in me. [2] I find then a law, that, when I would do good, evil is present with me. [22]For I delight in the law of God after the inward man: [23]But I see another law in my members, warring against the law of my mind, and bringing me into captivity to the law of sin which is in my members. [25]O wretched man that I am! Who shall deliver me from the body of this death?"*

The Apostle was not alone and neither are we. This is the struggle every human being goes through on a daily basis. One time the Holy Spirit said to me, "do you know the Old Man doesn't go or hasn't gone anywhere?" As I pondered over this, He said to me, "the Old Man is your soul and it is only subdued or kept in conformity with the spirit by the Word of God and prayer."

If the *old man*, the soul, leaves man, man will be incomplete and there will be no living simply because the mind, the will, the emotion and the intellect are what makes us live. At the same time, it is the soul that can cause us to sin if not kept under control by prayer and the Word. Paul, the Apostle, pleaded with believers to make a conscious effort to live right for the Lord in Romans 12. In verse 2 he tells us why and how to do that. *"And be not conformed to this world: but be ye transformed by the renewing of your mind, that ye may prove what is that good, and acceptable, and perfect will of God."* God desires for His people to live a holy and righteous life, which can only be achieved by constantly renewing our minds in the Word of God.

As a baby-Christian, I saw demonic manifestations in meetings and I saw what the devil does to people who he calls his own, his wives, or traitors. Some manifestations were so bizarre that in my mind, even as a baby Christian, I knew it was only the power of God that could deliver such a person. I saw and heard people speaking languages that they could not speak or understand in the natural. There were so many things that I witnessed with my own eyes and heard with my own ears.

Such spectacles only served to cause my own faith to grow both fast and strong. It was a miracle! In my Presbyterian background, I had never known or heard anything like it before. Just like my conversion; nobody can tell me it is not real. It is very, very real. The instant change and abandonment of things in which I was involved and engaged, was such a testimony to my work colleagues who were amazed at my instant transformation. This made many of them gave their lives to the Lord.

Thank God that I was born again in a place where I witnessed the deliverance of many who were oppressed, depressed, suppressed and possessed, by the devil and his demon spirits. Prior to my encounter with the Lord, I was a sceptic who would question anything that was strange. I would and even make jokes about such things. However, after many years in the Lord, I know exactly what to do now when I encounter demonic manifestations.

There are the extreme cases, and anyone who has come out of Satanism or witchcraft or any form of the occult, will tell you they were delivered before the Lord could use them. He now really uses them for His glory. Books like "He came to set the captives free" and others by Rebecca Brown M.D, "From witchcraft to Christ" by Doreen Irvine, and many others all correspond with what I had experienced as a *baby* Christian. It cannot all be coincidental that converted Satanists in Africa, America, Europe and other parts of the world all say the same things after their conversion. It shows the satanic realm is real, his rule in darkness is real, and his kingdom is real and not an imagination, as others would have us believe. If it were so the Bible would not have taught about deliverance.

So, why do we need deliverance? The answer is simple. We need to be totally free from the bondage or entanglement that we are or have been in. You and I may not have been involved in Satanism or any form of witchcraft but we indulged in many sins that opened the door of our soul for demons to enter. Remember what Jesus said in John 10:10, *"the thief cometh not, but for to steal, kill, and to destroy: I am come that they might have life, and that they might have it more abundantly."*

We need deliverance to have the *more abundant* life promised by Jesus. When we accept Jesus, we have life immediately. The Word of God says Jesus is the Way, the Truth, and the LIFE. The moment we receive Him, He comes to live in us. In other words, life comes into us, and so we have *Life*, but the *abundant life* comes when the thief is arrested by the Holy Ghost and cast out of our lives. Do not forget, he stole the heart of man from God the Creator, and enticed man to rebel against God as he, Satan has done.

God made us in His own likeness and image, and for His own purpose and design: to have fellowship with Him and to have dominion over His creation on earth. The devil stole this dominion from us and made man his slaves instead. The devil has a problem when we become born again. What he hates and resents most, is, when he is evicted from his "habitation".

Before we were saved, sin dwelt in our hearts, and where sin is, Satan rules, making us his subjects. In other words, Satan and sin both occupied the throne of our hearts. Becoming a Christian is a threat to his reign, but not as great as the threat of deliverance.

Deliverance totally strips him of every power that he has over the believer. One may say or think differently, but be patient as I explain this.

A man who once was a womanizer becomes born again and, for some time, seems to have overcome his habit, but is suddenly confronted by this problem again. I have known some men in the Kingdom of God who had this problem before coming to the Lord and everything seems to be going fine for them, until they suddenly find themselves in the same trap again.

One may easily say it is their fault and that they gave in to lust. What is lust? Besides its definition, it is a spirit. The devil will not tempt you with something that is not already in you. And how did he know that it is in you, if he did not put it there? I am not saying all lust is demonic even though it might be. What I am asking here is: why would a mighty man of God, who God has been using mightily, fall for lustful sin? It is because, on conversion, nobody took their time to counsel him and totally dethrone the enemy of our souls and fully enthrone the Lover of our souls? Think about that.

Everyone had, and still has, weaknesses in areas of our lives that require attention. I am referring to the prevalent sins that are literally overpowering. We seem not to have any control over such sins. I have seen people who were instantly delivered from drugs, alcohol and other addictions, and I have seen others who, after their conversion, continued to struggle with the same or similar issue. I have often questioned why it happens this way and have come to know that God, in His sovereign power and infinite wisdom, cannot be questioned. He does everything according to His plans and purposes.

I do not know nor can I explain why God does certain things the way He does. All I know to do is to trust Him even if it does not make sense. I have also come to learn that it is best left to God when it does not make sense. For He has said He will take the foolish things of the world to confound the wise.

The bottom-line is: let us apply what He has taught us and be free from oppression. Proverbs 3:5 says, *"Trust in the Lord with all thine heart; and lean not to thine own understanding."* I cannot even begin to try to question the Sovereign God concerning His ways of doing things. He is the Creator of all things, Master of all things and He knows all things. He does whatever He pleases with His own creation!

A colleague of mine was converted in a unique way that showed how only God could touch a man like him. Everything about this young man was a miracle. He had serious addictions with alcohol, cigarette, gambling and sex; just to mention a few. He hid these all very well from his wife and those of us who thought we knew him well. Yet, when God touched him, he was delivered instantly from them all. To the extent that, when he tried to drink wine, he vomited. Now God is using him mightily. Still, I have seen some men of God, anointed men of God for that matter, struggling with one addiction or another. What do we say to that? I do not know.

All I know and can say is they need help in the area of deliverance. Even within the secular world, it is accepted that people with any form of addiction require rehabilitation. Hence the formation of Alcoholic Anonymous (AA) and similar organizations. That is the world's way of weaning them off addiction.

So what is the Church's way? Deliverance! I am not speaking against Alcoholics Anonymous or Gambling Anonymous, but how often do we hear of a person returning to their addiction after a year or so of being "clean".

It is only Jesus who delivers and totally sets the captives free.

# CHAPTER 11

# Kinds of Deliverance

There two major kinds of deliverance:
1. Self–administered deliverance
2. Assisted-deliverance

What I call self-deliverance is acknowledging certain problems in our lives and crying out to God for deliverance. Examples of such problems are: extreme anger, lies, envy, jealousy, some kinds of lust, pride and many other works of the flesh. These are the basics for deliverance.

I remember, as a child who was very much abused, I grew up to be a very rebellious girl. I was full of anger and was always ready to defend myself in whichever way or by whatever means necessary. My slogan was 'if you hurt me, I will make sure I hurt you, double'. I built a strong wall around my heart to the extent that I said to myself; nobody is ever going to hurt me again. This was when I reached adolescence.

What I did not know was that inside of me was a well of anger and pain. For this reason, anyone who tried to hurt me received the shock of his or her life at the sheer venom that proceeded out of my mouth. Although I maintained a quiet exterior, I was very aggressive when provoked. I made sure to give a double portion in return if anyone hurt me. In my rage, I could have killed!

When I became born again, I was filled with the Holy Ghost, endowed with the gift of prophecy and much more, but this anger was still in me. I began to worry about it because I knew it was not godly. The problem was that I had not been taught that there was a problem. The Bible says *He is our present help in times of need*. I love the Lord with all my heart but I still had anger, wrath and bitterness deeply embedded within my soul.

One morning, as I settled down following my nightshift, I turned on my television set to the God channel and there was a man of God by name of Derek Prince. He was teaching on the topic, "The basics for Deliverance." Something caught my attention and I decided to stay awake to listen to him before going to bed. In fact, the teaching was all for me. It described the anger, wrath and other things that concerned me. From that day on, I began to cry unto the Lord for deliverance, as I understood it from the teachings.

It was a struggle. Let me tell you, God will always let you know if you have been cleared or not. At one point, I would rejoice that I am free only for something to happen to provoke me and my response would prove otherwise. It took a long time, but Jesus is my victor and today I can handle any form of provocation and go home and cry unto the Lord without fighting for myself. It is becoming easier after every attack, or should I say, every test or trial, I am learning to love those who do awful things to me. Hallelujah, for the Lord God, omnipotent, reigns! Indeed, He came to set the captives free. I was a prisoner of my childhood oppressors who abused me. Had I not received this teaching by Derek prince, the enemy would have embedded his demons in my soul, to torment me even though I am born again. This is an example of self-deliverance based upon the Word of God and prayer.

The Word of God works on its own because there is power in it. The application of the anointed Word of God can set the captive free. Try it, it works. Remember, the anointed Word is Jesus Himself. *"How shall they hear without a preacher, and how shall they preach except they be sent?"* Romans 10:15. God has sent (anointed) some people for specific work in the Kingdom, and that is why, when these release His Word, He honors it. That is, doing exactly that for what the Word was released. There is power in the Word.

This is just an example of self-deliverance. Confessing and praying the "deliverance" over the specific areas that seem to get the better of you, can administer self-deliverance. The Bible says in Hebrews. 4:12, *"For the Word of God is quick, and powerful, and sharper than any two-edged sword, piercing even to the dividing asunder of soul and spirit, and of the joints and marrow, and is a discerner of the thoughts and intents of the heart."*

God knows everything about me and in me, and if I sincerely call upon Him and not try to hide, He will come and save me. Anything that seems to make people question your Christianity, is worth looking at and seeking God's touch. The thing is, next to God, we know ourselves best. Let us not take all criticism as dislike. We should be able to take constructive criticism and not utterly dismiss it, but rather diligently consider what is being said about you. We have to be open to the Holy Spirit and His correction, which mostly comes in the form of conviction, or through our fellow human beings. When this happens, please do pay heed and cry out to the Lord for help.

I have learned from the Holy Spirit that we cannot be honest with God if we are not honest with ourselves first. 2 Corinthians 13:5, *"Examine yourselves, whether you are in the faith; prove your own selves. Know you not your own selves, how that Jesus Christ is in you, except you are reprobates?"*

You should be the best assessor of your own self, who you are and who you are not. You also have to acknowledge you have a need, before God can and will help you. Sometimes our first reaction is to be defensive when good friends tell us about those areas in our lives we need to address. We feel insulted, we feel we are being attacked, we feel people do not like us, but the truth of the matter is, we need help; period! If you find yourself being accused of the same thing over and over again by different people, then know that there is a problem there. Two, three or four people cannot all be wrong. Know then that it is time to seek God in prayer to reveal the *real you* to you.

One man of God says; if one person calls you an ass or a donkey, ignore him. If two people call you an ass or a donkey, begin to look for hoof prints. But if three people call you a donkey or an ass, get a saddle. This basically means the first time someone tells you something about yourself, you can choose to ignore it or dismiss it. The second time the same criticism shows up from different people, think deeply about it and begin to consider it seriously and, if necessary, seek God and counseling from your Pastor.

If nothing is done about it and you believe you are okay, you are deceiving yourself. When different sets of people point out the same fault or weakness, then know that you are what they say you are. No doubt about it. Get a saddle because you are a donkey.

Bear in mind that the Bible says in Proverbs 27:6, *"faithful are the wounds of a friend; but the kisses of an enemy are deceitful "* It is only those who truly love you who will lovingly point out your flaws. Your refusal to accept this shows there is a measure of pride in you which also needs to be dealt with. This pride is a spirit, which needs to be expelled from the believer's life. The Bible says in Proverbs 28:14, *"happy is the man that fears always: but he that hardened his heart shall fall into mischief."* This means, walk in the fear of the Lord and yield to His Spirit of Truth that convicts us of our sins and faults. *Mischief* is the consequence we bring upon ourselves when we do not surrender all to the Lord.

Self- deliverance is basically calling upon the Lord in all sincerity, and being prepared to co-operate with the Holy Spirit to deliver you through the Word and your obedience. I remember an incident that took place at work, years ago, when a particular co-worker set out to smear me with fabrications and lies. She could not stand me witnessing to some of our co-workers so she took it upon herself to discredit me. I was able to resist counter attacking her for three years. For these three years I suffered at the hands of this lady. I complained to the Lord repeatedly in my prayers and the Lord sustained me and strengthened me.

However, there came a day when she did the unthinkable. She stood in front of the staff in my section and cursed me. At this, I completely lost it. I felt overcome by darkness and I went after her to really beat her up. I know there will be a gasp from some readers but, yes, I did, and I was born again.

God used people to intervene at various points as I tried, in more than one way, to teach her a lesson. As expected, word quickly spread that set tongues wagging. The old devil was telling me, "You said you are a Christian. You preach to people. Your testimony is now in tatters."

I was tormented by the devil as he used various people to say hurtful things about my Christianity. On one occasion, a brother in the Lord approached me and handed over a bit of Scripture: 1 Thessalonians 5:22, thinking, I knew what that Scripture said. This made me angry because I felt he was judging me. I took out my Bible during my break time to confirm the verse and, behold, it was exactly what I thought it was; *"abstain from all appearances of evil."* One translation says flee from all appearances of sin.

As I read through this piece of Scriptures, I was boiling up with anger, preparing myself to confront this brother to find out why he gave me the reading. At this point, the Holy Spirit asked me "is it a bad exhortation?"

"No", I said.

He then asked me "If no, then why are you getting filled with this much anger?"

I felt like a balloon that had been pricked with a pin and immediately felt deflated and repentant. Now guess the first person I met on my way back from my break? The brother I was getting ready to attack for giving me the Scripture. I realised then the trap the enemy was setting for me to disgrace myself and my God again; but God worked it out for my good.

When I said to the young man, "oh, thank you for the word of exhortation, I really appreciate that", you could see the shock on his face and that was when I knew his intention was not to help me but to provoke me more into anger but glory be to God who causes us to triumph at all times if we listen to his voice of correction.

The Bible says in Psalm 19:12, *"who can understand his errors? Cleanse thou me from secret faults keep back thy servant also from presumptuous sins; let them not have dominion over me: then shall I be upright, and I shall be innocent from the great transgression"*

Cleansing is a form of deliverance. This is the cleansing of the soul. Remember this is the will of God for us, as He clearly tells us in the Word in 2 John 2, *"Beloved, I wish above all things that you may prosper and be in health even as your soul prospers"* God is interested in our well-being at every point and every level. At this stage, it is just you and the Holy Spirit. You do not need anybody to administer deliverance to you. Know that as you call upon Him to help you overcome, He will surely come to your aid.

Isaiah 35:4, *"Say to them that are of a fearful heart, be strong, fear not: behold, your God will come with vengeance, even God with recompense; He will come and save you."*

In some cases, you will need teaching and counseling. For instance, in cases stemming from an abusive background, you will have to be walked through the pain and be assured that nothing you did justified what you went through. This is especially important when dealing with childhood abuse. The devil has a way of making us feel that we are the problem, not our abusers and, for this reason, we live blaming ourselves and thinking something is wrong with us. The devil is a liar, do not take his lays on board and do not live and suffer in condemnation. Jesus Christ our Lord, who is our Strong Deliverer, took away our guilt and condemnation. So know that you can be set free. Yes! You can be free. Be free in the name of Jesus.

The second deliverance is the kind that requires someone who is anointed with authority for deliverance. There is a higher level of anointing required to have power over the demonic powers.

Do you remember when a man came to Jesus with a complaint about His disciples' inability to cast out the demons from his child? Although Jesus rebuked them, He concluded by saying in Matthew 17:21, *"...howbeit this kind goes not out but by prayer and fasting."* In this story you see the disciples, even though empowered by the Master, could not cast out this particular demon as it was too strong for their level of power or, should I say, anointing. This was a demon spirit of infirmity, and Jesus was teaching us through this episode that, as there are levels of demonization, different levels of anointing are required to expel them. I know this will raise a few eyebrows but it is simple and Biblical.

The Disciples had the Word outside them (Jesus) and not within then (Holy Spirit), and consequently their obedience was not complete. You see, when we accept Christ, we receive a measure of power to operate at some level of faith and anointing but it is our obedience to the Word of God that gives us authority in the realms of the spirit. As a minister you cannot live in disobedience and tackle demons. No. The demons will either expose you or even hurt you or your family. It calls for holiness and walking in the fear of the Lord.

Authority and power go hand in hand. You need both in order to operate in the anointing of God. There is nothing like, *I have authority and not power,* even though some try to operate in the power alone without authority, and that is dangerous.

The greater anointing I am talking about is the level at which you encounter weird manifestation, declarations of cursing, threats and even pleas from demonic spirits. The sceptics might attribute this to the fact that the person is suffering from a type of fever. Funny, isn't it? Where there is a power clash, the least will always beg for mercy or try to strike a deal with the strongest. If you have ever watched a wrestling match you would have realised this. When one wrestler is locked in an extremely uncomfortable position, he has to plead by raising his hand in surrender, before he is released. Until then, he continues to suffer at the hands of the stronger opponent.

The same is true with the Holy Spirit and the powers of darkness.

Demons will never manifest where there is no anointing of the Holy Ghost. It is only the presence of the most-High God that causes a demonic reaction or manifestation. In Luke 8:27, there is a power clash between Jesus and the devil and there is an immediate manifestation of the demons that tormented this man.

Let us see what the Bible says from Luke's account. *"And when He went forth to land, there met Him out of the city a certain man, which have devils long time, and wear no clothes neither abode in any house, but in the tombs. [28]When he saw Jesus, he cried out, and fell down before Him and with a loud voice said, what have I to do with thee, Jesus, thou Son of God Most High? I beseech thee torment me not. [29]for He had commanded the unclean spirit to come out of the man... [30]and Jesus asked him saying, what is your name? And he said, Legion: for many devils were entered into him. [31]and they besought Him that He would not command them to go out into the deep."*

Do you get the picture from the earlier illustration? Whenever the presence of the Most-High God shows up, devils react because they are overwhelmed and overpowered by the awesome power and presence of God. Is the same power that raised Christ from the dead, still operating through God's people today? The answer is a big, YES. So why are we allowing the enemy to deceive us so he can hold us prisoners out of our own ignorance? It is time for the Body of Christ to embrace the concept of deliverance and walk in total liberty. Jesus came to set the captives free!

In our everyday life, if you buy or move into a new house, you clean it to your personal satisfaction and standard. Sometimes the previous owner might even leave certain things in it, thinking you might like them. We throw them away and replace them with our own, even if we have to buy new ones. This is how God deals with us. Remember, He bought us with a price, a very costly price, (1 Cor. 6:20) and will not tolerate anything of the former landlord in us. He wants to get rid of the things left in us and replace it with Himself. Some may argue, saying a believer does not need deliverance because they have been bought by the Blood of Jesus and are therefore saved. This is true to a degree. Jesus said in John 10:10, "...*I am come that they might have life, and that they might have it more abundantly.*"

We have Life because we have been bought by the blood. As a result, if we walk in the ways of God and seek to please Him in all that we do, we will no doubt go to heaven. The *more abundant life* is when we are totally set free from our former landlord and the garbage left in us. We are able to enjoy all the benefits that come from being born again including walking in perfect peace, walking in good health, being victors in every area of our lives, overcoming poverty, experiencing victory in all situations and much more.

*"For He was wounded for our transgressions, bruised for our iniquities, the chastisement of our peace was upon Him; and with his stripes we are healed." Isaiah 53:5*

If we believe the above is true, then what do we say when we see a believer suffering one defeat after another, one failure after another, living in total despair and defeat; to the extent that he or she feels life is not worth living? Do you know the number of suicide attempts that happen among Christians? And we say deliverance is the thing of the past. I believe this generation needs it more than past generations because we are dealing with more sophisticated powers of Satan.

Let us wholeheartedly embrace what I call the 3Ds (three dimensions of Salvation, that is, Salvation for the spirit, soul and body. Deliverance comes in to totally evict the former landlord who has now become an illegal tenant. It paves the way for us to fully enjoy the benefits of the Cross. This is prosperity in every area of our life; prosperity in the spirit, prosperity in the soul, and physical and financial prosperity The Bible says in 3 John:2, *"Beloved, I wish above all things that thou may prosper and be in health even as thy soul prospers."*

Any vehicle owner will tell you that every year, at least, the vehicle will have to go through overhauling or servicing by replacing old and worn-out parts. It is foolish to expect that, once purchased in good condition; the vehicle will remain like that forever.. Similarly, even when we are delivered, we have to continually overhaul ourselves with the Word of God and prayer. The Bible says when a demon is cast out, he goes roaming about seeking a place of rest and if he finds no place to live, he says to himself, let me go back to my former house to see if it is still available for habitation. The Bible continues by saying when he comes back and finds the place swept clean, garnished and empty, he goes to find seven more wicked spirits than himself and they come to enter in to live...

Matthew 12:43-45, *"When the unclean spirit is gone out of a man, he walks through dry places, seeking rest, and finds none. Then he says, I will return into my house from whence I came out; and when he is come, he finds it empty, swept, and garnished. Then goes he, and takes with himself seven other spirits more wicked than himself, and they enter in and dwell there: and the last state of that man is worse than the first."*

There was a woman who would manifest almost at every meeting and, invariably, would be the first person I would pick to pray for. One day, I was asked by one of the other women why this sister always manifested demonically. I was not immediately able to respond to this, but the answer came from another sister who said, "Oh Pastor, it is her character that opens the door for demons to re-enter after she has been delivered."

Immediately it clicked. "That is it!" I exclaimed. She was an extremely angry woman whose mouth was full of venom. Some of the things she would say in anger to fellow Christians were unbelievable. She was also arrogant and very slanderous. These were the doorways through which the demons constantly entered. At that point, the Lord revealed why the action I was taking with her was not appropriate. He said to me, "You are doing things the wrong way round. First of all, teach the people about demonology, why they need deliverance, and how to maintain their deliverance once the demons have been expelled."

This, and other things the Lord taught me. He told me to record all the information into a book to bless His people. So, you see, we need to be educated on this topic so as to not wallow in ignorance. Ignorance will destroy us. Ignorance gives the devil a hiding place from where to command his evil forces to make sure that we never experience the *more abundant life*.

The one thing that Satan fears most is to be expelled or evicted as we see from Luke 8:31. The demons literally beg Jesus not to cast them out and when they realise that He was not going to heed their request, they plead with him not to be sent into the deep. He did this anyway. Jesus did not heed to their request but instead did exactly what they were afraid of. Demons are afraid of being homeless and so we need to do whatever we need to do to make sure we expel them from our homes, from our churches and from our lives.

Let me take your mind back to the Old Testament, to the book of Exodus. The Word of God tells us that God sent Moses to go to Egypt to deliver the children of Israel. In spite of the resistance from Pharaoh, God ultimately set them free, parted the Red Sea, fed them with manna and made sure that neither their clothes nor shoes ever waxed old. There were many miracles that He worked in the wilderness.

What was the response of the children of Israel anytime they were faced with a challenging situation? Complaining and murmuring became their daily food. Do you know why? They came out of Egypt but Egypt never came out of them. This is the reason why they pined after the garlic and cucumbers and the herbs of Egypt. Even though they had been saved from the slave masters, they were unable to rid themselves of them in their minds and so reflected this behavior and attitude in the wilderness. For this reason, they could not enter into the Promised Land.

Have you ever heard a believer say in despair that everything was fine with them until they became born again? Such a statement would come from someone who has supposedly left Egypt, but is still pining after his or her former life. If you are truly born again and totally set free from all demons, nothing of Egypt appeals to you ever again. The devil will make you long after the things of the world. Do you know that some people, literally, turn again to the world and its lifestyle? Oh yes, they are in the church, but still love the things of the world. They live a double life. In such instances, there is no difference between the unbeliever and churchgoer. That is exactly what they are. For these individuals there is no conviction of obvious sin. Even when it is addressed, they take offence. Jesus said you cannot serve two masters. You will either hate one or love the other Matthew. 6:24. *"No man can serve two masters: for either he will hate the one, and love the other; or else he will hold to the one, and despise the other..."*

It is impossible to serve two masters at the same time. This is what the Master, Himself, is saying. Essentially, you cannot be in Israel and love Egypt or desire the things of Egypt.

Consequently, if you recognize this desire in you, you need help. You need counseling first and then, having gained understanding, you must go through the process of deliverance. Let us get something clear here: deliverance is not always about commanding demons to come out of somebody but it also concerns teaching the Word of God to expose some ungodly mindsets and dark areas in our lives. The purpose is to pull down strongholds of false beliefs from wrong indoctrination or ideology. This will be elaborated in depths as we journey through the subsequent chapters.

As a matter of fact, we need to desire deliverance as much as we desire healing, as deliverance brings healing to the soul. (Psalm 41:4) Paul the Apostle said in Romans 7:19, *"for the good that I would, I do not: but the evil which I would not, that I do. Now if I do that I would not, it is no more I that do it, but sin that dwells in me."*

Let me pause here and ask a question. Who is the originator of sin? Satan is. In the same way that the Holy Spirit in us convicts us of sin and helps us to resist it, the devil does the opposite and lures us into committing sin. Whoever rules in you is the controller of your life. In other words, if the Holy Spirit is the one in charge, He controls you, The Holy Spirit will keep you in the fear of God, and shut out sin from your life. If, however, demon spirits are resident in you, or constantly hovering around you, they cause you to do the things that you do not want to do.

This is exactly what Paul is saying here. *"[21]I find then a law, that, when I would do good, evil is present with me. For I delight in the law of God after the inward man: but I see another law in my members, warring against the law of my mind, and bringing me into captivity to the law of sin which is in my members. O wretched man who shall deliver me from the body of this death?"*

This is the great apostle, Paul, speaking, crying out for deliverance for his soul. Was he not born again? Of course, he was. God had performed miracles through him, he had preached many powerful messages, but there was the old man and his influence still present in his soul, such that Paul had to cry out for God to deliver him. Even some Pastors may need deliverance. There is nothing shameful about this.

Are we ashamed of the Gospel of Jesus Christ? No! For it is the power of God unto salvation. Do not forget, Jesus bore all our sin, shame, guilt and condemnation on the Cross. Do not get me wrong, I am not trying to present myself as one who has attained everything, not at all; but rather, one who actually understands, because I have experienced the liberty that comes from being set spiritually free. Even now, like everyone else, I still I have areas in my life that the Lord is still working on, just like the Apostle Paul. This reminds us constantly of the sufficiency of the grace of God.

I am referring to the struggle with a particular kind of sin or weakness. I am talking about sin that extends beyond the *one-time.* I am talking about men in prestigious position sleeping with various women in the church, or vice versa. Do not tell me such members are not of God. Some are highly anointed. They love God, yet the spirit of lust controls them and they cannot seem to shake themselves free from it. They are firmly under the control of the demon spirit of lust.

What about people in the church struggling with homosexual tendencies? Are they not also Christians? We know of a number of ministers who have positively ministered to many for the Lord. These are truly genuine Bible-believing and teachers of the Word. What went wrong then? It was already present in them before they accepted Jesus as their Lord and Saviour, but nobody picked on it to deliver them. They thought being born again alone meant they were free. I believe that, when they saw the old demons revisiting them, they may have desired to be delivered but they had already attained some level of prominence. They were too afraid to seek help in case of betrayal or exposure. My prayer is that there will be more trustworthy ministers in the Kingdom that will support fellow ministers to talk through their issues without fear of betrayal.

What about pastors who lie easily, even from the pulpit? Some may have struggles within but with no one to talk to or trust, they keep their struggle within and suffer in silence. Some may genuinely want to be helped but where would they receive such assistance without the risk of being labeled. It is difficult these days to find genuine, discreet and trustworthy ministers who would walk alongside another minister through their struggle. These struggling ministers need deliverance. Do you think they feel comfortable knowing what they are doing in darkness? The answer is No! That was their weakness in the world. Being born again did not set them free and they still need deliverance for their soul.

I asked the Lord, why these men who are highly anointed, live in continual sin and yet remain anointed? His response was, "I keep them anointed for my children who come to sit under them to hear my good news. Also, I give them the chance to repent and turn away from their sins. But this is where they miss it. Because they feel my anointing, they think they can hide behind it and continue to sin, and that is when I move in to expose them."

God does not expose sins that easily. No, God is not in the business of disgracing His people. He pleads with us to forsake our sins and turn to Him in repentance. It is only when we harden our hearts and become iniquitous, girded by arrogance and pretense, that He exposes us. The Bible does not say if I *regard sins* in my heart, it says if I *regard iniquities* in my heart, the Lord will not hear me. Psalm 66:18. Iniquity is living continuously in sin.

# CHAPTER 12

# Who Needs Deliverance?

Who needs deliverance? We all need deliverance one time or the other, including Pastors. Larry Huck, a man of God, who is also a deliverance minister in the United States said in his testimony that, although he was a very successful Pastor, he was also hiding a secret. He had an uncontrollable temper that he hid very well from people in his church and others but at home he was a monster. He would beat his wife and kids until the Lord delivered him.

He talked about growing up with an abusive father who abused his wife, Larry's mother, and children. He said one time, after Larry had beat his son, he heard himself saying "I am just like my daddy." That was when he realised that it was the same demon spirit that had used his father to abuse him now operating through him. He sought deliverance and now he brings deliverance to God's people.

Seeing him minister side by side with the wife whom he used to beat, even when pregnant, demonstrates the power of deliverance and the very real need for it. They are now ministering, teaching and bringing deliverance to the Kingdom of God all over the world. I love watching and listening to them because of their openness and transparency of what many in the Kingdom may have swept under the carpet. I pray that more men and women of God would be that open and honest about their struggles. In this way they can encourage others to seek help and put the enemy to shame.

I once visited an inmate to ascertain why he battered my friend nearly to death. All I wanted to know from him was why he did it. To be clear, nothing can justify his action, but I felt compelled to pay him a visit nonetheless. The first thing I told him was that he should be grateful to God that he was not convicted for murder because with the injuries my friend sustained, he could have easily killed her if the Lord had not intervened. He gave me his reasons with tears in his eyes and I told him the truth; that it was due to demonic work. With my friend's permission, I made subsequent visits and attended his court hearings. To cut a long story short it emerged that he had abused several of his ex-girlfriends in the same manner. This confirmed what I suspected all along.

In a conversation with him after his release, he confided in me that, after listening to a message preached by a man of God whilst in prison, he came to the conclusion that his behavior stemmed from a generational curse that required deliverance. When he started narrating what the man of God said, I recognized him immediately as Larry Huck. I knew because I had personally heard this great man of God sharing his testimony. What I am celebrating here is the beauty of a preacher who is open about his own experience and is now helping others worldwide.

My friends abuser continued by telling me how, as a young boy, he saw his father physically abusing his mother. The worst moment that stuck in his mind was when, at the age of nine, he was admitted to the hospital. As it was an emergency situation, his mother had not had a chance to call his father to alert him. His father came to the hospital very furious and there slapped his mother so hard that she bled. Following that incident, he vowed to hurt his father but his parents divorced before he could get his vengeance.

I believe he still harbored the pain from that moment. He was bitter, and by keeping the bitterness of seeing his father abuse his mother meant he had never forgiven him. This opened him up to the '*spirit of his father*' to possess him. This same spirit was now causing him to abuse women just like his father did. This is not intentional, however, something in the bloodline had affected him. It is likely that his father had witnessed his own father abusing his mother just as this young man saw him doing.

In court, I met two of the mothers of his children from previous relationships and each of them described the same pattern of abuse, as had been meted out to my friend. There is hope for all of us if we reach out to the Lord in all sincerity.

As Christians, openness should be our lifestyle. There is nothing to be ashamed about. After all, Christ suffered the shame so we would be without any shame, guilt or condemnation. That is the Gospel of Jesus Christ. Remember, whatever we keep hidden has power over us but if we confess it openly to someone or unashamedly talk about it, it brings hope and deliverance to others, and yourself and the Lord is glorified. Please bear in mind that Satan is the chief blackmailer and will use things that we keep secret to blackmail and torment us such that some even commit suicide.

Do you find it difficult to control you temper? Do you find it difficult to control your tongue? Do you feel comfortable lying and exaggerating? Are you an extremely jealous person? Are you envious? Are you addicted to sex? Are you struggling with any form of addiction? These are some of the basics for deliverance.

Do you struggle with any form of lust at all? Lust is not only about sex. People can lust after food, some kinds of music, horror movies, pornography and many other pleasures. Lust is any unhealthy desire or obsession. You can seek God through fasting and prayer and, with determination and perseverance, the Lord will deliver you. The Word of God says in Galatians 5:19, *"Now the works of the flesh are manifest, which are these; Adultery, fornication, uncleanness, lasciviousness, idolatry, witchcraft, hatred, variance, emulations, wrath, strife, seditions, heresies, envying, murders, drunkenness, reveling and such like; of which I tell you before, as I have also told you in time, that they which do such things shall not inherit the Kingdom of God."*

The Bible is very clear about the consequences for those who indulge in these sins. One may say it is talking about unbelievers, no, and a big no! The Bible says that Scriptures are written for our edification and exhortation as believers. There are many in the church who are struggling with one thing or the other. Do not let the devil deceive us into believing that all is well when we know the opposite is true.

Any one of the sins listed above has a ruling demon spirit calling the shots. Will a totally surrendered, spirit-filled Christian fall victim to these temptations of the flesh, which are controlled by demons? My answer is, no. This is because a surrendered life is out of the reach of demons. That does not mean you are never tempted, but rather that the Holy Spirit is fully the ruler of your soul and in His strength you are able to say no to sin.

Jesse Duplantis, a man of God I admire and love, puts it like this, "I have had many occasions to sin, but I always turn my back and say

No, thank you to the devil, for I have made up my mind to keep my foot firmly on the devil's head all the days of my life." In other words, this man is determined to keep the devil, who is the orchestrator of all sins, under submission, refusing him any access whatsoever into his life. This is only possible once the devil has been expelled.

Jesse was the lead singer of a popular rock band. He talks of being delivered from drugs, alcohol and women on conversion. I do not know why God delivers some people instantly and others gradually. God works with others like that. I have seen a colleague born again and instantly delivered from womanizing, alcohol addiction, gambling and smoking. I have seen others who have to go through a process of deliverance and transformation. One may ask why the difference? All I can say is: I do not know and I cannot question God so I just leave it. He knows best what is best for us as His people.

After salvation, your spirit is automatically regenerated and for some there is instant deliverance. By co-operating with the Holy Spirit and choosing to walk in the fear of God, you can cast the devil out. This is what Galatians 5:1 says, *"Stand fast therefore in the liberty wherewith Christ has made us free, and be not entangled again with the yoke of bondage. Guard your soul with all diligence."*

Now, there is another level of demonic possession that requires a different level of anointing to administer deliverance. Remember the disciples of Jesus could not tackle a particular case of demonization and the father of the victim had to report to Jesus that His disciples could not help his son.

In Matthew 17:16, he said, *"And I brought him to your disciples, and they couldn't cure him."* After Jesus rebuked them and they asked Him why they could not cast the devil out, He answered and said in verse 20, *"Because of your unbelief... [21]However, this kind goes not out but by prayer and fasting."*

There are different cases and they require different levels of anointing. Even with the different levels, there are some cases that will take longer to completely deliver the person. You may ask, I thought we have all been commissioned to heal the sick and cast out devils. The truth is every believer should be able to pray for the sick and cast out devils at any given time. In such situations, God will surely honour the faithful prayers of the believer.

That being said, the Bible clearly states that, *"having then gifts differing according to the grace that is given to us, whether prophecy, let us prophesy according to the proportion of our faith. Or ministry let us wait on our ministering: or he that teaches, on teaching..."* Romans 12:6-7 We see here that, at any point in time, if anointed, anyone can prophesy. This is not their ministry and it does not make them a prophet. Some have been anointed for the ministry of the Prophets and these are called Prophets. Prophesying during a service does not make the person a Prophet.

In the same manner, men and women have been anointed for deliverance. They have the grace to operate in that area, and the anointing too. As a matter of fact, everyone in the five-fold ministry has the anointing to deal with any level of demonization. This level of anointing is vital for the higher level of demonization or demon possession. What is the higher level of demonization? These are some indications: visible signs of oppression, depression, obsession, possession, recurrence of failure and consistently not being able to finish anything one starts, repeated misfortunes, extremism, compulsion and the list go on and on. If you find that there is a cycle of events occurring in your life, bad things happening again and again even though you are a Christian and your walk with the Lord is good, then seek help in counseling first.

This may lead to actual deliverance to break this demonic cycle in your life. Have you ever wondered why very rich actors and so-called celebrities may shoplift items that everyone knows they are more than able to afford? They are what is called kleptomaniacs. This is a demon spirit of compulsive stealing. They do not even think of the consequences if caught. In recent times a renowned TV chef was caught stealing steak from a well-known supermarket. It emerged that he had been doing it for a long time. When arrested, he said whenever he was in that shop, a driving force compelled him to take a piece of meat without paying for it. He told the court he needed help to overcome that behavior, which the court obliged and suspended the sentence for him to seek help.

When in boarding school, I knew of girls from rich families who would steal items including knickers. This was shocking to us because, unlike some of us from poorer backgrounds, we were well aware of which girls came from wealthy families from the cars their parents drove and the items they brought to school. Some of the things some of them stole were ridiculously disgraceful and, not knowing what I know now, this was often the topic of discussion in our dormitory.

I also worked with a woman in one of the top international hotels in the 80s in the UK. She was a popular and well-known woman in her community. She carried herself as a high-class lady hence when I got to know she has been convicted for stealing a chicken from a supermarket, I gasped with shock as did all who knew her.

Chicken! Yes chicken! How much did it cost? This was nothing compared to her standard of living and yet she stole it. Years later her daughter with whom I also worked, was caught stealing a large sum of money from the company. She fled the country before her court appearance. What do you see here? This is a generational curse, which ought to be broken before her grandchildren also follow in their footsteps.

I had a cousin who was a thief. At first, we all thought it was petty stealing but, as time went by, I began to realise that a spirit was guiding him to objects and monies. No matter where you hid it, he would locate and steal it; but would also own up easily when confronted. This was long before I was converted but even then, I told my other cousins that he had a spirit guide which led him to the things without having to search for them.

Another thing I want us to look at is women who have excessive sexual drive or desire. This is called nymphomania. This is different from prostitution. The prostitute exchanges sex for money; it is a trade or a profession or so they think. However, the nymphomaniac just wants to have sex when the spirit takes him or her. I knew a colleague at work who disclosed to me during a conversation that there had been times when she would have strong sexual desires to the extent that she would go out to seduce a man. In other words, when she wants it, she has to have it even if she has to find a total stranger from the street to fulfill that desire. She was the same person who told me she has a spiritual husband and he is the only one that can satisfy her sexually. These people have a demon spirit driving them into this abnormal sexual drive and behavior.

There is also this crazy, filthy, and diabolical thing called bestiality. This is sexual intercourse between an animal and a person This is gross perversion of creation, an abomination, and insanity at its highest level. This can only be from the devil whose desire is to make man sin against God in the most insulting way. This is way beyond crossing the line of sin; it is provocation as far as God and His creation is concerned. What this is, is the devil is using man to insult God's wisdom and intent. He created animals for animals and humans for humans. Why should a human being even think of an animal in this manner?

I recall a story I heard as a child of about eight years old. The story was told of a girl who was paid by a white man to have sex with his dog. It transpired that the girl started barking like a dog and later died in hospital from rabies. What a wicked thing to do. The poor girl was enticed by the money to do this abominable act and ended up paying dearly with her life. This took place in Africa where poverty is eating into the very fabric of society. In her case, she was not possessed by demons but was deceived and lured into this hideous act.

I watched a program a while ago called Hollywood Pets and was horrified by some of the things I saw. In this program, a woman had about ten wolves living with her as pets, but had identified one as a sexual partner. Watching them kissing passionately made me sick to my stomach. She went on to say that she cannot have male friends because 'Jack', that her wolf lover, would attack any human male who gets too close to her. Have you ever heard a thing like this?

This is purely demonic. On the set, they kissed intimately like human-to-human and she unashamedly talked proudly about their intimate relationship. Anyone who ever does a thing like this, should they come to Christ, need to be delivered from these demonic activities.

I recently watched a television program called the Medical Detectives; a real-life investigative program. In this particular episode, the detectives were hunting down an arsonist who was going around neighborhoods in the early hours of the morning, setting houses on fire. After years of painstaking investigation, he was eventually caught and arrested. It is what he told detectives that caught my attention. He told the investigators not to say it out loud, but he hears voices telling him to burn down houses. When they said to him, "you have set several dozen homes alight" he said, "it is over two hundred going back a decade."

You see the devil increases the desire to do evil if it is not dealt with. Prison is a punishment but not a solution. In Christianity, we have to believe in both punishment and solutions. The world believes in punishment and this may perhaps offer no or limited solution, but as believers we have to go beyond punishment and find out what compels man to behave in certain abnormal ways or commit crimes. With some of these issues, we have to look for the underlying factors in order to pray for deliverance for them as the Spirit leads. We have to do this as this will set people free. As a matter of fact, anything that is extremely abnormal needs to be well investigated.

I have come to the conclusion that all excesses, recurrences and extremism are demonic and have to be dealt with through counseling and deliverance knowing that for this cause was the Son of God made manifest that He might destroy the works of Satan. Let Him set you free for He came to set the captives free and you will be free indeed

# CHAPTER 13

# What is Demonisation?

Having laid the foundation about deliverance, will can all agree that without demonization, there would be no need for the topic of deliverance at all? What then is demonization?

The word stems from the word demon. The Oxford dictionary definition of Demon is: *An evil spirit or devil, esp. one thought to possess a person, b. the personification of evil passion.* Another definition is, *an evil spirit with the power to harm people; a messenger and a servant of the devil.*

Demons are fallen spirits. The Bible says when Satan was cast down following his rebellion against God; the 'one-third' that he drew after him were also cast down with him. Revelations 12:4, *"and his tail drew the third part of the stars in heaven, and did cast them to the earth...v. 9 and the great dragon was cast out, that old serpent called the devil and Satan which deceives the whole world: he was cast into the earth, and his angels were cast out with him."*

The devil has assigned his messengers and put them in strategic positions in continents, nations, cities, towns and villages. Some rule over the oceans, seas, rivers, waterfalls and streams. Others rule over mountains, hills and caves and not forgetting rain forests around the world. According to the Scriptures, in *Ephesians 6:12,*

*"For we wrestle not against flesh and blood, but against principalities, against powers, against the rulers of the darkness of this world, against spiritual wickedness in high places."*

This is the hierarchy of the kingdom of Satan. Just like in the army, we are dealing with ranks here. There are generals, lieutenants, sergeants, and corporals and demons are the messengers of these evil forces. The devil, though an Archangel, is also an unseen being, but is not omnipresent, so he employs demons as his messengers. He sometimes reveals himself unto servants of his and even unto some servants of God too.

Do not forget that he, the devil, imitates the things of God. Jesus, the Son of God, sometimes reveals Himself to both believers and unbelievers who later turn their lives to Him. So, the devil does the same, using his demons.

The late Myles Munroe puts it beautifully in his book "*The principles of the Kingdom of God.*" He states that it is illegal for spirits to operate in the earthly realm except they have a body to possess. This explains why the devil had to possess the body of a serpent to deceive Eve in the Garden of Eden. The same is true with God. God who set this principle will not violate His own principle. That is why He had to come to earth in human form, as Jesus, to wrestle with the devil to take back what he the devil stole from man, dominion over the earth realm and all that is in it. So then, these demonic spirits have to do things to human beings at the command of their officers who answer to their commander-in chief, Satan. In order to effectively do this, they need to possess bodies, mostly that of humans. This is what we call demonisation in its highest form, demon possession.

Just as God uses human beings to fulfill His plans on earth, so does the devil. Unlike God, the devil forces his way into the human life. This starts subtly and sometimes innocently too. I have heard testimonies of people who were invited to "church" by friends; only to get there to realise it was a satanic gathering and not a church

The woman felt this compelling obligation to continue because her so-called friend would not let her quit. She witnessed both animal and human sacrifices. It took the Lord Jesus to deliver her from being close to be slaughtered by the group one Halloween night. There is no choice at all where the devil is concerned! Once he is able to lure you into his web, it will take the Lord Jesus to deliver you and even then, you have to make up your mind to stay under the Lord's feet permanently with continuous deliverance.

God does not force us in any way whatsoever. Everything with Him is a choice. He gives us the freewill to choose whether we accept His son, Jesus, as our personal saviour and to obey Him. It is all about choices when it comes to the Kingdom of our God. Joshua, the servant of God, echoed His voice to the children of Israel in *Joshua 24:15-16, "And if it seems evil to you to serve the Lord, choose you this day whom you will serve; whether the gods which your fathers served that were on the other side of the flood, or the gods of the Amorites, in whose land you dwell: but as for me and my house, we will serve the Lord."*

As you can see, the choice was given to God's people. God Almighty does not force us to do anything at all; everything is 100% by choice. It is not so with the devil. He leaves his victims with no choice at all. Jesus described him very well for us to understand the way Satan operates in *John 10:10 as, "the Thief.* He comes to steal." No thief asks permission to steal. Never! *"He comes to steal, kill and destroy."* No killer asks permission to kill, and neither does a destroyer seek authority to destroy his victim. In fact, if you resist a thief, he is likely to harm or kill you. Although a trespasser, the thief has the ability to make you feel subject to him when you accidentally interrupt his illegal activities in your own home, office or streets. We have heard about killings that were eventually discovered to be mistaken identity. Should the victims have been given the chance, the killers would have recognized that they were the dealing with the wrong people.

This is how the devil operates. He leaves his victims with no choice at all. *"the liar and the murderer" "You are of the devil, and the lust of your father you will do. He was a murderer from the beginning, and abode not in truth, because there was no truth in him. When he speaks a lie, he speaks of his own: for he is a liar and the father of it."* John 8:44

From the description of Satan by Jesus, we can conclude that there is no justice from a liar's point of view, nor is there any mercy from a murderer. Many liars have put innocent people in jail; others have been executed because of false testimony. Such individuals have no conscience and will lie to make themselves look good, bear false witness against innocent people that may lead to punishment, without any consideration for the ultimate destruction of their victims.

They are possessed by the devil to do his bidding. This goes to conclude that as far as the devil is concerned, humans have no choice at all. He calls the shots. **BUT** thank God for Jesus! Satan no longer has the right to call the shots in a believer's life except we allow him.

AMEN!

# CHAPTER 14

# The Characteristics of Demons

A little information first about demons, and their operation. Demons are fallen spirits. They are messengers of the devil. They are sent by their master to carry out his evil plans on earth. Listed below are some of the characteristics of demons.

1. They are very intelligent beings.

2. Very disciplined as their kingdom operates a strict regime.

3. They are liars like their master,

4. They operate in deception.

5. They have a great deal of knowledge in all their assignments. This is what the Bible calls familiar spirits or spirit of divination. They take time to gather information on their victims and use that information to deal with them. As a matter of fact, I would not be wrong if I were to describe them, among other things, as spiritual journalists who work for the secret service of the kingdom of darkness. *Psalm 64:5-6, "They encourage themselves in an evil matter: they commune of laying snares secretly; they say, who shall see them? They search out iniquities; they accomplish a diligent search; both the inward thought of every one of them, and the heart is deep."*

Demons go about gathering information like military intelligence, before they attack. Psalm 56:5-6, *"Everyday, they wrestle my words: all their thoughts are against me for evil. They gather themselves together, they hide themselves, and they mark my steps, when they wait for my soul."*

These are monitoring spirits that have been assigned to harass individuals and to pick up information about them in order to effectively oppress them.

6. They are extremely stubborn and are never driven off easily. They know that at the mention of the name of Jesus they are in great trouble and danger of becoming "homeless" still they do not quit easily. One has to be well equipped by the Holy Spirit to handle them.

7. When confronted by the highest anointing, they are very fearful. They will be pleading with the minister just as they did with Jesus not to send them away.

These are just a few of the many characteristics of demons, which I have learned over the years in the field of deliverance. They claim ownership of their victims. Some will say "I have married her so I will never leave her; I have lived here for eighteen years so I cannot leave; she was given to me by her mother/father so she's mine and some other funny things they will say to make you stop and laugh. When they realise that they are surely going to be evicted, then they will start pleading and telling you about the punishment awaiting them if they fail in their enterprise.

To be demonised is to

1. make into or like a demon.

2. represent as a demon.

My own definition is to be under the influence of demonic or satanic powers to the degree that you cannot control yourself. There are also levels of demonization.

One can be oppressed, influenced, suppressed and possessed by demons. Whichever way they can use you to do their bidding, one way or the other. This is why you need help to be able to take back control over your life and live a submitted life unto the Lord.

# CHAPTER 15

# Signs of Demonisation

Some of the signs one must look out for are, lack of self-control and when someone behaves in a way which is embarrassing to their family and yet this person sees nothing wrong and keeps behaving in the same way. Other indicators include compulsive behaviours like lying without any necessary cause, continually doing bad things with no explanation or control. When confronted, all they can say is, "I don't know why I did it or a voice in my head told me to do it."

There are certain behaviours that start from childhood and if it is not addressed, become a stronghold. I know of situations where parents will say their child enjoys his/her own company. Yes, there are kids like that, but when they grow up and become a recluse, it is only a matter of time before it becomes apparent that something is not right. Other signs to look out for are, when an adult who is supposed to go to work, refuses to do that, and is always sleeping and sometimes does not even bath. If this is not a one off but a lifestyle then this person needs help. Often even believers do not see these signs as evidence of demonisation, but take it to be laziness. All extremism is demonic. This means this person is controlled by an internal force that he cannot control.

Extreme anger and rage.

Violence, which can cause someone to kill or cause grievous bodily harm to another person.
Reclusiveness
Restlessness.
Suicidal thoughts and/or attempts
Self-harm and/or self-cutting
Compulsive behaviour

As I pointed out earlier, spirits cannot operate without a human body on earth even though there are instances where the devil makes his presence felt by moving objects around in places that he has occupied for a long time. This could be a house, an office or even a church. This is what we call "Haunted Places". People have spoken of organs playing in the church halls without anyone being present. We can say that it might be an angel but my question to this is: is the Holy Spirit in charge of this denomination? If yes, then we might agree. Then again why would heaven allow the playing of instruments when there is no gathering?

Satan gets angry when his control over an individual is being broken, violated or his control over a territory is being threatened. He hates being evicted, as demons will always claim their right of abode in a person's life. Unlike Satan, the precious Holy Spirit does not come to live in someone without an invitation or permission. The devil, on the other hand, forcibly takes over a person's life and ultimately ruins it.

The Holy Spirit comes to live in us from the very day we become born again and uses us to fulfill the plans and purposes of God, if we continue to walk with Him. God will always use human vessels to do

His work on earth. There are also times that the Holy Spirit does things without any human intervention or interference at all. The devil has counterfeited God's power and operations.

As said earlier, and according to the gospel of John, the Holy Spirit comes to dwell in us on conversion. *"Even the Spirit of truth; whom the world cannot receive, because it sees Him not, neither knows Him: but you know Him; for He dwells with you, and shall be in you."* John. 14:17.

*This* is written for everyone who is born again. You may have people questioning; if this Scripture is true, then how can the Holy Spirit dwell in the same body as evil spirits of the devil. The Holy Spirit deals with the regeneration of our spirit man and the devil deals with our soul. Remember, it is the spirit that is born again and not the soul. The Bible says it takes the Word of God to separate the soul from the spirit of the believer as the soul can affect the spirit that is void of the Word of God. Hebrews 4:12 (NIV), *"For the Word of God is alive. Sharper than any double- edged sword, it penetrates even to dividing the soul and spirit."*

Do not forget that sin is always lurking in our soul according to James 1:13-15 *"Let no man say when he is tempted, I am tempted by God: for God cannot be tempted with evil. Neither tempts He any man. But every man is tempted when he is drawn away of his own lust, and enticed. Then when lust is conceived, it brings forth sin: and sin when it is finished, brings forth death."*

One thing I want to point out is, Jesus was with the disciples, He dwelt with them even as the Holy Spirit dwells with us now. On occasion, He warned Simon Peter of Satan's intentions to deal with him. In *Luke 22:31, "And the Lord said, Simon, Satan hath desired to have you, that he may sift you as wheat: ...[32]But I have prayed for thee that thy faith fails not:"*

One time, as I was going about my daily chores, the Spirit of the Lord said to me, "Do you know the Old Man doesn't go anywhere from you?" I asked Him to explain it to me, and He asked me, "Who is the Old Man?" As I was pondering over it carefully, He said the Old Man is your soul. Before one becomes born again the spirit was dead and when something is dead, it is dead so it was the soul that was in control of the sinner's life not the spirit.

Remember sin is not committed by the spirit but by the soul. The Bible says in Romans 12:1-2, *"Therefore I urge you, brothers and sisters, in view of God's mercy, to offer your bodies as a living sacrifice, holy and pleasing to God- this is your true and proper worship. Do not conform to the pattern of this world, but be transformed by the renewing of your mind. Then you will be able to test and approve what God's will is-His good, pleasing and perfect will."*

When the soul or "Old Man", is in control in a believer's life, he or she is very carnal or fleshy and can easily fall into sin. But, when the soul is kept in submission to the Word of God and the Holy Spirit, it is not easy for a believer to yield to sin, let alone be easily influenced by demons. Sometimes we have to look back to where we came from, and give God the glory as it is not by might nor by power but by the Spirit of the Lord that we are kept from falling as we cooperate with Him to work in us and on us. It takes the Word of

God in our hearts for us to say no to sin.

The all-knowing Jesus knew there were areas in Peter's life that would open the door for Satan to come in to attack him. What happens after an attack is, if God does not intervene, the devil takes his victim as a "prisoner of war." This is because after most of his attacks many of us tend to lose faith and throw in the towel. Jesus went on to say to Simon Peter in this same Scripture that, *"when thou art converted, strengthen thy brethren."* In other words, I have prayed for you, that you will not fall a prey to the evil one, and when you are totally set free from the influence of the evil one, be there for others, pray the prayer of deliverance for them, make sure that the devil will not have dominion over them.

Do you recall that on another occasion Jesus addressed Peter as Satan personified? In Mark 8:32, He spoke that saying openly. *"And Peter took Him, and began to rebuke Him... [33]But when He had turned about and looked on His disciples, He rebuked Peter, saying, get thee behind me Satan:"*

This statement was made immediately after Simon Peter through the Holy Spirit had declared "thou art the Christ." We note from this Scripture that a Christian can be influenced or be used by the devil at any given time. He also has to have something in you to create the doorway for him to be able to use you. There has to be a doorway for the enemy to come through to use or influence a believer.

Another example I want us to look at, is Judas Iscariot. Was he a disciple of Jesus? Yes. But the Bible says in Luke 22:3, *"Then entered Satan into Judas surnamed Iscariot, being one of the twelve."* I believe it is now becoming clearer that a believer can be demonised. There is always a doorway or something in the individual that opens a person's life so demons can enter.

Demonization is a thing of the soul. The Holy Spirit dwells in the spirit realm while demons can operate freely in the soul, depending on the spiritual strength of the believer.

Remember Judas was upset and moaned when Mary came to anoint Jesus' feet with the expensive ointment, saying the oil could have been sold and the proceeds given to the poor. John 12:6 Note what Jesus said here: *"This he said, not that he cared for the poor; but because he was a thief, and had the bag, and bore what was put therein."* (Underlining mine) Judas was a thief before he became a disciple according this statement of Jesus. You could say that being with Jesus, did not change him as a thief. This is because there was a doorway that was not dealt with. I do not know why Jesus did not deal with it, but I know from the Scripture that Judas was called the son of perdition whose destiny was sealed before time.

As a result of this doorway, it was very, very easy for the devil to enter into Judas and influence him to betray Jesus for money. Clearly the doorway in Judas' life was greed and the love of money, which the Bible says, is the root of all evil. The difference between these two disciples, Peter and Judas, is that Jesus prayed for one. A prayer of deliverance was what the Master prayed for Peter, *"… when thou art converted…"* Converted? Yes, converted. I thought he was a disciple. Yes, Peter was a disciple who needed to be converted, saved and delivered from the old taskmaster, just like all of us today.

Most Christians are followers of Jesus like Peter. Yes, we are Christians but, like Peter, we need deliverance. Peter needed some spiritual work done in him and that is the reason why Satan desired to *sift* him. Satan felt strongly that Peter had things in him that gave him (Satan) the legal right to torment him.

Our High Priest is interceding for us as He did for Peter. The *old man* has to be dethroned before the throne of our hearts can be occupied by the Lord Jesus alone. For two kings cannot occupy one throne. It is just not possible nor is it practical.

I know that our God is not a partial God so why would He deliver one and not the other? Do not forget, He sees the heart of man and, as Jesus said, our motives are laid bare before Him. Jesus knew exactly why Judas was upset about the oil. Judas had an attitude that stunk in the nostrils of the Master. He had no fear of God, hence was able to question the use of the oil.

Whatever you do, seek for the truth as you confront certain issues in your life. God desires the truth from our inward parts. If you are honest with Him, all things will work together for your good. Do you know why Peter was delivered and Judas was not? Simon Peter was genuinely repentant but Judas was not. He felt ashamed of what he had done and wanted frantically to undo it. When that failed, he committed suicide.

Child of the Most High God, hear me clearly today, there are some things you cannot do for yourself God will have to use someone else to bring deliverance to you. All you have to do is to acknowledge that we have a Deliverer and we do not have to suffer alone. Judas thought of the reputation he did not possess, but his nakedness was showing all the time. He had been oblivious to this fact. He was even called a thief by Jesus in John 12:6, *"Not that he cared for the poor, he was a thief, and since he was in charge of the disciples' money, he often stole some for himself."* NLT.

The devil continued to deceive Judas until he finally killed himself. Friend, what you often try to cover up is wide open all the time. People see and notice certain things that do not add up but who would tell you? And if they did, would you accept it or you will think they are criticising you?

Please, from now on, do not try to hide anymore but seek help. Cry out to God and He will send help your way. Remember what we try to hide has power over us and will ultimately destroy us if we do not seek help. God, in His infinite wisdom, teaches and encourages us to confess our faults one to another to be healed.

Is deliverance part of the Gospel of Jesus Christ? Yes! I am not ashamed of it for it is the power of God to set me free. And whom the Son sets free, is free indeed. Why should we be ashamed of any aspect of the Gospel? One time, in prayer, I saw, in a flash, Jesus on the Cross and my attention was drawn to the linen wrapped around His lower parts. I asked what this means. The Holy Spirit spoke clearly to my spirit and said, *"See, I gave up my Royal apparel and chose to be wrapped in this for you. I gave it up to cover your nakedness so you don't have to be ashamed any more of your nakedness."*

Do you understand this? Oh, please try to understand that He did not have to do this, but He did it anyway; to cover our nakedness, our shame, our reproach, our guilt and condemnation. Do not try to hide anymore. Jesus knows your name and your pain, He understands why you do the things you do, about which you are ashamed to talk. Call on Him and, most assuredly, He will deliver and save you.

In the early nineties, a well-known UK footballer, described as a born-again Christian by the press, committed suicide. His younger brother was also a well-known footballer who played for the same club and also for England, and for this reason the story was all over the news and tabloids. In my view, it was a very sad story.

As the story of his life began to unfold, I realised that he had died a needless death. I do believe he was a Christian who was confused by his sexuality and was judged by those who did not understand his struggles, He was offered no help from the church. His suicide note said it all. According to the press, he ended his note by saying he hopes to find forgiveness from the Lord Jesus whom he loved. Very sad indeed, there was no-one to reach out to this young man, who loved the Lord but had a struggle with his sexuality. He did not have to commit suicide just because he was struggling with homosexuality. He loved the Lord but was not connected with people who would have helped him to overcome the struggle that tormented him and to live for the Lord to fulfill his purpose on earth.

Many of us have been exposed to one thing or another before we came to Christ. These things have given the devil the right to do things to us and with us. It is about time the Body of Christ woke up from their slumber of deception; that deliverance is a thing of the past. Rise up to set God's people free for the purposes of our God to come to pass in our lives. I am talking about the more abundant life that Jesus promised. I have personally seen the manifestation of these Scriptures in my ministry; where after I have administered deliverance to some members of the church, the Lord has opened doors that had been shut for years in their lives.

Praise God, Jesus saves, delivers and heals. He restores as well. He has said it and He will perform it. Hallelujah! Thank God for sending us His son, Jesus, the Mighty Deliverer, the Strong Deliverer, the Lion of the Tribe of Judah who is still in the business of saving, healing and delivering and restoring His people.

Indeed, He came to set the captive free.

# CHAPTER 16

# Ways of Demonisation (Entry Points)

There are diverse ways whereby one can become demonised or demon possessed. Coming from an African background, I have come to understand many things since I became born-again. I come from a district associated with the practice of witchcraft and idol worship. There is a large shrine of which it was said, could possess people as far as United States, including Caucasians.

According to observers, the possessed, would dance barefoot and unharmed through the fire when the spirit took them. There would be no burns, blisters or bruises. This was an amazing piece of satanic work. I witnessed people make yearly pilgrimage to my town until I left and moved to the city. Years after I left for the UK. I was told it had continued until the High Priestess died. I guess she died with her demonic powers.

As a child growing up in an area where we did not have running plumbed water, we had to fetch water from some rocky wells. During what we call the *harmattan* or the dry season, the flow of the water decreased or dried up making it increasingly difficult to get water. For this reason, we had to wake up in the middle of the night to fetch water to avoid the morning rush. Living with a grandmother who did not have a clock, we were woken up randomly at any time she chose.

On a particular morning we were woken up to fetch water. We had to drag our sleepy selves out with our buckets and lamps as there was also no electricity in the town in those days. As we turned the corner near our house, we saw some lights and as the leader of the group, I urged my cousins to pick up pace thinking others had already taken the lead. As we doubled our steps, we observed something phenomenal. The light we saw rose higher and higher. It would then disintegrate into particles like fireworks and then gather back into a fireball. This went on for about one or two minutes. I immediately remembered a story my mum had told me years ago about how she encountered witches in display. What she described to me was exactly what I was seeing. Without a second thought I shouted "it's a witch" and we all run back home. Thank God grandma did not make any fuss at all as she would normally have, but rather allowed us back to bed to sleep.

The dark world is real, it is very real. Oh yes, the devil is real, his messengers are real, his world is real. Demons are very, very real. I believe that everything that has a name exists, seen and unseen, natural and supernatural, physical and spiritual. Even atheists, believe in something. In my opinion, they walk and live in denial. Growing up, there were numerous pagan activities in my town such that this town has a reputation and it is now well-known for its idolatrous activities. I saw too much, which I later understood to be the works of Satan. I thank God that my strict Presbyterian upbringing was a good foundation, though not a perfect one. I look back and say, thank God for godly grandmothers.

My grandma was a very strict and God-fearing woman. There was always punishment for anyone of her grandchildren, if we did not go to church. If we were caught anywhere near demonic festivals or celebrations, we would be severely punished. Obviously, as children, we were very inquisitive, wanting to know why we were forbidden to watch such activities. This caused my cousins and me, rebellious at the time, to go and watch what I now know to be demonic displays of satanic powers.

I witnessed with my own eyes when demonic spirit arrest young ladies against their will to be fetish priestesses. Their transformation was beyond belief. The devil always went for the most beautiful ones and destroyed them. This is what convinced me that this thing is indeed evil. I decided not to watch any more of those activities. The above is one of the ways that one can be demonised or demon possessed. If we ignorantly attend demonic or satanic celebrations or activities, we can be taken captives.

There were times also when people would dance to the rhythm of the beating drums during the celebrations and become possessed by the evil spirits. I also witnessed instances when the fetish priestesses would throw some white mixture of white clay and talcum powder on the crowd; causing as many as that substance fell on to manifest like demonised fetish priests or priestesses. They became possessed! This is known as to as Transference of spirit.

# CHAPTER 17

# Transference of Spirit

This is an instantaneous action that causes a quick transmission of demons from one person into another. Demons always want another place to go to when they are being expelled. Their best targets are human beings.

I have witnessed a demon spirit targeting and pointing to a place where a believer was fast asleep during an all-night service. She was vulnerable, not because she was asleep, but because, when the instruction was given for us all to cover ourselves and the children with the blood of Jesus, she did not hear it and, therefore, did not do it. Sometimes believers dispute such events and I wonder why they find it hard to believe these things. Let us see what happened when Jesus had an encounter with a demon in Luke 8:27

*"And when He went forth to land, there met him out of the city a certain man, which had devils long time, and ware no clothes, neither abode in any house, but in the tombs. When he saw Jesus, he cried out, and fell down before Him, and with aloud voice said, what have I to do with thee, Jesus, thou son of God Most High? I beseech thee, torment me not. For He had commanded the unclean spirit to come out of the man... [31]and they besought Him that He would not command them to go out into the deep... [33]Then*

*went the devils out of the man, and entered into the swine: and the herd ran violently down a steep place into the lake, and were choked."*

Here is a clear biblical example of transference of spirits or demons as you may term it. What has changed? Absolutely nothing! The same tactics the devil used in Jesus' day is the same tactics he is using today. The only thing we can say is, as God of all creation has given man wisdom to advance in technology and is using it to spread the gospel of Jesus Christ, so is the devil who is always stealing God's ideas and corrupting it. Satan has also advanced and mobilized his demons with such sophistication that is unbelievable. He has never been able to create anything and he never will. He steals God's ideas and perverts them.

Transference of spirits is real. Even in the church, it is happening. Why do you think gossiping can bring about division and ultimate breakaway by factions in a congregation? All it takes is for the enemy to sow a seed of discontentment in one person and for that person to spread the seed around; selling it to anyone who is receptive. This is the evil spirit of confusion and division, aimed at destroying the church of Jesus Christ.

Our daily walk with the Lord must be solid to avoid this manner of demonization. People of God must be taught how to resist these moves in the church universal. There has to be education on what to do when demons are being expelled. The best way is to be praying and covering one's self with the Blood of Jesus. Bear in mind that one thing that frightens demons is where they will go after they have been expelled. I have heard demons asking where do you want me to go, seeing I have lived in this person for maybe sixteen or twenty years? Some demons will bluff, saying, "I have married A or B for several years and I am not leaving." Sounds familiar? Remember in Luke 8:27, the demons begged Jesus not to send them into the deep.

This teaches me that demons are scared of where they will go after being cast out. It is interesting to see the demons begging Jesus concerning where they will be going after they are expelled? Look at what Jesus did. Initially it looked as if they had their request granted by the Lord but looking at it closer, that was not the case. Jesus still sent them to the place they feared to go, the deep. *"[31]and they besought Him that He would not command them to go out into the deep. And there were a herd of many swine feeding on the mountain: and they (demons) besought Him that He would suffer them to enter into them. And He suffered them. Then the devils went out of the man, and entered into the swine: and the herd ran violently down a steep place into the lake, and were choked."*

Did they have their request granted by the Lord? No, they ended up in the place they had feared to go in the first place. The Lord Jesus dealt with demons with no mercy whatsoever because the devil shows no mercy when it comes to human being that God has created in His image and likeness. He comes to steal, kill and destroy.

This is the reason why demons must be directed to where to go when being expelled. . I have heard demons asked after being commanded to come out in Jesus name, where should we go? If they are not properly directed, they find and enter any available human being who is not properly covered, living in sin, walking in disobedience or other things the Bible speaks against.

Transference of spirits can also take place when you touch unclean things without godly authority. I know of a young man whose family was heavily involved in paganism and had a shrine in their home. This young man, following his University education, decided to burn the family shrine. He was warned not to, but did not pay heed. He went mad afterwards. I mean, totally insane. We watched him deteriorate over the years. He never regained sanity.

The Bible tells us that aprons and handkerchiefs from the Apostle Paul were laid on the sick and they recovered, Acts 19:11-12, *"And God wrought special miracles by the hands of Paul: so that from his body were brought unto the sick handkerchiefs or aprons, and the diseases departed from them, and the evil spirit went out of them."* The same is true with demonic spirits. Powers can be transferred from items dedicated to the devil. The Bible says in the book of 1 Timothy 5:22, *"Lay hands suddenly on no man, neither be partaker of other men's sins: keep thyself pure."*

There can be transference of spirits through laying on of hands according the above Scripture. You have to be in a place of spiritual authority to lay hands and, even then, the Bible says not to do it suddenly. I quite remember, years ago, I was just praying over people in church and as I stretched forth my hand towards this particular woman, she started manifesting like a snake; hissing and spitting. A tiny bit of her saliva landed on my arm and a day later that spot was darkened; and for weeks it remained dark. I anointed that part and prayed against any effects of it, in Jesus name. This could have significantly affected someone who was not anointed or authorised.

Remember the seven sons of Sceva? "Jesus, we know and Paul we know but who are you?" In other words, by what authority are you casting us out?

Acts 19:13-16, *"Then certain of the vagabond Jews, exorcists, took upon them to call over them which had evil spirits the name of the Lord Jesus, saying, we adjure you in the name of the Lord Jesus whom Paul preaches. And there were seven sons of one Sceva, a Jew, and chief of the priests which did so. And the evil spirit answered and said, Jesus I know, and Paul I know but who are you? And the man in whom the evil spirit was leaped on them, and overcame them, and prevailed against them, so that they fled out of the house naked and wounded."*

Demons can be transferred in many ways from man to man, through sex, food, drink and interactions. Proverbs 22:24-25, *"Make no friendship with an angry man; and with a furious man thou shall not go. [25] Lest you learn his ways, and get a snare to your soul."*

# CHAPTER 18

# Paganism and Idol Worshipping

This is an act of worshipping anything besides God Almighty. Some do not think they worship Satan, but whichever way we look at it, if it is not God, the Creator, through His Son Jesus Christ, we are worshipping the devil. John 14:6, *"[Jesus is]… the way, the truth and the life. No man comes to the Father but (except through) by Me."*

The first of the Ten Commandments is not to worship any other gods besides God. *"You shall have no other gods before me. You shall not make to you any graven image, or any likeness of anything that is in heaven above or that is in the earth beneath, or that is in the water under the earth. You shall not bow down yourself to them, nor serve them: for I the Lord am a jealous God, visiting the iniquity of the fathers upon the children to the third and fourth generation of them that hate Me."*
Exodus 20:2-5

The Bible is clear about what constitutes idol-worship. It opens doors to demonic oppression, possession and harassment. It also makes anyone involved, a slave to Satan; knowingly and unknowingly. What happens afterwards is that the person possessed is empowered by the devil. Whether you go looking for protection or power, the consequences are the same. Demons automatically come to live in you in the same way the Holy Spirit does with those who accept Jesus Christ as their Lord and personal Savior.

In the case of someone who once worshipped Satan, but is now born-again, is that the end of the story? No. There needs to be some sort of deliverance to overthrow the former master of his soul. Acts 19:18-20, *"And many of those who believed now came and openly confessed what they had done. A number who had practiced sorcery brought their scrolls together and burned them publicly. When they calculated the value of the scrolls, the total came to fifty thousand drachmas."*

This is a biblical example of what needs to take place after an idol worshipper, or Satanist, is converted. The old has to be totally destroyed and renounced. In other words, every entanglement and link to the past must be severed. This is deliverance! The subject of deliverance must be taught in every segment of the Christian setting and church. We need to bring awareness to the body of Christ.

Idol worship is setting one's heart to seek help from, or worship other gods instead of the Creator. In these last days, we see many false and demonic pastors that are not Christ's anointed pastors at all, but have chosen the profession to deceive the simple–hearted. Jesus warned us of such. Many of them are satanic agents whom Satan has employed to deceive and take as many as they can, down to hell with him. Such "pastors" use demonic powers to work fake miracles, signs and wonders, against which the Bible warns us.

The sad news is, even the elect are falling prey to these satanic agents and their "churches". They are deceiving and destroying lives and yet people are flocking to these "churches." Many Christians have fallen into the hands of these wicked men and women, simply because the church is not teaching us to equip them. Remember we are destroyed because we lack knowledge.

Awake, awake church of Jesus Christ, let us awake from our sleep and slumber, and tackle this issue. The day of our Lord's coming is drawing closer and closer. It was His love for the souls of men, and the desire to save man from eternal damnation, that drove Jesus to the Cross. He has given us a charge to do the same; to save as many as possible. Jude 18-23, *"How they told you there will be mockers in the last time, who should walk after their own ungodly lusts. These be they who separated themselves, sensual, having not the Spirit... [20]But ye, beloved, building up yourselves on your most holy faith, praying in the Holy Ghost. [21]Keep yourselves in the love of God, looking for the mercy of our Lord Jesus Christ unto eternal life. [22]and some have compassion, making a difference: [23]And to others save with fear, pulling them out of the fire; hating even the garment spotted by the flesh."*

This is what the Word of God is saying; the Lord has given us this charge as followers of Christ. We have to love each other enough to pull some out of the fire.

If the believers in Acts 19 had not taken their occultist books and other items to be destroyed, they would have continued to be tormented by the devil even though they were believers. The reason for their destroying all manner of things was to completely disconnect themselves from anything to do with their past, as Satanists, idolaters and occultism. This is necessary because anything that is used in the days of devil worship remained a point of contact between you and Satan. No matter how we look at it, demons still have a legal doorway to continue to torment or harass you if such items are not destroyed and proper counseling administered.

The temple of God, as the Bible refers to as our bodies, was once the temple of Satan and needs proper cleansing before it can function spiritually as it ought to This is why deliverance is so necessary. As previously mentioned, there are levels of demonization. Therefore, we need have levels of deliverance. *"Howbeit this kind goes not out but by fasting and praying."* Matthew 17:21

There is a need to discard the old in order for the new to work effectively. These days, we see or hear testimonies of men and women who were deep in devil worship and paganism. These people were actual workers of darkness who took direct instruction from Satan to kill, destroy and steal from their victims. All had their apparatus immediately burnt after their encounter with the Lord Jesus Christ. You see, they know first-hand that they have to do this before they can have the freedom to follow Christ. This "cleansing" is the beginning of the process of the journey into total liberty called deliverance.

When the children of Israel were leaving Egypt, God Almighty permitted them to take gold, silver and raiment from the Egyptians. Lo and behold, the gold taken from the Egyptians, became the very first object of rebellion and sin in their lives. The gold collected, was used to mold and mount up a golden calf to be worshipped as their god. Exodus 32:2 *"And Aaron said unto them, break off the golden earrings, which are in the ears of your wives, of your sons, and of your daughters and bring them unto me. 4. And he received them at their hand and fashioned it with a graving tool, after he had made it a golden calf: and they said, these be their gods, O Israel, which brought you up out of the land of Egypt."*

This is what is missed in the story; both the gold and raiment belonged to the Egyptians but the raiment was instructed to be washed and not the gold and the silver. Washing signifies cleansing or sanctification but this was not done to the gold or the silver. Hence, the spirit of Egypt was able to influence the Israelites to rebel and sin against God, their deliverer.

I trust a clearer picture is being formed in the minds of God's people, my dear brethren in Christ. Let us look at another scenario in the New Testament.

In Matthew 21:12, *"And Jesus went into the temple of God and cast all that sold and bought in the temple, and overthrew the tables of the moneychangers, and the seats of them that sold doves. [13] And said unto them, it is written, <u>my house shall be called the house of prayer</u>; but you have made it a den of thieves."* (Underlining mine)

This was the cleansing of the temple of God before the work of the Holy Spirit could begin - clearly shown in *verse 14, "And the blind and the lame come to Him in the temple; and He healed them."* After expelling them, Jesus declared the place wholesome enough to be a house of prayer. This is deliverance, and clearance.

Brethren, we need to shout it out from the rooftops that deliverance is for now as much as it was then. The church needs to understand and administer deliverance so people of God can be totally free from the claws of Satan. This will help the advancement of the Kingdom of our God.

# CHAPTER 19

# Witchcraft

Witchcraft is the use of magic or sorcery. This is done under demonic powers and influences of the devil. This is another way that we invite demons in; knowingly or unknowingly.

I know this because I attempted to witness to a colleague of mine at work who emphatically told me and these were his exact words, "Oh my dear, I know there is God and I also know there is the devil, but I have chosen to serve the devil." I learned later on that he was president of the witches and the wizards in the area where he lived.

You see, some people love the power of evil they can exert over others inflicting hurt and destruction. I believe that this man loved that. He even told me how he went to his home country, and a known witch from his village brought him meat. He knew the meat was to hurt him so he paid this woman back by killing her son in the United States. He said he did this through a car crash. He then proceeded to tell me that African witches are not as powerful as those in the Western world are.

There were a few witches at my working place. I started to witness to them but they quickly changed the topic of conversation. They proudly told me they love the power, even still, I told them about the Savior, Jesus Christ. The interesting thing is, they all acknowledged Christ but it is all about their choice. What they do not know is that there is a higher power above all powers and that is the power of God Almighty who created all things including their master, Lucifer. The sad thing is that they have chosen to serve the creature instead of the Creator.

Another witch tried to convince me to come to his "church" after he had told me what they stand for and their practices. He actually told me I would be made a High Priestess if I join them. I declined and made all every effort to let him know that he was a Satanist and needed to repent and come to the knowledge of the Truth. This man was far-gone; a high priest in their cult. He told me things that blew my mind but I knew were also true. He could do astral projection to go anywhere in the world including other horrible things like human sacrifice. He was really taking me deep into their deeds when the Lord warned me to stop flirting with the spirits.

During one of my conversations with him, I found myself passing out. Yes, I was fainting and I shouted the name of the Lord Jesus to regain consciousness. Later on, I asked the Lord what that was about and that was when He told me to stop flirting with the spirits. Yes, that is the word He used "flirting." Up until then, I had never heard of this phrase being used anywhere in preaching or in teaching. God is merciful.

When I withdrew from having anymore further conversations with this co-worker, the Satanist, he asked his other friend also from the same cult, to try to convince me to join their sect. I overheard him saying to his friend, "this is the lady I am trying to win to our side."

One day, after I had withdrawn from him, he came to me and said, "Oh I came to visit you last night but I met someone else in your bed."

So, I asked, "who was it?"

He answered, "It was salt."

I then told him that it wasn't salt but my Lord Jesus Christ and he said, "The Christ"

I challenged him again to give his life to the Master and that was when he told me he used to be a Methodist preacher but something happened which made him choose this pathway. He became embittered by what others did to him, did not handle it properly and ended up in the satanic cult. Here he loved the power given to him by Satan over others and did not want to relinquish it.

Such people have literally sold their souls to Satan in exchange for power. Power to be famous, power to be rich, power to do evil and to cast spells over people in order to destroy or kill them. Some say they are white witches and they do not do evil things. That is a lie from the pit of hell. There are no demonic powers that are not used for evil things.

There is no good thing in the devil according to John 10:10 so why are we deceived into believing that white witches are good. Practicing witchcraft is a choice. Every witch knows he or she is a witch and knows the scope of his or her operation. As is the character of the devil, so are his subjects. They are all liars. There is no truth in them. Therefore, my brother and my sister do not be deceived, the devil is a liar and so are his demons and messengers.

There are different kinds and levels of witchcraft in operation in the world. We see children practicing how to cast spells on others, thanks to books like Harry Porter and other Television programs. There is witchcraft taking place even in the church, with some Pastors manipulating and controlling members. Disobedience is as sinful as witchcraft and yet the church of Jesus Christ is wallowing in rebellion and many have become disobedient and disrespectful of even God's authority.

I once had a work colleague that was also a friend until I was restored from my backsliding. On one occasion, she simply told me, "Do you know I have a spiritual husband?"
I asked her what she meant by that.
She repeated, "I have a spiritual husband and he is the only one who can satisfy me sexually." She continued by saying she faked orgasms during intimacy with her physical partners. Yet, with the spiritual husband, she really enjoyed it and was able to participate fully.

I then said to her, "You must be extremely lucky to have had children."
To this she answered, "I know, it is an arrangement between us (herself and her spiritual husband) that I can have children but I am not allowed to marry."
I told her that it was not good and was the reason she kept having one failed relationship after the other. She agreed with me on this so I suggested to her that she accept Christ and go through deliverance, She flatly refused the suggestion, saying, "Why should I allow him to be expelled? I love him."

Such a person has knowingly sold her soul to the devil. She is a willing captive in this case as she knows and enjoys the intimacy with this spirit. This is a form of witchcraft. She knows exactly what she is doing and she enjoys it as well. I know that this must sound weird and strange to some Christians; but I have met a few who were totally oblivious of the existence of demons and their operation until they read the book by Doreen Irvine, <u>From Witchcraft to Christ</u>, which I offered and pleaded with them to read.

There are others who have inherited witchcraft from their forefathers who had sold themselves and their descendants to the devil. This is not by choice. The Bible declares in Lamentations 5:7, *"our fathers have sinned and are not; and we have borne their iniquities."*

For such, Isaiah 52:3 says, *"For this is what the Lord says, you were sold for nothing and without money you would be redeemed. You ask yourself, how it will be done. The answer is, by His Blood we are redeemed."* 1 Corinthians 6:20, *"You were bought at a price. Therefore, honor God with your bodies."* 1 Peter 1:18, *"For you know that it was not with perishable things such as silver or gold that you were redeemed from the empty way of life handed down to you from your ancestors. [19]But with the precious blood of Christ, a lamb without blemish or defect. [20]He was chosen before the creation of the world, but was revealed in these last times for your sake."*

Dear reader, Jesus saves! Oh yes, JESUS SAVES!

Remember, the Bible says in 1 John 3:8. *"For this purpose the Son of God was manifested, that He might destroy the works of the devil."* Know that He came to set the captives free and if you desire of Him, He will surely set you free. You do not have to remain in bondage or a prisoner of the devil forever.

The question most people ask is why I should be punished for the sins of my fathers. God is not the one punishing you for the sins of your fathers; it is the effect of the covenant between them and the devil. That covenant gives the devil the legal right to oppress you, and do things against us even more now that you have accepted Jesus as you Lord. One might say but I am born again! Yes, you are.

Let me give an example. A married woman walks out of an abusive marriage and meets a man who by all standards looks like the perfect husband. Her investigations into his background bring more good news about him, so she decides to give it a go. After a while, he asks her to move with him in to another country where they decided to marry. Let us say the law of that land allows this and she gets married, even though she is not divorced from her first husband. Does her new marriage annul the first marriage?

The answer is, no. The first husband still has a hold over the woman. She is still his wife. She needs a clean bill of divorcement in order to be totally free of the first husband and marriage.

Another scenario is if this same woman had children with her first husband. Does her marriage to her current husband remove the first from her life completely? No, he will forever be in her life unless he signs over his paternal rights to the current husband or the woman does the same by giving him the sole right over their children. Only this would mean there is no reason for either to be involved in each other's life.

The same is true with our new life. It is either we renounce the devil and exclusively follow Christ or the devil will always have a legal hold in our life. Every bit of our sinful past has to be renounced and properly dealt with. Jesus went through all the legal procedures to secure our total emancipation so, therefore, we need not miss out on anything that is the truth; for we as human beings have a role to play to bring it to completion. You ask if the death of Christ is not enough to set us free. I say no. Did He not die for all mankind? Is all mankind saved automatically? The answer is, no.

Then next question then is, is being born again not enough? The answer is another no! Why would a true born-again believer struggle with certain works of the flesh? Not only do ordinary believers struggle, but ministers as well. Do you think they do not love God or desire to do what is right in the sight of the Lord? They do, but there is a war between good and evil raging within them. This is because there is something of his (devil's) left behind, which could give him a doorway into our lives, and cause us to go against the ordinances of God. This is where we then need to consider either self-deliverance or ministration from an anointed man or woman of God.

The book of Colossians makes this clear to us in Colossians 2:14. *"Blotting out the handwriting of ordinances that was against us, which was contrary to us, and took it out of the way, nailing it to His cross."*

Jesus went to the cross so we could be born again by His shed blood so that we can enter the Kingdom of God. The process to our total emancipation however starts from the moment we openly confess our sins and accept Him as our Lord and Savior. John 1:12, *"Yet to all who did receive Him, to those who believed in His name, He gave the right to become children of God. [13]Children born not of natural descent, nor of human decision or a husband's will, but born of God."*

These Scriptures led me to understand that everything in our lives as Christians is part of the process of being sons and daughters of Almighty God. At every step of the way there is some requirement from us to fulfill in order to meet the criteria of our eternal glory with Christ Jesus. This is the reason why the Bible clearly warns us in 1 Corinthians 10:12, *"Wherefore let him that thinks he stands take heed lest he falls."*

This verse tells me it is only by God's grace that we are who we are at any given time. We should not be complacent, but examine ourselves daily to see if all is well with our walk with the Lord. This pertains not only to our spiritual walk but to our emotional walk as well because the soul plays an equally important role in our Christian life.

I can always tell when my prayer life is not up to the level that feeds both my spirit and my soul. I see myself getting angry quicker and at the slightest thing. Something that I would normally let pass now irritates me easily. On reflection, I come to learn my prayer life has been affected for one reason or the other. Do you know why? The enemy is always lurking around us to catch us in our vulnerable state, to attack us emotionally in order to weaken us, to overtake us in our soul.

Please watch what you read, watch, touch or where you go. Be careful when friends invite you to "church" or any kind of meeting. Ask questions about what is done there, what you should be expecting and how it will benefit you in the long-term. Do not settle for anything that is not well explained to you. Many people have gone into places they did not know or understand anything about only to be forced into the occult with the threat that they will be killed if they attempt to leave.

A former witch, a high level one for that matter, who is now a minister of God, spoke about how her dear friend in their coven was killed before her eyes, simply because they desperately wanted to leave.. She pleaded with them but to no avail. According to her confession, three witches "travelled" through the walls of this woman's apartment, killed her and left the same way. There was no trace of force entry.

The demonic realm is real and its evil operation is as real as in the physical. The difference is that it is unseen at times. Demonic forces operate under cover of darkness; they are referred to as the kingdom of darkness.

It is never too late for one to seek help if you unwittingly did any of the above; even if you led yourself into it Our God is more than able to deliver you if you seek Him. He is not mad at you because you did that. No, he loves you, but He hates your sin. All we need to do is cry out for His help. He is that merciful. Do not let the devil triumph over your life. Jesus shed His precious blood for you so you can be delivered.

Remember He came to set the captives free!

# CHAPTER 20

# Mediums

Many Christians are very ignorant concerning mediums and this entire aspect of sorcery. This includes palm reading, tarot cards reading, tea leaves reading and horoscopes? Any means by which another person can 'read' and tell you about your past, present and future is demonic except he or she is a true prophet of God.

People do not stop to question things enough, and simply go with anything and everything. Ask yourself from where the person gets their power to know and tell you things about yourself you know to be true. If power to know comes easily and freely, just like that, we would all have such powers.

Do not be deceived, these people have signed pacts with the devil and, for their part, they have sworn to initiate as many as would come to them, into devil worship, one way or the other. The moment you give these agents of Satan access into your life, you are marked for destruction. Do not be deceived, Satan does not give free gifts; you will pay for it in whatever way he chooses.

Some 'medium' powers demand human sacrifice in order to gain more power from Satan. Sad to say, many Christians are ignorant of these things and permit palm readers by the roadside to read their palms. Many Christians read their horoscope on daily basis. I do not blame them because they have not been taught that it is demonic. I listened to a testimony of an undergraduate who used to be a high-ranking officer in the satanic kingdom. She confessed to having killed thousands of people including babies. She had rendered men and women impotent and barren during her reign by sleeping with them in the physical and in the spiritual... In her confession, after the Holy Ghost arrested her, she said it all began by reading her horoscope every day, which then led to her writing to some magazine in the U. S. for more materials on astrology. This is when she started having demonic visitations and then her final initiation into witchcraft.

Beloved, these things are real; do not be deceived by the devil that these are harmless fun. If you have been reading your horoscope or tarot cards, or have ever had your palm read, please go before the Lord in repentance and seek deliverance. Someone will say, "I did it before I was born again so I do not need to." Yes, you are a new creation old things have passed away and all things have become new, but it does not cost anything to take it to the Lord in prayer and thoroughly purge your soul.

Let me pose a question. If a prostitute contracts a sexually transmitted disease and afterwards becomes a Christian, does her new birth automatically bring healing and deliverance? In some cases, the answer is, yes, but in most cases the answer is no. Why is that? I cannot tell. It is God who chooses on whom to have mercy I do not have any knowledge on who or why. I have often wondered why some get instantly delivered from all forms of addictions in their life the very moment they are led to Christ, yet others have to go through a process for several years. Eli the priest said *"It is the*

*Lord: Let Him do what seems Him good"* 1 Samuel 3:18.

Being born again does not automatically bring deliverance from the effects of  the things in which we have indulged or been involved in. Cry out to the Lord and He will deliver you. Isaiah 52:2-3, *"shake thyself from the dust: and sit down. O Jerusalem: loose thyself from the bands of thy neck, captive daughter of Zion. For thus says the Lord, ye have sold yourself for nough t: and ye shall be redeemed without money."*

Our God is waiting to deliver us if only we cry out to Him. Do not let the devil fool you into thinking you do not need deliverance. What have you to lose if you cry out and you did not need to? God will bless you, or deliver you.

# CHAPTER 21

# Covenant

The Oxford Dictionary defines this as:
1 - *An agreement; a contract.*
2. - *Law drawn up under a seal esp. undertaking to make regular payments to a charity.*
3. - *Bible. The agreement between God and the Israelites (see the Ark of the Covenant.*

From these definitions the conclusion can made that believers enter into a covenant with the Lord from the very moment a choice is made to follow Jesus. This decision does not affect only us. Our families are automatically drawn into it according to the Scriptures. The jailer in the book of Acts 16:31 saw the power of God and asked, *"What must I do to be saved?"*
*"And they said, believe on the Lord Jesus Christ, and you shall be saved, and your house"*

Now look at this, it was only the jailer who accepted Christ, in other words, he entered into a covenant with Christ Jesus and the terms of that covenant were swiftly executed. The terms meant his whole household was automatically drawn into it. Paul and Silas were quick to spell out the terms of the covenant in its simplest way, that is not only you shall be saved, but your entire household.

He made a decision and immediately his whole household became beneficiaries.

Another Scripture in Luke 19 tells about Zacchaeus, the chief tax collector who joyfully accepted Jesus. He was told by the Lord in verse 9, *"This day is salvation come to this house."* In Acts 10 similar thing happened in Cornelius' house. Would I be wrong in saying the same is true if the head of the family decides to serve Satan? This is where generational issues come into the equation.

In life, I have come to know that every decision I make affects my children one way or the other. They may be totally innocent of the consequences of my bad decisions, but will their innocence stop the effects on them? No. When Achan sinned against God through disobedience, he was severely punished. His decision to yield to temptation affected the whole nation but the punishment to this sin affected his whole household. Joshua 7:24, *"And Joshua, and all Israel with him, took Achan the son of Zerah, and the silver and the garment and the wedge of gold, and his sons, and his daughters, and his oxen, and his asses, and his sheep, and his tent, and all that he had: and brought them to the valley of Achor.* [25] *And Joshua said, why have you troubled us? The Lord shall trouble you this day. And all Israel stoned him with stones, and burned them with fire, after they had stoned them with stones."*

Did Achan's household know about his decision to commit this forbidden act? Definitely not! Did they suffer with him? Absolutely! Covenants affect generations. The devil steals God's principles and uses them to accomplish his evil desires. God is a covenant-keeping God and so is the devil. Let us not ignorantly dismiss this basic truth.

Jesus took our sins and curses upon Himself. Curses are the penalty for our sins. However, He also gave us the keys to deal with certain things. The Bible informs us that Jesus rebuked the disciples when the father complained to Him about the inability of the disciples to cast the devil out of his son. Jesus later on confirmed that, *nevertheless this kind only goes out by fasting and prayers.*

That is the key right there for the believer to use in expelling demons. The full Gospel of Jesus Christ must be taught and applied in order to set God's people free.

What do we see in a marriage when the covenant is broken? The effect is not seen only by the couple who signed or made the pact; if there are children then they are likely to pay the price too. More often than not, the children pay more for a divorce more than their parents do. Was it their fault the divorce took place in the first place? No. Some children may well have been too young to understand what was happening, but they grow up suffering the effects of it anyhow. Some even carry the wounds into their future relationships, unless they receive counseling for it.

In the Garden of Eden, God made a covenant with Adam and everything was fine until the devil entered in with one purpose in his heart, to cause man to break the covenant with God. The consequences are still evident. Christ dying on the cross has now revoked the curse declared by God. As far as the believer is concerned, and for everyone that will come to believe in Him,

Jesus took the curse upon Himself so that we are no longer under the curse of God that was declared over man. Instead, we have the new covenant. However, the devil causes man to break this by assuming the identity of God and, unbeknown to man, formed a covenant between man and Satan.

Unlike God, Satan took the holy covenant and polluted it to make man worship him. Satan became the god of this world. The blood automatically removes the curse and we do not have to do anything more about it. Jesus did it all for us yet, as far as the satanic covenant is concerned, we need to renounce it to be delivered.

The reason for this is that we took on the nature of Satan, yes, every human being. Are we then at fault? No. We were not present in the Garden but our father, Adam, was, and as he sold himself to the devil by eating the forbidden fruit, we were all brought into the covenant even though we were yet unborn. Remember the Bible says Abraham paid tithes to Melchisedec and Levi who receives tithes paid tithes whilst he was in the loins of his father. (Hebrews 7:10)

This was a covenant that affected generations. This makes me aware that covenant is not just revoked but has to be broken by renunciation. This is a principle that God will not interfere with. He is a God of principles. There is a principle for sowing and reaping in life. You sow good deeds, you will reap good harvest. He is a just God who will not interfere with ma n's will including any demonic pact made by the fathers who have kept the children bound.

What I believe and know He will do is, offer knowledge of how to cry out to Him for deliverance. The moment we cry out, we are telling the devil, I no longer want your influence in my life anymore. I am born again and I have chosen to give my life to Jesus. One may ask if it is not enough to believe you are free from the powers of the enemy. No, that is not enough. The journey has just begun and so has the process.

An example is found in Acts 8 and the story of Simon the sorcerer. Acts 8:13 *"Then Simon himself believed also: and when he was baptised, he continued with Phillip, and wondered, beholding the Miracles and signs which were done. [18]And Simon saw that through laying on of the apostles' hands the Holy Ghost was given, he offered them money, saying, give me also this power, that whomsoever I lay my hands he may receive the Holy Ghost. But Peter said to him, your money perishes with you, because you have thought that the gift of God may be purchased with money. You have neither part nor lot in this matter: for your heart is not right in the sight of God."*

The Bible clearly indicates that Simon who was a sorcerer came to believe and was even baptised. In modern times, we would say he became born-again, baptised and, moving with the flow, is now enjoying the euphoria and the hype that comes along whenever there is a supernatural occurrence. He was probably speaking in tongues and all.

I am convinced that Simon was born again and going through the process. I also believe that the Apostle Peter treated him harshly considering where Simon was coming from, a sorcerer, who was saved but has not yet been delivered. I think Peter should have been a little more considerate with him as he himself was rebuked by the Lord Jesus Christ, referring to him as Satan. *"Get thee behind me Satan."*

The issue was that the devil still had a hold on him because of his previous involvement with him and his demon spirits. You can see from his response to Peter's sharp rebuke that he was unaware of the fact that, after he had believed and been baptised, the devil could still speak through him. I believe he was shocked at himself and fear gripped him. He quickly repented and was quick to do what Peter said. *"Then [he] answered Simon, and said, pray ye to the Lord for me, that none of these things which you have spoken come upon me."*

Would you say Simon was not born again? I believe he was sincerely born again but as he was not delivered, the devil was still in control over his passion for the supernatural operations including taking money for demonic operations. I also believe he sincerely thought things remain the same when it came to the power of God. The reason I believe strongly that Simon, the sorcerer, was saved is, the soul that is not yielded to the Holy Spirit cannot repent let alone entreat Peter to intercede for him. In this context, we need to know our family history if things are not going according God's will for our life. I know, without a shadow of a doubt, that you will trace the root cause to one thing or the other that took place in the family even before your birth.

In my case, much of what my grandmother and mother told me about certain family histories made proper sense to me the moment I understood the concept of deliverance. I came to understand why my grandmother buried all but one of her male children, eight of them before she died. It was very sad watching Mama burying all her sons one after the other. She died leaving only her two daughters and youngest son alive. I believe he was left because he was so highly involved in Satanism.

It was long after I became born again, that the spirit of the Lord reminded me of a story that Mama had told us grandchildren, about a cousin of hers who placed a curse on the house we lived in. Mama defiantly said she believes in God and that no evil would befall her from the curse. After the death of my grandfather, his family drove her and the eleven children out and she returned to her family home. She described the house as desolate and uninhabitable but she took it upon herself to make it habitable for herself and her children. She brought the house back to life.

Grandma was a staunch Presbyterian who would have nothing to do with anything demonic or pagan. One thing I have come to know and believe is, *what you do not know can actually kill or destroy you.* This is in stark contrast to what the world says: *What you do not know will not kill you.* Unknowingly, Mama brought her children to a demon infested, toxic environment that claimed her sons, one by one, including my own father.

I became born again in 1981, the first on both my paternal and maternal sides. It took me over two decades to know and understand what I am talking about now. It began to dawn on me after Mama died and all the members of our immediate family had left home, that the tide had turned towards the family of my grand uncle who had placed the curse in the house. They, too, began dying through horrible circumstances. There was an accident that claimed two of his grandchildren at once; both were buried the same day. Another one shot himself on a hot summer's day, something that is very uncommon to our culture. The devil pounced on his descendants with a vengeance.

The only way for the devil to be stopped in his tracks is for at least one family member to give their life to the Lord and stand in the gap for the rest. Beloved, the demonic realm is very, very real. A demonic stronghold in a family can only be broken by the power of our Lord Jesus Christ and His Holy Spirit through the shed blood of Jesus Christ. Some old-time altars have to be dealt with as the Lord told Jeremiah in *chapter 1:10 "See I have this day set you over the nations and over the kingdoms, to root out, and to pull down, and to destroy, and to throw down, to build and to plant."*

God gave this assignment to the Prophet Jeremiah. This is the voice of the Lord speaking to us, the body of Christ. There is a greater need for us today than ever before due to the increase in demonic activities and the open and acceptable display of witchcraft in our society. We need to root out, pull down and destroy the very foundation of family generational altars.

Almost every home in Africa had an idolatrous foundation before the missionaries came to introduce our forefathers to the God of the Bible. For this reason, we all have to apply the Word of God to root out and destroy this demonic root. We need to pull down the satanic strongholds in our lives just as we need to destroy the demonic altars in our families. We must seek God for guidance for deliverance.

Demonic covenants can be broken in the name of Jesus by the power of the Holy Ghost and the Blood of Jesus through deliverance. There are people who have gone into blood covenant with former lovers without thinking about the consequences. Those people require deliverance to break the demonic covenant before they can be happily married. The marriage will always be a rocky one because there is always another entity involved. This is because the blood covenant has bound two people together; referred to as a soul tie. We are blessed to be saved, so let us make the most of our salvation. Jesus paid in full with His precious Blood. Let not the shed Blood of Jesus be in vain in your life and mine. Remember, Jesus came to set the captives free. Do not allow the spirit of error rob you of something that Jesus Himself dealt with when He was on earth. You can be delivered today by the Lord through His servants who have the heart of the Messiah to break the yoke of bondage and the chains of the devil off your neck, feet and hands. I am not talking about physical hands and feet but the spiritual. I am talking about total emancipation.

Today, men break covenants easily, but our God is a covenant-keeping God. The covenant of marriage is a good example. See how easy it is for men and women to break this covenant. It is the ploy of the devil to cause chaos in our world today. If the home is on fire, the community suffers. This is because the children, suffering from the effects of a broken covenant, go out filled with bitterness and pain and most end up hurting others as well. The result is there for all to see. Men are killing each other because of a broken covenant. Bad business deals, or when one feels cheated out of an agreement, have resulted in death because there was a breach of covenant or contract. These are the doings of the devil and yet he is hiding behind the smokescreen of deception concerning deliverance. He wants to keep his covenant with you alive so he can steal from you. The devil is a liar; you will be delivered in the Name of Jesus! Desire your liberty, break the covenant of evil pacts and be free.

Another area is the pouring of libation in most African cultures. This is an act of pouring alcoholic drink or sometimes water on the ground to invoke the spirits of the departed to bring "blessings." During this act, some declarations are made that are highly demonic. This ritual is usually performed during a child's naming ceremony, traditional marriages, cultural festivals or funeral ceremonies. It is also performed during the annual pagan festivals and enthronement of chiefs. This is done to invoke the spirits of the departed.

So, many a child starts his or her life already dedicated to the devil unknown to him or her. This child grows up not knowing that there is a demonic covenant made by his parents without his consent. During sessions of deliverance, I have heard demons repeatedly say *"she is mine; I have married her for eighteen years so I will not go."* Some say, *"I have lived here from since she was born and now you are casting me out, where should I go? I am not coming out!"*

During a deliverance session for a woman in the church I was pastoring at the time, the demon spirit asked me, "Is she your child? Did you give birth to her? I gave birth to her so I have authority in her life.”

I said to her, “No, you do not; Jesus has all authority in her life so be quiet and come out of her, in Jesus name.”

It seems that demons understand the concept of covenant better than many believers do. Demons will make you understand that they have the legal right to remain in a person. The only way they will be evicted is by the application of the Word of God and the blood of Jesus. Revelation 12:11, *“And they overcame him (Satan) by the blood of the Lamb, and by the word of their testimony.”*

I want to announce to all believers that the devil has no legal power over you anymore because Jesus paid the price for your salvation in full. All we have to do is speak it out aloud to him. He thinks we are ignorant. Have faith in God that you are born again and, as a born-again Christian, the price for your deliverance has already been paid. Remember Jesus came to set the captives free, you can and you will be set free, in Jesus Name.

Where I come from; some children are dedicated to rivers, shrines and other things. Whatever you may have been dedicated to besides God Almighty is the devil and the Word of God clearly states, *“Thou shalt not serve any other god besides me.”* If you were dedicated to anything at all besides God, and you become born again, you will need to be delivered from those demons otherwise, they will forever harass you.

# CHAPTER 22

# Soul Ties

A soul tie is a form of bond created between two people. Usually, this is formed with a deeper feeling beyond the norm. This can be a spiritual or emotional connection. In our world now the first thing that comes to mind when the subject is mentioned is sexual intercourse but I do not want to limit it but put it into two categories with biblical examples.

There are two kinds of soul-ties. A Holy or Godly one and an ungodly one. In 1 Samuel 18:1, the Bible declares that, *"And it came to pass, when he had made an end of speaking unto Saul, that the soul of Jonathan was knit with the soul of David and Jonathan loved him as his own soul. ...³then Jonathan and David made a covenant, because he loved him as his own soul."* This is a Godly approved soul tie, that works together for our good as God intended.

Another Scripture in Colossians 2:2 states, *"that their hearts might be comforted, knit together in love, and unto all riches of the full assurance of understanding, to the acknowledgement of the mystery of God, and of the Father, and of Christ."* This is the desire of God to see His people in holy and godly soul-ties that binds us in unity and perfect love in the body of Christ. There is always peace and harmony wherever there is this kind of soul-tie; power and strength are released from our God to live a victorious life. The Bible commends us to live in this bond of unity and peace.

The second type or kind of soul-tie is the unholy and ungodly tie. This kind is based on fleshly relationships. A biblical example is when Solomon married wives from the forbidden nations that led him into idolatry. He served the idols of the foreign women and caused the covenant between God and his father, David, to be broken. 1 Kings 11:9-13, *"And the Lord was angry with Solomon, because his heart was turned from the Lord God of Israel, which appeared unto him twice, and had commanded him concerning this thing that he should not go after other gods: but kept not that which the Lord commanded. Wherefore the Lord said unto Solomon, forasmuch as this is done of thee, and thou have not kept my covenant and my statutes, which I have commanded thee. I will surely rend the kingdom from thee, and will give it to thy servant."*

Solomon suffered loss and it affected not only him but also the generation after him. Ahab married Jezebel and died horribly as a result of a soul-tie with a Baal worshipping queen, which resulted in the whole nation being led into idolatry.

Another story I want us to look at is story of David and Jonathan, two young men who entered into a covenant. 1 Samuel 20:14, *and thou shall not only while yet I live show me the kindness" of the Lord that I die not: But also, thou shall not cut off thy kindness from my house forever: no not when the Lord hath cut off the enemies of David everyone from the face of the earth. ...[16]so Jonathan made a covenant with the house of David, saying, let the Lord even require it at the hand of David's enemies v. [17]And Jonathan caused David, to swear again...."*

From this Scripture we form a picture of what I was referring to earlier on. When a covenant is cut, both sides are bound by its terms. Jonathan was killed in battle and David bitterly mourned his dear friend and brother. Later, he ascended to the throne and perhaps forgot about the covenant as it was reported that the entire household of Saul had been wiped out.

One thing we must know is that covenants are binding to all parties involved and any breach of the contract can be very damning. We see this from the consequence of Adam breaking the first covenant between him and God in the Garden of Eden. This brought the separation between man and his Creator; the line of fellowship was severed and man was driven away from the place of intimacy with the Lord.

David, as an anointed king, knew the importance of covenant. A day came that King David remembered the pact made between Jonathan and himself. I believe the Spirit of God prompted him and he quickly called into remembrance the terms of the pact. Remember, it went like this: even if I should die, the terms still hold for my entire household forever. 1 Samuel 20:14-16 *"And you shall not only while I live show me the kindness of the Lord that I die not: [15]But also you shall not cut off your kindness from my house forever: a, not when the Lord has cut of the enemies of David everyone from the face of the earth. [16]So Jonathan made a covenant with the house of David, saying, let the Lord even require it at the hands of*

David's enemies. [17]*And Jonathan caused David to swear again, because he loved him: for he loved him as he loved his own soul."*

King David, now in 2 Samuel 9:1, was burdened by the spirit of the covenant and without being sure if there was anyone left in the house of Saul asked, *"And David said, is there yet any that is left of the house of Saul, that I may show him kindness for Jonathan's sake?"* Note the word 'yet'. This means David was not sure if there was anyone left. In response to this question, it was revealed that there was one person left, Jonathan's own son, by name Mephibosheth Everyone seemed to have forgotten about him because he was in Lodebar due to his disability. He was lame. David, the King sent and fetched Mephibosheth. *In* chapter 9:7 *"And David said unto him, fear not: for I will surely show thee kindness for Jonathan thy father's sake, and will restore thee all the land of Saul thy father; and thou shalt eat at my table continually."* This was a covenant that was made as a result of a holy soul-tie.

Another biblical example of a holy soul-tie is the bond between Naomi and Ruth whereas the relationship between Samson and Delilah and others such as Ahab and Jezebel are examples of unholy alliances and soul-ties.

The same goes with any intimate association that we may find ourselves in, especially sexual relations outside marriage. The Bible says if you join yourself to a harlot, you become one body, 1 Corinthians. 6:16 *"Know ye not that he which is joined to a harlot is one body? For two saith he, shall be one flesh."*

This means if you knowingly or unknowingly sleep with anyone who indulges in occultism, witchcraft, or practices any form of spiritualism, you are bound to be a recipient of the demons that are in him or her. For this reason, even long after the relationship is over, you cannot seem to get over him or her because there is always a pull towards this person even if they are married and getting on with their life.

In some cases, the victims could not form any positive relationships let alone marriage until after deliverance when the covenant is broken by the power of the Holy Ghost and the power of the Blood of Jesus. Soul-ties are not only made through sexual relationships, but in ordinary friendships as well. Sometimes, something that we view as casual can develop into a serious soul-tie. The enemy of our soul is very subtle.

One time I was in a 'Women Aglow' meeting where the speaker shared her testimony to show from where the Lord had taken her, and the things He had brought her through. Among other things, she made mention of her acquaintance with a work colleague. This started as a co-worker relationship but she soon noticed that she was developing a strong physical attraction towards this man. As a happily married woman and a woman of God, she told her husband. They started praying about this. Each day at work was a strong test for her. She kept her husband informed of the struggles, and the prayers intensified until victory came.

It became evident that the colleague and worker for the couple, was stealing from the company's coffers. Being in the occult, he had cast a spell on the woman in order to subdue her for sex, which was to have become a blackmail ploy if ever his offence was exposed. This plan failed however; it was discovered after his departure from the company that he had stolen over $30,000 from their coffers. It is only the grace of God that saved this couple. She would have been a recipient of demons from the spells of this man, which would have destroyed her marriage and her credibility as a woman of God.

Watch this now, no one is immune from such things, it is all down to the grace of God that keeps us from falling prey to the evil forces of darkness operating through human-beings, who have yielded themselves as instrument of the devil. If this precious woman had slept with this man, not only would he have blackmailed her but also there would have been transference of demons that would have resulted in a demonic soul-tie. Thank God that this story ended victoriously by the grace of God through His divine intervention.

Still on the subject of soul-ties, the woman in the next story was not as fortunate as she was struggling in her walk with the Lord. A very dear friend of mine, working in a big organisation did a large amount of business while travelling with, and in the company of a male colleague. She confided in me about having an affair with this colleague. Their sexual involvement only took place whenever the pair travelled together.

She was extremely troubled and wondered if she should tell her husband. I counseled her and told her to break free from this man.

She told me it was hard since they worked in the same office and she was not a strong Christian then. I prayed with her and, during my prayer time, the Lord revealed to me that the man was using demonic powers on her, in order to climb the promotion ladder since she was in a senior position to him. He figured the only way to do so was to sleep with her and use it as intimidation and to blackmail her.

I prayed a prayer of deliverance over her and broke the soul-ties and told her to observe one or two things at work. One of these was not to drink the water that this man had decided he would provide to the office, out of his own pocket. I also told her to plead the Blood of Jesus on her chair and desk every morning before she sat down. I told her to always get to work earlier to pray and plead the Blood of Jesus in the office taking authority over every power that is operating there. I further advised her to stop taking orders from him and to assume her position as his boss in the office.

When she did all these religiously, the man became confused and afraid and started calling her "Madam." In short, the man was reduced to nothing, virtually powerless where my friend was concerned. All the intimidation ceased immediately by the power of the Holy Ghost. Praise God! Jesus is our victor. Hallelujah! The snare was broken. Now she is a very strong woman of prayer and she is growing fast in things of God.

The devil is a liar. Deliverance is for us today and forever. Can you see the difference between the two stories? The first woman was spirit-filled so she escaped from the snare of the fowler. The second was a weak Christian and so it was easy for demons to overpower her. I later discovered that there had been much witchcraft in her family and also in her husband's. There were serious demonic doorways that made her vulnerable to the evil forces of darkness. Thank God for Jesus! There is power in the blood of Jesus.

The Bible says in the book of Colossians 2:14 *"Blotting out the handwriting of ordinances that was against us, which was contrary to us and took it out of the way, nailing it to His cross; and having spoiled principalities and powers, He made a public show of them openly, triumphing over them in it."*

Jesus took care of our deliverance on the Cross so we do not have to suffer any needless pain. All we need to do is embrace the concept of deliverance as part of the full Gospel of Jesus Christ. From the cross, He declares, "it is finished." Everything was done, signed and sealed with His blood. Does this mean we do not have to do anything at all? No. We have to take action to be saved, right? That is, to confess with our mouth and believe in our hearts that Jesus is the Son of God. He came to the earth, lived, died and was resurrected to reconcile us back to our Creator. It is only through Him that we can be saved from eternal damnation and separation from God forever.

Salvation does not just walk to us; we have to take steps to walk into our salvation. If we need healing, we are instructed to call on to the Pastors or the Elders to pray with us, according to James 5:14, *"Is any sick among you? Let him call for the elders of the church; and let them pray over him, anointing him with oil in the name of the Lord"*

Why is it then that when it comes to deliverance alone, some ministers have a problem? Deliverance also needs a corresponding act, seek help, for God has anointed men and women to help us come out of bondage and to enjoy the full benefit of the Cross. Teaching, yes, but teaching alone will not bring deliverance, there has to be a corresponding action, and that is to pray over the person, casting out the demon spirits by commanding them to come out of the person just as Jesus did. Jesus did it, so why cannot we? Everything He did was to show us and teach us how to go about things in the exact way Jesus did it.

Please bear in mind that one has to desire to be delivered as no one can force any one to go through deliverance if he or she does not want to. As in all cases, God does not force anyone to do what they do not want to. Everything we do, even as believers, is all up to us. God will not overrule our freewill, He works with us based on our cooperation with Him and this is a choice.

I know a woman who has been close to me and still is. I came to the realisation that the Lord had connected her to me for mentorship. I was not a minister then, just growing up in the things of the Lord but very fervent in the things of God as I was very hungry for Him. Before she drew closer to me, she had a friend, a very dear friend for that matter.

I admired their friendship as it seemed there was this closeness and love between them. I will call the other woman, Maria, and my protégé, Cherie. Seeing them together always reminded me of the story of David and Jonathan.

Since Cherie and I went to the same church, we invited Maria to come with us, which she did few times. I put it down to the fact that she was not ready to commit her life to the Lord Jesus. Nevertheless, I continued to witness to her in the simplest unconventional way. She would always confess that I made it easy to understand Christianity.

However, after perhaps a year, I began having some awkward feelings about her, and then later on about their relationship. This troubled me to the extent that I had to question my own motives. The feeling grew stronger and stronger. I confirmed my motives determining that there was no reason why I would want Cherie to separate herself from Maria.

It was during this time that the Lord gave me a dream upon which I questioned Cherie, and she made some shocking confessions to me. I became angry with Maria but Cherie defended her. This made me to realise why I was feeling the way I felt. The Lord God Almighty wanted a total separation.

At this point, I told the Lord He would have to do what He thought necessary. During one conversation with Cherie, multiple revelations were coming to light and the Spirit of the Lord said to me that an Esau spirit had taking hold of Cherie. "Esau spirit?" I asked. I had never heard anything like that before. He went on to explain what an Esau spirit is and what it does.

I instructed Cherie to go and pray and listen to what the Lord would say to her and whatever He said, to do it. A whole month went by. One day, she came to work (we worked in the same office), and I looked at her and asked, "What have you promised the Lord?" Before she could answer, I said, "Go ahead and do it immediately." She had promised the Lord to embark on a twenty-one day fast for direction. She started the following day and, lo and behold, the Spirit of the Lord told her to inform Maria that from that day onwards she would be spending her break time with the Lord.

All hell broke loose and Maria, like the devil, tried to negotiate with Cherie. "That's fine," she said. "But how about spending the first break with the Lord and the second one with me?" Cherie said no. That was when her hidden agenda became exposed. Maria was conducting witchcraft and was subtly controlling Cherie, using her as a servant.

Cherie was five or six years older than her, and our culture would expect the younger to serve the older. The Esau spirit was set in motion against Cherie and instead, the opposite was happening.

I have left a great deal of the story out, but just to show you that there can be unholy soul-ties that can ruin the believer's life or steal his or her destiny if God does not intervene or if we do not seek to know Him and His Will for our lives. This relationship was broken and, of course, I became a target for malicious attacks from sympathizers of Maria who blamed me for the breaking up of the friendship. This was an unholy and an ungodly soul-tie.

The Bible clearly tells us to flee from darkness and it became clear that the two women had nothing in common. People operating through witchcraft look for easy and vulnerable targets to attach themselves to, so they can control or destroy them. Let us be vigilant, even in the church, for not all that is in Israel, is of Israel.

There are some who have soul ties with their church. A common thing they say is, "It is my grandma's church, and I have been going there since I was born. I was baptised there so I cannot leave even though they know there is no knowledge of the Scripture and obviously no understanding. When you hear this, you know there is a soul-tie with the church.

Begin to earnestly seek God if you find yourself in a dead or a cultish church and you discern in your spirit that something is not right, yet you find it difficult to leave. I believe there is something holding you back and it is definitely not the Holy Spirit but another force. Manipulation and control are forms of witchcraft. These are used by some Pastors to keep people from leaving their church. If the Holy Spirit is the one in charge of His church, then He will build His church and you do not have to manipulate or coerce people to stay.

On the other hand, if you are the one in charge, then obviously, you are leading in your own strength and will need to employ bullyboy tactics because of the fear that people will move on once they realise the absence of the Holy Spirit.

If you have realised this and still stay, you are under the influence of this person who clearly is not submitted to the Holy Spirit. In this case, just be aware that you are under the influence of the spirit of control and manipulation and are bound by it. You will need deliverance to break this kind of soul tie. Why would one want to leave a healthy church? I know that we have the nomadic Christians who go from one church to the other. I am not talking about those ones. I am talking about those who have been in a church for years and are not growing in the things of God.

You hear other preachers or teachers and you know in your heart of hearts that this is what is missing in your church. Why continue to stay? You see everything wrong in this church, you murmur and complain about it and yet, you cannot leave. This is a clear indication of a soul-tie!

Note that someday you are going to stand before the Lord and give account of yourself, not the church you attended or the Pastor whom you chose to follow instead of the Lord Jesus who died for you. Always seek to please God and not man. Fear God and not man. I am not advocating that people leave their church for just any and every reason. Seek the Lord while He may be found and, if He is not in your church, then seek Him elsewhere.

A serious example of soul-ties was what took place in Waco, Texas with David Koresh and others like Jim Jones who lured their followers to death. Their 'disciples' would not see the warning signs that were right before them. Even when family and friends tried to warn them, they still did not pay heed until finally, it was too late to wake up from their spiritual slumber. This is an extreme case of a soul-tie; we still have people with their souls tied to ministers and are reluctant to leave those churches or ministries.

Our loyalty must not be tied to man but Christ and Christ alone.

I have witnessed to people who have told me "I was born a [denomination] and I will die a [denomination]." This is a soul-tie. This is the church my grandma, my mum and dad and basically the entire family had attended since before I was born; I cannot leave.

Look! Salvation is an individual matter. Grandma will stand before God to give account of herself to God. On that day, God is not concerned in your generational soul-tie to a church. This is because He has not called you into a denomination; He has called us unto fellowship and relationship with His Son Jesus Christ. God wants you to forsake all and follow him.

You need help? Call for help to break the soul-ties. You do not have to wake up to the naked truth in hell. Deliverance is for now and forever just like healing and salvation. As long as we live in this world, salvation, healing and deliverance will forever be needed.

Jesus said in Matthew 10:35, *"For I am come to set a man at variance against his father, and the daughter against her mother, and the daughter in law against the mother in law. And a man's foes shall be they of his own household. He that loves father or mother more than me is not worthy of me: and he that loves son or daughter more than me is not worthy of me."*

Does this mean Jesus cause confusion in families? No! It simply means our relationship with Him should be our top priority in everything we do and in every decision we make. We should first of all ask ourselves if it will please my Lord. Is this what He would have me do? Is it in line with the Word of God? It simply means seeking to please Him and Him alone at all times.

It also means no compromise whatsoever, no matter with whom we are dealing. The truth should always be what we seek and observe to do. Of course, Jesus wants us to have peace in our homes with our families but this can sometimes affect our faith in Christ. Choose to please God no matter what the price is.

When you choose to follow a family tradition contrary to the ordinances of God just to please your family, then the Lord is telling us that we are not worthy of Him. We follow these ungodly ways because we do not want to offend our father or mother or uncle or auntie at the expense of our loyalty to our God. I heard about people disowned by their entire family all because they chose to serve our Lord Jesus Christ.

It can be a painful experience but it is worth anything and everything. On the Day of Judgment, my mother or father or any other person, will not and cannot take my place before the Great Judge, God Almighty at the White Throne or the Judgment Seat of Christ. The Bible is clear on this in Hebrews 9:27, *"It is appointed unto man, once to die and after that judgment and so shall each and every one of us give account of himself to the Lord."*

Everyone will take his or her punishment or reward individually. Husbands and wives cannot stand in for each other; and neither can parents stand in for their children if they have reached the age of accountability. Do not drag your feet for anyone because it is only when you have life that you can save others. Stand up, stand up for Jesus!

This brings me to my favorite illustration, the cockpit drill. Prior to take off every airline is required to do this so people are acquainted with what they are supposed to do in the case of any emergency. Passengers are always advised to put on their oxygen mask before attempting to help even their babies or children. Initially, as a young mother travelling with two kids under three years of age, I thought my priority would be to fix the kids' before mine.

One day as I was pondering over this drill, the Spirit of the Lord explained it to me that I can only help my babies if I have life, but if I do not fix my mask first, they will be helpless in case after I have finished fixing theirs I lose my life. He likened it to what I have just explained to you above. Everything about our walk with the Lord is you first; then you can be of use to others.

You soon realise that every ministration of the Word is directly pointed at you as an individual and not a part of group.

Will you seek to break the soul-ties and dare to take a stand for Jesus? Remember, He took a stand for you, even to the death on the Cross. Was it easy? No. In the Garden of Gethsemane, He cried unto the Father to take away the cup if possible, but He chose the Will of the Father over His own feelings.

Some men have to break soul-ties with their mothers. This is a very delicate subject as it is not always admitted or accepted by the men involved. Something is wrong when their mothers are unable to stay out of the affairs of their marriages. This kind of mother dictates the way her son should run his marital home. She freely comments on her daughter in law's ways of doing things as being wrong. She wants things to be done as she did in her family home when her son and siblings were growing up.

You know there is a soul-tie there when a son does not stop his mother but rather wants to enforce her desires in his marital home. This is not right; it is not healthy and has to be broken. There should be a healthy line drawn between giving respect and honoring one's parent.

I know of a young man who when he first was converted, he was on fire for the Lord. He told me how he feared his mother so much so that, whatever she said, had to be obeyed. This is not right on any level; a grown, married man "terrorised" by his mother. He was prayed for and was set free from this soul-tie with his mother. Praise God he was delivered and he now has control over his own life and family for that matter.

If you find yourself in a relationship where you cannot keep anything to yourself but are required to tell your partner everything while he or she will not say anything to you about himself or herself, be on the alert, pray and walk in wisdom. If you find it difficult to do the above, then seek God through fasting and prayer. Ask God to deliver you and He surely will.

You see, these things may seem like harmless everyday things but they might not be that to the spiritually alert person. I always encourage believers wherever I go, to pray for the gift of discerning of spirits so we are not taken unawares. The devil is smart and we have to be on constant alert to discern his subtle ways of hurting us lest he destroys us.

# CHAPTER 23

# All Forms of Spiritual Consultations and Operations

The Bible warns us about this in the book of Deuteronomy 18:10, *"There shall not be found any one that makes his son or daughter to pass through the fire, or that uses divination, or an observer of times, or an enchanter, or a witch, or a charmer, or a consulter of familiar spirits, or a wizard, or a necromancer. For all that do these things are abominations unto the Lord!* Let us look at these individually and see what it entails.

## Fire-walking

I know of demonic activities that require participants to walk on red-hot coals, and they do this without suffering burns or blisters. This is against even the law of nature. If any part of any living thing comes into contact with fire, there is supposed to be burns and blisters, if not severe burns. In this case, in order to prove their satanic powers, the demon spirits take over the person's body so that they do not suffer any burns whatsoever. Anyone who practices this is heavily possessed by the devil.

A Christian must not be anywhere closer to such celebrations, let alone participate in these. The reason being, there can be transference of demonic spirits during this display. Moreover, what has light got do with darkness?

I witnessed this practice first hand in my hometown where white men had travelled all the way from the US (we were told), to take part in the annual celebration of pagan activities dedicated to the gods of the land. There were supernatural displays of magical powers, which I found out after my conversion to be highly demonic.

## Charmers

A charmer uses charms to lure people into devil worship. A charm can be an object, act, or words having demonic or magical power or a spell. Some may dismiss this as mere acts of trickery. Well I have news for you. This is exactly what the devil wants you to think or believe so you will be lured in. By the time you realise it is real, the demons of the charm are harassing you.

I know of a magician who used to cut people into two, removed their intestines, chew them and returned them back to life. This was performed in various cities around my country of birth. There was this occasion when he performed this magic trick but was unable to bring the person back to life. He got arrested and died shortly afterwards in prison.

The devil is a deceiver who only possesses a limited amount of power, but the God of all creation has all power over all His creation. Joshua told the children of Israel to choose this day whom you will serve.

## Hypnotism

We see acts of hypnotism on primetime television. The devils have gained entrance into the media in such a way that nobody questions anything anymore. Let a Pastor go on secular television to preach or conduct a deliverance service and all hell breaks loose

Hypnotism is a demonic act; not just acts of illusion, as those who conduct this act want you to believe. I read in one of the leading newspapers in London, that a volunteer for a television hypnotism act later on experienced hallucinations and suicidal feelings. I know that these were demons harassing this man and telling him to kill himself.

All this was after he allowed himself to be a guinea pig for the devil. He sued the hypnotist and lost the case. The reason being he was not forced to participate but had volunteered. I strongly believe that some Christians do not even know the depths of these things and can easily be fooled if they happen to be around such practices.

Wake up people of God! There is an unseen realm that has dark hidden secrets. God has revealed these to us so we do not have to suffer needlessly. Deuteronomy 29:29, *"The secret things belong to the Lord our God: but those things which are revealed belong to us and to our children forever, that we may do all the words of this law."*

There is help in the Lord. The world says that what you do not know will not kill you, but in the Kingdom of God, what you do not know is what will kill you. Hosea 4:6 *"My people are destroyed for lack of knowledge."*

My dearly beloved, what you do not know will kill or destroy you. The devil feeds and thrives on our ignorance. Do not be ignorant, seek information and seek help; for remember, He has come that we will have life and have it more abundantly. (John10:10)

## Divination

This is insight into the future or the unknown gained through supernatural power. Bear in mind that the devil tries to counterfeit every gift of God. As a matter of fact, the devil is the chief counterfeiter. He imitates everything that God does and uses it adversely.

As God Almighty has His Prophets as His mouthpiece, so too has the devil got himself people whom he uses to tell the future or the unknown. They seem to have some measure of knowledge about people. This information is released to them by demons, so that people will believe in them and be lured into destruction. Today we see people are hungry for the unknown and the unseen, which is the supernatural. They are fascinated by miracles and they go to any length to seek information.

The sad thing is that many believers are ignorant of the fact that the devil has unleashed his agents, some of whom have found their way into the Kingdom of our God. They are not there for fun but are on a mission to infiltrate and contaminate God's people to ultimately destroy them.

Divination is closer to the real thing and, quite frankly, it sounds very real to the hearer. Most times it takes a spiritually trained ear to sift the information and its discharge to determine that it is of the devil. This is what is referred to as the discerning of spirits. Jesus warned us before He went on the Cross that all these people would arise, and we should always be on our guard. (Paraphrased)

The Apostle Paul warned the church in Acts 20:29, *"For I know this, that after my departing shall grievous wolves enter in, not sparing the flock. [30]Also of your own selves shall men arise, speaking perverse things, to draw away disciples after them.* [31]*Therefore watch, and remember, that by the space of three years I ceased not to warn every one night and day with tears."*

This is the burden that the Apostle has for believers, warning us to be spiritually vigilant. We are experiencing the same today and even worse than in his days... The worst part is that it is not only the wolves that have infiltrated but also those from within that have been corrupted by their own ambitious drive to make a name for themselves. Whatever their motives are and whichever way we look at it, they are of the devil. Jesus declared that if you are not for Me, then you are against Me. If you are against Him, then you cannot be operating in His Spirit.

My sincere desire is for the Kingdom of our God to arise and resist this move of demonic infiltration in the Body of Christ. The church seems to have become too tolerant and that is not good; you cannot change what you not willing to confront. People of God, we have a charge to keep, a God to glorify and we need to make the purpose of the Cross a driving force in all that we do, so we do not lose sight of the fact that He died to set the captives free. We need to fight for every soul the Lord has placed in our care; be each other's keeper, looking out for one another, and hold the hands of the fallen to help them rise again. This goes for all of us and not only for ministers. The days of being laid back should be over as we see the day of our Lord fast approaching.

The songwriter says, *"Rescue the perishing and care for the dying..."* We must see them in Heaven and great will be our reward. It is not too late to change the atmosphere in our homes and in our churches; beloved, we can do it. It is not by might nor by power but by the Spirit of the Most High God. We need the cleansing of the church of Jesus Christ now more than ever, from the pulpit to the last pew.

On our prime-time television, we see people consulting the dead through mediums who claim to speak with the dead. People go under hypnotic powers to quit smoking or lose weight. Why? The devil does not give free gifts. He cures you of something and he leaves his demons in you to take away your peace, money or your marriage. Even that, which we call cure or healing, is a temporary fix.

It is only the original manufacturer, our Creator, who gives lasting and permanent healing and answers our needs. The truth is that Satan is not all-knowing. It is only God Almighty who knows all. I remember how before the late Princess Diana died; it was reported that she had consulted a medium concerning her relationship with Dodi Fayed. It was in the newspaper a week before she died. My question was how come she was not warned against the impending accident that claimed her life?

Trust only in God who created you and let Him have your life and your future in His hands. Any form of medium used in telling the future and other things, aside from the Holy Spirit and real prophets who deliver God's Word, are demonic. 1 Timothy 4:1, *"Now the Spirit speaks expressly, that in the latter times some shall depart from the faith, giving heed to seducing spirits and doctrines of devils."*

We are now in the 'latter days' the Bible is talking about. The devils have infiltrated the churches with the spirit of divination, which is operating through false prophets. We need discernment and *discerning of spirits* in the Church of Jesus Christ now more than ever before.

Have you ever asked yourself how the woman in Acts 16:16 nearly got away with the spirit of divination by declaring who they were (the disciples or Apostles) and their mission in that city? This to the ordinary ears might appear to be from God but was actually the spirit of the devil trying to deceive the people to believe her power is authentic and from the Lord. This was because she was speaking what appeared to be the truth but was not; what appeared to have come from the Holy Spirit was not from Him at all. It took several days for the Apostle Paul to discern this in his spirit, to rebuke and cast out the spirit from the woman. I believe they may have been caught up in the euphoria with their guards down, hence taking several days to detect the demonic power under which she was operating.

This is also happening in our days and even worse as there is no detection, let alone confrontation or casting out of these demonic spirits that are trying to hijack the church of Jesus Christ. We need to bring back the power of the Cross and of the Word into the church in order to make the church a place of habitation for the Lord and refuge for us.

A consulter with familiar spirits fuels and feeds on divination. Divination is the practice, and the consulter is the one who makes the trip to enquire from the diviner. So, you see, whether you are the doer or the seeker, you are both abominations unto God and there are consequences for both according to Romans 1:32, *"Who knowing the judgment of God that they which commit such things are worthy of death, not only do the same but have pleasure in them that do them."*

## Wizards

A wizard is a sorcerer or a magician. Both are demonically empowered to do the devil's bidding to deceive and to destroy people's lives. The devil does not have your best interest at heart; in fact, he hates you as much he hates our Lord for coming to take the authority to rule the earth realm from him and giving it to us.

Do not be deceived; the enemy will lure you with riches and all the good things you can think of. This is temporal and it will not be long before you see the falsehood when the riches turn into something unforeseen. One thing I have learned and believed is that the devil does not give free gifts as our God does. When the devil gives you something, know that he will require from you; something of worth in return. Not only that but he will use it to destroy your life and home.

Every gift of God is free and He adds no sorrow to them, but Satan adds sorrow to his. In short, Satan will add interest to what he gives you and this interest is not something that you can simply pay off. It is an everlasting debt unless you cry out to the Lord to intervene. Nevertheless, He will come and save you. Isaiah 35:4, *"Say to them that are of a fearful heart, be strong, fear not…He will come and save you."*

Jesus loves and cares about you.

## Necromancy

This is the predicting of the future through supposed communication with the dead. It is also a form of witchcraft. Some practitioners literally make midnight trips to the cemetery to invoke the spirits of the departed to obtain powers to destroy others. There is no demonic power that is for the good of humanity, in fact, it can only lead to death and destruction.

All who practice necromancy and other consultation methods are empowered by the devil, though some want people to believe otherwise. If you ever go to seek help or information from anyone else apart from God and His anointed servants, know that you are selling your soul to the devil; be it knowingly or unknowingly. The Bible says whosoever or whatsoever we yield or succumb to, we become slaves to. Therefore, if anyone consults any form of medium, he or she is expressing their faith and trust in that and whatsoever you trust in, you definitely tend to depend on it for your spiritual and physical needs.

Meanwhile the Bible says in the book of Exodus 20:3-4 *"Thou shall have no other gods before me. Thou shall not make unto thee any graven image, or any likeness of anything that is in heaven above, or that is in the earth beneath, or that is in the water under the earth. ⁵Thou shall not bow down thyself to them nor serve them: for I the Lord thy God am a jealous God, visiting the iniquity of the fathers upon the children unto the third and fourth generation of them that hate me."*

From this Scripture we know that anything we yield ourselves to, or surrender to, apart from God the Creator, is an idol and there are both spiritual and physical consequences for doing that.

These days there is more and more openness about abominable activities. Television has become a channel for both good and bad activities. The internet has taken things to another level while political correctness has given an open forum for all to advertise and market their 'products'. Witches are openly and proudly declaring their vocation, hypnotism is being carried out on primetime television, mediums are consulting the dead for their audience and the list goes on and on.

Meanwhile, in the not-so-distant past, these were considered an abomination by society. Godliness has diminished in our westernized culture. Liberalism has given way to a more demonized society and there is no fear of God. As a matter of fact, Christianity is losing its grip on society. There is open hostility towards Christianity, whilst other religions are allowed to 'flex their muscles' in the land that is considered to be a Christian nation. Men like John and Charles Wesley, Charles Spurgeon, Smith Wigglesworth, and others paid the price to help establish this nation in the faith of our Lord Jesus Christ. The United Kingdom is considered to be a Christian Nation but the voice of Christianity is slowly fading away as other religions gain ground. May the Good Lord help us!

The Bible says whilst men slept the enemy came to sow tares among the wheat. The universal Church has fallen asleep and needs a rude awakening. The church has lost its voice in the world, but there is still time for us to get it right before the Lord Jesus returns.

All the points I have mentioned are only some of the doorways the enemy uses to invade an individual's life or even a nation. It is time us, Christians, wake up from our long sleep and begin to pray for the universal church and the nations we live in. The Bible says, *"righteousness exalts a nation but sin is a reproach to any people."* (Proverbs 14:34) If we do not pray for deliverance for the nations, for a fresh move of God and stay where we are debating the Word of God ignorantly, the demons will destroy the land and the Lord will hold us accountable.

# CHAPTER 24

# Legal Doorways We Open for Demons

There are so many ways the devil can use to mess up our life. The enemy can gain access into our lives through sound, sight, smell, drugs, sex and ignorance, bitterness, un-forgiveness and resentment. All these can open legal doors to the devil to come in to attack us.

## Sounds

Sound is a sensation caused in the ear by the vibration in the surrounding air or other medium; an idea or impression conveyed by words; (audible or not.) Every born-again, Christian knows that God speaks and so does the devil. Some have heard the audible voice of the Lord; others the inner voice picked up in our spirit. He speaks in visions and dreams. He speaks through His servants the prophets. God also speaks to us in hymns, songs and in His Word, the Bible. He also speaks to us through doctrinal books and wholesome movies, both secular and Christian movies.

Satan also uses these methods and media to propagate his mission of destruction. Sounds have become the greatest asset for the satanic kingdom. Music is playing a major destructive role in our fast deteriorating society. The devil is using music to lure people, especially our youth into suicide, murder, sensualism, promiscuity and many more anti- social behaviors. Blasphemy is top in his arsenal, especially through music. I am privileged to have had teenage children who furnished me with some lyrics that they themselves can easily identify as demonic.

It is no secret what Hip Hop has done to our society. Heavy Metal is another genre often used by the devil. The violence portrayed in the videos and the sensual enactments are clear to see. Unfortunately, this is a perverse generation so nobody seems to condemn anything because nobody wants to become a 'scapegoat'. It is all about being politically correct and diverse. That is to please people and not to do anything to step on any toes.

The devil infiltrates our minds and lives through the sounds and lyrics; these flow into the soul and begin to exert their influence in the life of the hearer. This slowly begins to eat into the very fabric of the soul and that is when the spirit behind the song takes over and possesses it fully. The Bible tells us to resist the devil and he will flee from us. You cannot resist him if you are cooperating with him, so, at this point; the unfortunate soul begins to do whatever the words are suggesting. Do not forget that Satan's strategy is to first suggest his intentions as we see in the temptation of Jesus in Matthew 4:3, *"And when the tempter came to him, he said, if thou be the Son of God, command that these stones be made."*

This was a suggestion. The devil did not push it at that moment. So, Satan will initially only suggest and the weak will soon be ensnared. Once ensnared, you are under his demonic influence and for that matter, in bondage. This is where the battle begins for your mind. He appeals to your mind and if you do not resist him, he engages you with challenging thoughts and images. The Bible says, we are to resist the devil and he will flee from us and, if you pay too much attention to him, you will fall into his snare, just as Eve did in the Garden of Eden.

Do you know what people say when you try to point out the spirit behind certain kinds of music? "Oh, you are over spiritualizing everything, this is just music." Well, that it is another lie of the enemy to lure you into his web of destruction and if, at this point, you still have not realized that Satan is in control of your mind, then you are in serious trouble.

Wake up! It is not just music, there is a spirit behind the lyrics and even the sounds, and the more you listen to these songs, the more you open yourself up to demonic invasion. I have listened carefully to some of the lyrics of some of Michael Jackson's songs and was shocked to hear him singing, "*I sold my soul to the devil*" and many other similar lyrics. This is an artist that I have enjoyed listening to as far back as I can remember, until I understood for myself not to listen to secular music.

The Hip Hop genre is full of hate, violence and blaspheming and yet, some believers do not see anything wrong with it. From this moment on, after absorbing all these unwholesome music into your soul, know that you have been ignorantly enslaved by the devil. Your life begins to take a new turn; your attitude and your mood begin to change for the worse. You easily become agitated, aggressive and vicious. Some people also become extremely withdrawn, spending more time indoors in their own rooms and in their own company, and yet, in the company of the demons which have taken over their lives. Such people sometimes do not even bath or shower for days.

Sometimes people around you may comment on the changes in you. Please do not just dismiss or ignore this; consider their sayings and seek help. When the devil entered into the Garden of Eden, he did not just stand by to watch Eve. He approached her with a sound, the sound of his voice bringing suggestion. Be careful what you or your children listen to in your homes. If you are reading this book and you are not born again or you are in transition or, in the valley of decision, and you are a music lover; I recommend you listen to songs that are uplifting and not songs that talk about murder, hatred, and devils.

Do you know, and some of us from Africa can tell you, that serpents love music? Satan was created with every musical instrument in him and he was the anointed Cherub that covered God Almighty with worship. Satan was cast down from heaven and that is why he has hijacked the music industry and is perverting this generation with it.

There have been many incidents that I know of when serpents have been found at places where music was being played; even in some church houses. Serpents love the sound of organs/pianos.

Saturate your homes with godly stuff. Fill the atmosphere with praise and worship songs. One might say it will be boring. What is boring? Where the Holy Spirit is, there is no boredom; there is excitement and joy. What a place to be!

In the presence of the Most High there is joy, peace, hope and righteousness. Create an atmosphere in your home for the Lord's habitation. Demons can never be comfortable where the presence of the Lord is. These days the devil has comfortably come into the church. There is hardly any difference between the believer and the unbeliever. Even our praise and worship have become a time of entertainment. Performing has replaced true praise and worship.

Satan is very pleased yet we are not in the least disturbed by the state of some of our churches today. May the Good Lord deliver us! Everything goes in the church of Jesus Christ today. We want to befriend the world for the world to be converted. This is fine to a degree, but we should not allow the world to take over the church. That is not what Jesus taught us. This is very dangerous. We are dancing with wolves, and if things do not change sooner rather than later, some of us will be devoured.

Yes, we will become like prey to the teeth of the evil one. You wonder why some Christians cannot worship God in the midst of His congregation, let alone in their homes? The answer is simple; someone else has taken residency in their soul and it is not the Holy Spirit. There is an entrenchment in their soul and it is only when deliverance is administered that their souls shall be free again to worship their Creator.

What we call praise and worship today is no longer ministration but performance and entertainment. We go to church to be entertained by loud noises created by instrumentalists who want to show off their prowess but are spiritually depleted. Christians who are leading praise and worship are living in sin and there is no reproving or correction for fear of them leaving the church. In fact, some of them are highly demonized.

These days every manifestation is described as 'the anointing'. There is no discerning of spirits any more. Do you not know that the devil also 'anoints'? Some of what we see in our churches today is performance and not ministration. They minister in the flesh and not in spirit: to the flesh and not to the spirit. Performance entertains whilst ministration exalts God and edifies the believer.
It is acceptable and proper that churches should make accommodation for the youth but we should not be consumed by their way of doing things in order for them to fit in. Back in the day, when I got converted, the church did not change to accommodate me; I changed according to the Word of transformation I experienced when I encountered the Messiah.

The Bible says Jesus Christ is the same yesterday, today and forever, so has Jesus changed that we should change His way of doing things? No! We, the church, have to get back to basis; to His way or nothing else. There have been many young men and women who have been used by God Almighty from their youth, yet the standards of their fathers were never compromised. Samuel, David, Jeremiah, and Timothy were all very young when God raised them up and used them. There was no mention of the standard being lowered for them.

My prayer is that we will get back to basis to align our deeds to the Word of God. Anything done outside the principles stated in the Word of God is not His way and we, the church, should repent of the way we have made it.

People are dying and eternity is crying out, seeking a people to stand in the gap, to bring deliverance and healing to the souls that are perishing day by day. The saddest thing to happen to the body of Christ is to hear that someone in the church has committed suicide, especially if they were a young person. That young person must have been in and out of church and may have even been a member of the choir. Did it just happen? No. I believe there were signs which were ignored simply because they had an angelic voice, performed very well, were present at every meeting and seemed to be doing well.

The telltale signs were never picked up on. Why? We are worshipping ourselves in the church now and not Jesus. We are too busy taking care of things that are not as important as the soul of the people sitting in the pews for whom Christ shed His blood. Matthew 25:43 *"I was a stranger, and you took me not in: sick, and in prison and you visited me not. [44]They also will answer, "Lord when did we see you hungry or thirsty or a stranger or needing clothes or ill or in prison and did not help you?" [45]He will reply, Truly I tell you, whatever you did not for one of the least of these, you did not do for me."*

As long as we focus on building big cathedrals and lose sight of the well-being of the people, we are not doing the Lord's will. We need balance in the Kingdom of our God.

Sound can cause an entire home to be infested with demons when particular songs and lyrics are continually played. One woman of God, Marilyn Hickey, wrote "<u>Satan proof Your Home</u>" This book really blessed my household and I in my early walk with the Lord. At that time things were happening in my home. There were footsteps in my corridor at odd times when I was by myself. My daughter was having nightmares, which I knew were demonic attacks. A cane patio chair I had would sometimes rock back and forth as though someone was sitting and rocking in it.

My husband thought I was being paranoid and over spiritualizing things until one night whilst I was at work, he just Wenham gone to put our girls to bed when all of them heard the footsteps in the corridor. According to him, both girls sprang up and asked, "Who is it daddy?"

He said to me, "Now I believe what you have been saying all this time." Oh, now he believed!

Please pay attention to family members at home when they tell you of their weird experiences, even if you are skeptical. These things are real, they are very real. I watched a true movie back in the nineties where a family bought a property and as soon as they moved in; their older son started receiving visitations from a being.

Nobody, including his parents, believed him when he told them. This went on for weeks and months and his parents started accusing him of seeking attention.

Anyway, after a while his younger brother also started experiencing similar attacks from this being. He was once yanked from his bed and thrown on the floor. When he complained, his parents moved him out of the room he was sharing with Paul, his older brother as they felt he was influencing him. Paul was left alone to accept this creature and the visitation. He would wake up with visible scratches on his body but his parents remained in denial.

One day their niece came on vacation and while they sat at table for dinner, the girl was whisked and slammed into the wall. This petrified them all. That night Paul attempted to rape his cousin and that was the breaking point for his parents. They now checked him into a psychiatric home. After that, the being turned on the younger brother, yet still the parents were in denial until one night the father woke up with scratches around his midriff. This time they believed and send for an exorcist who could not handle the situation and so abandoned it. Someone introduced them to a church and the minister came to pray for them from time to time and things became quiet for a while but not completely. It was later on revealed that their house was formerly a funeral home.

Folks, these things are not imaginations as some of us may think, they are very real. We are dealing with a real devil here and that is no joke. Everything that has a name exists. That is why it has a name and it is as simple as that.

The Lord used my little girl's nightmare episodes to teach me and fire me up into prayer and spiritual warfare. This is the moment the Lord began to teach me how to wage war against the demonic forces that seemed to have invaded my home. All this while, I did not know anything of what I am writing about today. It all came together after years of battling in prayer, and my desire for information about the subject both from the Word and from the teachings of the late Derek Prince, a renowned man of God.

I still did not have the full picture of what it was all about. One thing I thank God for, is my daughter, and I began to learn how to use the Scriptures to pray. As I was teaching her, I was learning as well and very quickly, for that matter. I believe the Lord orchestrated it to be so and thank God, He did.

A member of a church I attended was admitted to a mental hospital. Her case was clearly a demonic case, but when dealing with systems in the Western world and when the family is not well vested in the things of the Lord, one has to tread cautiously. She was allowed to be hospitalized, and the church prayed for God's mercy and divine intervention. God, in His mercy, answered us and she was released within a week.

I am not going to delve into her case but want to look at something we overheard during one of our visits to the hospital. During this visit, we heard this loud cry from a woman and to tell you the truth, had I not been told it was a woman, I would not have believed it until I saw her. Her body frame and size, and the sound I heard, did not match at all.

What do I mean by that? The woman was tiny and petite and the sound was as though it was from a male with a loud speaker. What was very strange about this was, the sound filled the whole place and even carried to the large waiting room where we were, and it hit my spirit like a bolt. I felt a great sound wave hit me in my stomach; and this is no exaggeration. I stood up and asked, "Who is this man?"

That was when we were told it was a woman. If I was not strong in the Lord or experienced with what I had experienced, I know without a shadow of a doubt that I would have returned home with some demons in me. I knew what to do as soon as I got out of the hospital. The place in itself felt heavy with demonic presence. You could even tell that some of the workers in this mental hospital were affected by the way the patients behaved. May the Lord have mercy on His people who work in such an environment.

Still on the subject of sound, God works through sounds and Satan does as well. What you continuously listen to, can affect your spirit-man irrespective of you being a Christian or not. In 2 Kings 4:6 *"For the Lord made the Syrians to hear a noise (sound) of chariots, and a noise (sound) of horses, even the noise (sound) of a great host… ⁷Wherefore they arose and fled in the twilight, and left their tents, and their horses and their asses, even the camp as it was and fled for their life."*

This sound from the Lord created an atmosphere of fear and terror. The spirit of fear took hold of a whole army including their commanders. This was God's act of defeating the enemies of Israel and also to bring instant provision for His people. This is what I call the sound of producing an atmosphere for the impossible and miraculous. It was sound that brought down the walls of Jericho.

Beloved, every sound carries a spirit, and these spirits have specific assignment in the hearer's life. I use the word hearer because I have come to know that there is a difference between hearing and listening. When you choose to pay attention to what you are listening to, that is when you are hearing what is actually being transmitted and then you act on what you hear. We are living in a world that so much is going on around us but it is what you hear that can and may affect you. I can be in a place where worldly song is being played and since I do not have the right to turn it off, and I cannot block my ears from listening to it. I have a choice to hear what the song is saying or not. My ears have no choice but to listen to the sound but I have a choice to give attention to what I am listening to or not. Listening can proceed to hearing and this is by choice.

As I said earlier on, every sound carries a spirit, either the Spirit of the Lord or demonic spirits. The wonder of sounds is the fact that there have been testimonies of people in coma who have had healing Scriptures played over them day after day will come around from that state. Others respond to healing songs recorded and placed by their bedside.

I was conducting a Friday night prayer service and the power of God hit me when I was reading a Bible verse, I felt the surge of the anointing of the Holy Spirit come upon me at the time and there came a violent manifestation to this from one of the members. This lady reacted violently and began to literally sweep the floor with her hair. This went on for some time and when the service was over, still being in shock of what had happened to her, she came to me for help. What had happened was the demons in this lady heard the sound of my voice reading the Scriptures and it was not just that but there was also an anointing upon me when I did that. I felt the surge of the anointing and obviously, the demons in her felt it too and reacted through her.

Someone who had visited us in church invited me to his church and I went just to reciprocate his gesture. As soon as I entered the church, I knew within my spirit that it was not the Holy Spirit in charge of operations in the church but demons. I wanted to leave but the ladies I took with me were separated from me and I could not locate them to motion them for us to make our exit. I first of all invoke the blood of Jesus on my ladies and myself. As the service progressed one of the Ministers took to the podium and began to breathe upon the congregation through the microphone. In response to this, there were some serious manifestations with people making all sorts of funny noises. Others were flapping their wings like birds and falling down. I became vexed in my spirit and began to decree things as I prayed in tongues. I made a declaration like this: "Lord I am very sorry for not asking you permission or enquiring from you before making this trip here, and not just me but I brought these precious daughters of yours as well. Lord, the

Bible declares that whatsoever I shall decree shall be established by you therefore in the Name of Jesus I forbid any spirit from operating in this place as long as I am here. I also declared that I block every spirit from their exhibitions and manifestations here in the Name of Jesus." Do you know that the atmosphere became diffused immediately and this is no exaggeration! I say it to the glory of God. As I was in the front row, the "Minister" turned and looked at me and our eyes were now fixed and locked in each other's. At this point I knew he had identified me as the one responsible for the change yet not I but the Spirit of the Most High God. Beloved we have power through Christ Jesus and His Precious Holy Spirit. There is also power in His Precious Blood. He tried and tried and could not rise to the occasion so he abandoned the so-called ministration. I left the place shortly afterwards. Ladies and gentlemen, there is power in the Name of Jesus; we just have to take the authority to use it and every knee will have to bow and every tongue will have to confess that Jesus Christ is Lord of all to the glory of our God. What happened here was, there was a sound that troubled my spirit and I counteracted it with a super sound from the Lord. Note this; the demonic realm is as real as the heavenly realm. They are unseen but very real, as real as the earth realm.

Drums are often beaten during pagan festivals to invoke demonic spirits and to open people up to be possessed by demons. Likewise, trumpets can be sounded in the house of God and there will be the manifestation of the power of God with evidence of tangible healings and other notable miracles. Sound, beloved, is very powerful in both worlds. Mark4: 24b Jesus says, *"Take heed what you hear:"*

What you hear can affect you in either a good or a bad way. The Bible often says, *"Hear ye this O Israel"* which means listen and give attention to what I am about to tell you - sounds can affect us indeed.

When children and adults too, play their computer games, it is the sound effects that excite them and they get lost in it; such that some will not even take a break to eat. The sound effect is used to captivate the mind and soul of the individual and eventually, they become addicted to some of these demonic games. In the book of *2 Kings 7:6-7, "For the Lord had made the host of the Syrians to hear a noise of chariots, and a noise of horses, even the noise of great host: and they said one to another, Lo the king of Israel has hired against us the kings of the Hittites, and the kings of the Egyptians, to come upon us. Wherefore they arose and fled in the twilight, and left their tents, and their horses, and their asses, even the camp as it was, and fled for their life."*

It was sound that God used to put fear into these enemies of God such that they had to flee. Sounds have power to affect the hearer, whether for good or bad. In short, sound can open the doors to our souls for demons to enter in. The devil knows this only too well. This is why he has hijacked the music and cartoon industries. The cartoons have been hijacked to captivate the very young children and the music for the young adults and old folks alike. He is not stupid. The devil is a very wise angel of darkness and he starts with the young at a very early stage of their life; seeking to destroy them with sound, is one of the many of several ways he comes after us. Parents, let us monitor what kind of music our children are listening to and advise them. Sometimes they will see this as intrusion of their privacy but you have to patiently explain the truth about these songs and their effect on their minds and souls. We, the parents have the God-given right and authority to control what takes place in our house. Music has the power to change the atmosphere in the house so choose what kind of atmosphere you prefer and educate your kids before it gets out of hand.

## Sight

This is the faculty of seeing with the eyes: 2. a way of looking at or considering a thing. This is the dictionary meaning of sight. I want us to consider the way we look at things as Christians. This is very important, as the eye is the doorway to the soul and the spirit, spiritually speaking.

The Bible says in John 3:3, Jesus said, *"Except a man be born again he cannot see the Kingdom of God."* This means one cannot perceive or understand, let alone consider, the way the Kingdom of God operates. You can only do that by the opening of your spiritual eyes that is, sight, given by the Spirit of the Lord. This is when one gets connected to the Spirit of God and one is able to understand clearly what the Kingdom of God is and what it is all about.

What we see can affect the way we think and behave. I believe seeing involves paying attention to something that one happens to set their eyes on; whether consciously or subconsciously and in stages. When you pay attention to it then, you can see what that thing is all about. In the Garden of Eden, Eve looked around her everyday as she and Adam walked through the Garden, until the day the devil called her attention to something. The Bible says in Genesis 3:6 *"And when the woman saw (gave attention to, and considered and decided) that the tree was good for food, and that it was pleasant to the eyes, and a tree to be desired to make one wise, she took the fruit thereof, and did eat, and gave also to her husband with her, and he did eat."*

The sight of a thing can scare you to death or can excite you. One of the ways the devil enters our minds is through images. In the Garden of Eden, the devil pointed out to the woman, the object of contention, which was the tree of knowledge of good and evil. She looked and saw. There is a way of looking that will cause you to be ensnared by the evil one. We have just read Genesis 3 but let us go over it again and see the picture as it is. *Genesis 3:6 "And when the woman saw that the tree was good for food, and that it was pleasant for the eyes, a tree to be desired to make one wise, she took the fruit thereof, and did eat..."*

Eve paid too much attention to what was said by the serpent about what she was looking at (The Tree) and the suggestion from the devil. She was trapped in the web of deception of the devil. Adam and Eve had always strolled in the Garden and had no doubt walked past this tree numerous times. Is it possible they had walked past day in and day out and not seen it? It was visible to them at all times but had never considered eating it until the serpent came in and caused Eve to give attention to the tree in question. In this same way, we could also be ensnared by what we see.

Images are powerful. Have you ever heard the saying that a picture is worth a thousand words? That is exactly that. People watch horror movies and become possessed by the spirits of that particular movie. People often say, "Oh! It's just a movie." Let me sincerely tell you something; behind every movie there is a spirit and this is true.

Ten and eleven-year-old boys who watched Chucky, a movie about a doll who went on a killing spree, then went on to commit murder in exactly the same way as this possessed doll had executing his victims in the movie. This is a true story that happened in England in the early 90's; a crime that shocked the whole nation. The victim was a two-year-old boy. What on earth got into these two children? That is exactly what they were, children!

The content of the movie fed their imaginations and the devil moved in swiftly to suggest to them what they had to do with the information gathered from the images that had been fed to their souls. Once the spirit had possessed them, it led them to find a victim. No matter what, they would have murdered somebody that day; it was only unfortunate that it happened to be a child who had strayed from the mother's sight when she stopped to buy something.

Another movie, on the other hand, is the Passion of the Christ. How can people watch this movie, and surrender their lives to the Lord

Jesus? It was the Holy Spirit who was the director of the movie and not Mel Gibson. Gibson himself confessed to this in an interview. How would someone shoot a movie, *"The Queen of the Damned"* and be damned in truth by dying in a horrific plane crash immediately after shooting the movie?

In this case it was the evil spirit that directed the film that killed her after using her to fulfill his agenda. She became damned indeed, when she was killed in that plane crash. The spirit of death that killed her is still alive to either kill or destroy anyone who watches it.

A friend of mine told me she loved horror movies and I could not lecture her about the demon spirits behind such movies because, at the time, I did not have the knowledge I have now which would have enabled me properly explain things to her even though I knew it was wrong. For a believer, her life seemed quite weird. As I began to grow in the Lord, I realised that she lacked understanding and was comfortable to remain a 'baby Christian.'

The Bible tells us that the devil comes to steal, kill and destroy. He might leave you to do well in certain things just to stop you from growing in the things of God. Let us keep our temple clean enough for it to be a habitation for the Holy Spirit.

We know from reports and Police investigations that most rapists feed their minds with pornographic materials and other sex magazines prior to their deed, until their minds are saturated with sex, sex and more sex, very often associated with violence. They go out fully charged up by the spirit of perversion and lust, and lie in wait for their prey. We know this from what has been found on their computers, Laptops and other devices. Indeed, what you look at and see feeds your imagination, and imagination out of control is acted upon.

This is the reason why the Bible says to cast down imaginations. *2 Corinthians 10:5, "Casting down imaginations and every high thing that exalts itself against the knowledge of God..."* Basically, do not entertain any imagination that is contrary to the Word of God or the Will of the Lord for your life. Imaginations fueled by filthy thoughts will lead you to a world of sin. This is the reason why many men and some women, too, can be addicted to pornography.

What we call addiction is a spirit driven desire to do something that can be harmful to you, and yet you seem not to have control over it. This is demonic and can lead to destruction or death as one spirit will let several others in, which can lead to several addictive behaviors.

There are good and bad imaginations and you cannot stop thoughts rushing through your mind, but you have the choice to ignore them or pay attention to them. The Bible says resist the devil and he will flee from you. (James 4:7) Apostle Paul says in his letter to the *Philippians 4:8, "whatsoever things are true whatsoever things are honest, whatsoever things are just, whatsoever things are pure, whatsoever things are lovely, whatsoever things are of a good report, if there be any virtue, if there be any praise, think on these things."*

Feed yourself with good imaginations, godly imaginations. Hope for God's best. The Word of God makes it clear to us how powerful imaginations can be. In the book of *Genesis 11:6 says "And the Lord said, Behold, the people is one, and they have all one language; and this they begin to do: and now nothing will be restrained from them, which they have imagined to do."* Here you clearly see the power of imagination.

Satan has a way of getting into the minds of man through what we feed our eyes on and what we hear. It is all about paying too much attention to something you are looking at or hearing. Have you ever seen a person walk into an object or trip and fall as a result of being fully captivated by something he was looking at? This is a practical illustration of how the devil will catch your attention onto some destructive image and eventually cause you to stumble and fall. It might look harmless at a glance, but if you give it too much attention you will be drawn into his snare.

 Some Christians still read their horoscope. Do you understand what this means? If a believer had to read his or her horoscope to determine how his day is going to be, then where is our faith in God to keep us from all evil and to supply all our needs, including everything that pertains to both our spiritual and physical life? Anyone who does this, is telling God that He is not capable to do what He has said He will do for us. This is called doubt and also going against the commandment that says, *"You shall not have any other gods besides Me."*

Reading your horoscope means you are depending on the

clairvoyant who is being used by evil spirits to tell you your future. Who knows you better than the One who created you? The moment you do this, you are opening yourself to demons to come into you or to be near you to supply information to the dark world and that can be dangerous.

This is as sinful as going to consult a medium. As the name sounds, so it is: horoscope. Horror movies have become an obsession in some believers' life. They say it is harmless and fictional. Do you think the devil will allow you see anything wrong with it? No. He is subtle, from the beginning until now, and will be until Jesus comes again. That is why the Bible warns us to be vigilant and sober and not to be ignorant of the devices of the devil. Most evil outcomes start with a hint of innocence.

I know of a woman who started innocently reading her 'stars' in the daily newspaper and was soon hooked to the extent that she begun ordering books about stargazing, horoscopes and other associated materials to feed her desires and quest to know more about the subject. It was not long before she started receiving visitations from dark spirits, which then led to her to be recruited to work for the devil for many years before she was saved.

Friends, these things are not as innocent as they appear, they are devilish and destructive. What about cartoons? In the distant past cartoons such as Tom and Jerry, Roger Rabbit and Pink Panther, to name a few, were appropriate for children to enjoy. Horrid Henry, The Simpsons and Ben Ten among others have slowly and subtly replaced these. These can corrupt the young minds of the children and lead them to try out some of what they see.

Some parents will say "Oh it is just a cartoon; it does not mean anything." Dear one, it means a lot. Destiny can be destroyed by one silly mistake; allowing a child to watch that cartoon. On one occasion I was watching a cartoon, I do not even know why I was watching as there was no child with me at that time. It was later on that it dawned on me that the Lord wanted me to listen to some of the things said by the characters in this episode. The main character sends his subjects to go and deliver a message to a group of young children. They could not get the kids to do what they wanted them to do. They then reported back to the boss that the children did not pay any attention to what they were saying. The boss told them, "I know what to do. You just have to get into their minds with images and then the message will be pushed through to them."

The saying that a picture is worth a thousand words indicates how one image can mess up a person's mind. Most murderers have an obsession with horror movies and magazines. As they watch these movies or read these magazines, the evil spirits of murder invade their thoughts and then, as they enter in, they begin to operate from within. Within is far more powerful than without.

Nowadays video games have captivated both young and old. Parents are buying these for their children; even Christian parents. I ask myself, "Do they sit to watch these games with the children to at least get to know what they are about?" Is there any more discernment in our homes, let alone in the church? God help us.

There is a wealth of Christian literature for kids and this is something in which I recommend both parents and church invest.

A good example is CBN Super book that is taking the world of kids TV by storm. The Super book series and apps can be downloaded for Sunday schools and for home courtesy of CBN, the Christian Broadcasting Network. These materials are changing the lives of many kids around the world.

You literally become that which is within you. If you eat healthy food you become healthier and if you eat bad food you will suffer ill-health. The same principle applies spiritually. The Lord commanded in *Ezekiel 2:8b, "Open your mouth, and eat that I give you. [9]And when I looked, behold, a hand was sent to me; and, lo, a roll of a book was therein... 3 [1]moreover He said to me, son of man, eat that you find; eat this roll and go and speak to the house of Israel. [2]So, I opened my mouth and He caused me to eat that roll."*

This made Ezekiel, an able minister, a great Prophet of God. Similarly, people who are used by the devil had also told about things that were given to them to either eat or drink that made them spiritually strong. The principles are the same. This is simply because the devil stole the principles of God, perverted them and is using them against God and His people. If you read and study the Bible, you become strong in the things of God.

Books and magazines that we read can also affect us. I worked with a young man in the early nineties who, after reading a certain book became demon possessed. According to him, he picked this book from his local library. His case was so serious that in his own words, the demons would come into his room at night, pick him up from his bed and throw him against the wall. He would literally feel his bed being lifted up and suspended in the air. There are times he would be levitating.

All these demonic activities were taking place in his life because of a book he picked and read. This caused a demonic invasion of his home and also his body and soul. He felt the demons were eating up his brains. He would walk around continuously brushing the top of his head with his hands. Things were so bad that, one night, he called a man of God during one of these episodes. When the minister arrived and saw what was happening, he could not do anything to help the poor man because he, himself, froze in fear.

He said to me, "I ended up praying deliverance for myself before the demons left me." This may sound strange to some believers who have not been taught about the real world of darkness but my dear one, believe me it is as real as the physical world. These days, both young and old alike, are flirting with the spirits by reading occult-filled books like Harry Potter, and other mystical books on how to cast spells. Someone may say but these are harmless fiction! No, they are not. Behind every book there is a spirit, it is either God's spirit or the devil's spirit.

Have you ever read a book about the Holy Spirit and literally felt His presence filling your room? I have. So is the case when we read things of the devil and are not filled with the Holy Spirit. We have to pick and choose what to read and what not to read. Do not let curiosity lead you to destruction. Do not be inquisitive into things that you are not sure about and be mindful of your level of growth or maturity in the Lord. You can always confer with an elder or a Pastor.

Rebecca Brown's (MD) books, "<u>He came to set the captives free</u>" and "<u>Prepare for war</u>", are serious books exposing the satanic world in the medical field. She starts by praying for the reader. You will need to cover yourself with the Blood of Jesus if you are a believer before you read any book that exposes the dark world of Satan and his demon spirits. There are some very good books from renowned men and women of God. Why not invest in them to equip yourself properly from the onslaught which the enemy has unleashed in the world today. Invest to equip yourself with very good doctrinal books that will benefit your walk with the Lord and prepare you for eternity with Him.

The early church knew that people could not hold on to books of idolatry once they came to the knowledge of the truth. Converts were moved by the Spirit of the Lord to bring their books to be burned. Acts 19:18-20, *"And many that believed came, and confessed, and showed their deeds. Many of them also which used curious arts brought their books to be burned before all men: and they counted the price of them, and found it fifty thousand pieces of silver. So mightily grew the Word of God and prevailed."*

Where there is cleansing, there is growth. Where there is growth, there will be maturity and fruitfulness. When a plant is pruned, it becomes healthier and more fruitful. The true church of Jesus

Christ needs cleansing in preparation for the coming of the Lord. The Bible confirms this. He is coming for a glorious church without blemish, wrinkles or spots. We need to promote deliverance and implement it to liberate the people of God by not only preaching and teaching partially, but also rather the full Gospel of Jesus Christ. In Luke 4:18, Christ spells out His mission as commanded by God, His Father aided by the Holy Spirit; the Prophet Isaiah prophesied this in chapter 61:1-2, *"The Spirit of the Sovereign Lord is on me, because the Lord has anointed me to proclaim good news to the poor. He has sent me to bind up the broken-hearted, to proclaim freedom for the captives and release from darkness for the prisoners, [2]to proclaim the year of the Lord's favour and the day of vengeance of our God, to comfort all who mourn"*

I know that some of us Christians will be quick to say, "Oh, but this is in the Old Testament and we are in the New." Check Luke 4:18 and you will find the same there. I want to point out that most of Paul's preaching contains quotes from the Old Testament. Jesus said He did not come to abolish the Old but that He came to establish it. We have to be careful how we interpret the Word of God.

One occasion when I was pondering on this controversy, the Holy Spirit told to me to ask anyone who proposes this if they quote the Scripture in their prayers, which says, *"No weapon formed against me shall prosper. I will contend with those who contend with and save your children; but upon Mount Zion shall be deliverance, and there shall be holiness."*

"If the Old is done away with then why are they using it in their prayers?" He said."

Jesus was clear about His mission when He stood up in the synagogue in Luke 4:18 and declared, *"The Spirit of the Lord is upon me, because He has anointed me to preach the gospel to the poor; He has sent me to heal the broken-hearted, to preach deliverance to the captives, and recovering of sight to the blind, to set at liberty them that are bruised. [19]To preach the acceptable year of the Lord."*

You see that? It is clearly part of His mission and He actually did exactly that. Jesus cast out demons from people several times and so did Paul. All that Jesus did, we will do as well, and even greater things as the Lord promised us.

So then, my question to those who oppose the concept of deliverance is, why would this be in the Bible if it was not going to be relevant for our lives today? Awake, awake people of God, for the enemy is doing these things to divide us and to deprive us of the truth that will set us free so he can overpower the church of Jesus Christ. I have witnessed people who once indulged in devil-worship and witchcraft bringing their stuff to be burned after their conversion. This is important because these items, if not destroyed, can become a point of contact for demons to freely harass and torture those involved even though they have been born-again and are in Christ Jesus.

Derek Prince, one of the best Bible teachers of our time, tells in one of his books of a time he went through serious financial challenges. It was so severe that he sought the Lord for answers. The Lord pointed him to artifacts that he had bought whilst on holiday in Japan. These were large fans that he displayed on the wall in his living room. I think he said there were three or four of them. The Lord told him the enemy is using them to blow away his money. He listened to the voice of God and got rid of them all.

The result was unbelievable. Immediately his finances were restored. What if he had said it was in his mind and not the voice of God? To the untrained spiritual mind, the devil will say that it is ridiculous. This is where a lot of us have suffered loss; we equate some things to our thoughts and imaginations when God speaks to us, and as a result, we do nothing and continue to suffer. As long as we are in possession of the 'accursed things', we can pray until Jesus comes and nothing will shift.

All we have to do is to obey the Word of God and it shall be well with us. Nobody is immune to these things. Remember, Derek Prince was a great man of God whom one would have thought should have known, but we do not know it all. God teaches us as we go along and mistakes are made. It is for us to walk with Him in total surrender and obedience to His Word, to make it work for us.

I say to any Christian who thinks he can read whatever and watch whatever, to think again. Satan is not stupid; he knows how to deceive and lure us into his evil web of destruction. It is all a matter of choice, isn't it? The Bible says in 1 Corinthians 6:12 that, *"all things are lawful unto me but all things are not expedient: all things are lawful for me, but I will not be brought under the power of any."* God does not force anyone to do anything but we have to choose what is beneficial and profitable for both our spiritual and physical well-being.

It is all right if God instructs you to read certain articles or books, surely, He has a reason for that, and then you can be rest assured you are fully covered and protected from any attack of the devil. I know there are times when God may send you on a certain errand, just to show you certain facts and operations of the spirit realm. Be sure He is the one who is asking you to touch or read that book. Ask Him for His instruction and make sure you understand the rules of engagement. Do not just take anything for granted. He is faithful!

Be careful what you read and what you allow your children to read. Also take heed what you allow into your home. What you watch is equally important. Do not take anything for granted; even the music you allow in your home. The evidence of demonic possession may not be visible immediately but who knows what is building up inside of you or in your children.

When my son was a teenager, I went to his bedroom and on his walls were many large posters including a well-known hip hop artist, covered in tattoos. All I knew about him was what I had heard from my kids about his songs. I was moved to rip his poster and others from the wall and, as you may well guess, my son was very upset with me and vowed to replace them.

At the time, I did not know anything about the Hip Hop culture or some of their lyrics but my spirit was not in agreement of those images on his wall. That rapper was shortly shot and killed and that further aroused my interest about that sub-culture. I was shocked to discover seriously blasphemous, murderous and highly demonic lyrics. I immediately went on the warpath by secretly and slowly getting rid of my son's collection of music. To God be the glory he never once asked about any of the missing CDs, until he left home.

Why did I bring this up? I want to remind parents that we have authority over our homes and have the power to permit or not to permit certain things. The question then is what if the parent does not know about 'demonically baptised' goods or products? My answer is, once in a while, pray and anoint the house, asking the Holy Spirit to expose things that defile your home and help you to get rid of them without fuss. Remember, whosoever seeks will find and if you ask, you shall receive. The Holy Spirit is our greatest Helper. Bear that in mind that when you call upon Him, He will always come to your aid.

Recently I was listening to a great man of God and his divorced and soon to be remarried wife on TV. She made a statement about her mental state, which was made worse after reading a certain book. She did not want to make known the author or the title of the book, at least not on air.

She talked about a demonic invasion after she read the book, which played a part in her torment and finally led to her filing for divorce. She went on to say she should have known better as she is a third generational preacher's daughter and also a minister's wife. Beloved, these things are real and we need to guard against these 'innocent' materials. They may sound or appear to be good for reading and the title may even appear to be godly, but the Bible teaches us to test every spirit and see if it is of God. Do not be fooled. If you flirt with demonic spirits whether by reading, listening or watching, you will fall into their nets. It calls for spiritual vigilance in our everyday walk.

We cannot be overly alert but we have to be conscious that we are in the last days and things are hidden from us naturally as Satan tries hard to push his agenda and his wicked deeds to catch us in his evil nets. How many times have I walked into a bookstore and bought a book that caught my attention because of the title? Perhaps I even read the back and thought it is ok, only to get into it and realise it is not ok after all. Many things become questionable when things I read did not tally with the word says in the bible.

In short, some truths have been twisted. The moment the red flag went up, I stopped reading. Let us not forget that the Scriptures warn us about doctrines of devils and doctrines of men, so let us all be vigilant in all these things as the day draws nearer and nearer.

Fill your bookshelf with Christian books and materials that will help you grow in the Lord. I am not saying you should not read any books besides Christian books, by all means do, but be careful what you read. I remember my youngest daughter, as a ten-year-old used to read heavy stuff. She would pick up books like Rebecca Brown's "Vessels of Honor" and read and I was wondering if she actually understood what she was reading but I did not stop her. As she was growing, I realised that sometimes she would make references to some of the things she had read. Remember, the Bible says to train a child in the things of God and when he grows up, he will not depart from it. This does not mean they will be perfect kids, but no matter what befalls them, the seed of God which have been sown in them, will guide them. No matter how far they go, God Almighty will bring them back. Praise God!

Our God is faithful; the Word of God is faithful and sure. Isaiah 49:25 says *"But thus says the Lord, even the captives of the mighty shall be taken away, and the prey of the terrible shall be delivered: for I will contend with him that contends with you, and I will save your children."* That is our God speaking these assuring words unto us and we have to trust Him that that is exactly what He will do.

## Smell

The faculty of perceiving odor or scents 2. It is the act of inhaling to ascertain smell. This is one of the five senses of man. Inhalation can tell you what is either a good or a bad odour. In the Old Testament, the Priests burnt incense in the temple of God to invoke the presence of the Lord but in the New Testament, it is the Holy Spirit, Himself, that fills the temple of the Most High through the praise and worship of the saints.

As the devil is a good imitator, his worshippers, by his command, use incense and other perfumes to invoke his presence. Some Satanists use incense, some particular perfumes; some scented, colored candles and many other scented products to invoke demonic spirits for their spiritual operations.

If your spiritual sense of smell is trained you can pick up demonic scents just like that. This makes you aware of any demonic presence when you enter into a place. What happens when non-Christians go to such places to consult the mediums is, the demons in operation enter into the person or begin to follow them wherever they go and eventually end up harassing them.

Paul in Acts 16:16-18 picked up the demonic scent from the woman who followed them proclaiming what seemed to be true, but not the truth. *"And it came to pass, as we went to prayer, a certain damsel possessed with a spirit of divination met us, which brought her masters much gain by soothsaying. The same followed Paul and us, and cried, saying, these are the servants of the Most High God which show us the way of salvation. And this did she many days. But Paul being grieved, turned and said to the spirit, I command thee in the name of Jesus Christ to come out of her. And he came out the same hour."*

This is what I am talking about, Paul was full of the Holy Spirit and for that reason his spiritual sense of smell was very sharp.

I was once invited to come and pray in a member's house so I went with my teenage daughter and a six-month old baby we had in our care at that time. The reason I went with them is that the baby was used to me so, as long as he could see me, he was fine. If I had known what I was to encounter or I walk into, I would have found a way of not taking the precious little one with me.

As I entered into the house, right at the door was a strong demonic presence. This was a very peculiar smell and it spoke volumes about the spirits dwelling in the house. When the woman started narrating her story, it just confirmed things to me. There was serious demonic activity going on in the house, especially in her children's bedroom.

As I looked around, I began to pin point certain artifacts that needed to be removed, which she did immediately. I prayed and sanctified the house and left. When we left the place, my daughter said to me, "Mummy the house was full of demons so I started pleading the Blood of Jesus on Baby J and myself." I was amazed as to how sensitive she had grown to the things of the spirit but I was grateful to the Lord for the works He was and is still doing in her life.

There are also some other kinds of smell that can be picked up only by the spiritually trained nose. An example relates to a very peculiar, foul and Sulphur-like smell. Personally, when I enter into a place with strong demonic presence, it is either the smell or a reaction in my spirit that warns me and prepares me to take the necessary precautions. I liken the spiritual smell to discerning of spirits. Paul the Apostle picked on the spiritual scent of the spirits in operation in this particular woman, but it took him several days to pick it up in his spirit.

I believe the Apostle Paul took his time to act because he was waiting to see if any of the other Apostles might pick up the scent as well. However, after days of waiting with no one else having done so, he decided to deal with it and there it was; he was spot on with his discernment.

If there be any headway for the church of Jesus Christ to deal with the influx of demons in the church today, we need discernment with an ability to discern spirits. This is because it is not just enough to discern that something is not right but also, we need to be able to identify the spirit in order to deal with it effectively. Everyone must pray for the Holy Spirit to endow them of the gift to discern spirits. This is very important for ministers. Do not be fooled by all manner of manifestations and attribute them to the anointing. Jesus warned us that the devil would appear sometimes like an angel of light. Without this operational gift of the Spirit, the devil will hijack the reins of the church simply because you will not know who is who and what is what.

Few years into ministry, everything seemed to be going well and the power of God was dominant in every meeting; I love the Presence of the Lord, The Lord began to show me in dreams a particular lady who had drawn closer to me over the years. I made her to sit next to me in church, and please do not ask me why, I was drawn to that. I, by the grace of God came to realise that what I called the "prophetic gift" which she operated in was actually divination. Lo and behold this lady would prophesy the things the Lord would tell me in my private prayer times in church meetings. At which times I thought it was the Holy Spirit. She also showered me with expensive gifts including Louis Vuitton bags and shoes, eighteen carat gold chains and bracelets and other things. As a matter of fact, I am not moved by such things at all and would not compromise the things of God for gifts; this I had always made plain to the congregation. I do not beg for things and therefore if one came to me and said God has laid it on their heart to bless me, I would take it and pray God's blessings upon them and use it. She told me the Lord had told her there is something she needs to get from me. I had thought maybe I needed to mentor her in the things of God and help her in expounding the Scriptures to her.

The dreams I had were very detailed and also regular. The woman started criticising me, trying to undermine my authority and to sow seeds of confusion in the church. I called a meeting with her to address the issues and took steps to ground her. It was during this time that the Lord showed me that she was actually a witch. She manifested and said a whole lot of nasty things, and after that she never set foot in the church again.

Prior to all this, I had seen something during one of our retreats and had offered to pray deliverance over her but had to let it go when she refused to cooperate. Another time, I had offered to help again to pray deliverance for her, but she wanted me to come to her house to do that, which I declined. God has called us into wisdom and it is essential that we walk in it. Do it as Jesus did it and walk like He walked; that is what we are supposed to do. Jesus never cast out any demon in a private home. Certainly, He was never alone with the demonised person.

If you happen to find yourself in a situation that needs urgent action, know that the Lord is with you and He will send His angels to help you. Do not just decide to go on this trip or invitation alone with the person. Jesus always had His disciples with Him. I need to have my team with me wherever I go and whatever I do concerning visitations.

This is not an isolated incident; the universal church is now full of her kind and they are thriving because the church is slowly losing the fire. The Lord is calling upon His people to wake up from our sleep and slumber and let the House of the Lord be filled with fire once again. Revival!

Let us keep the house of God clean and demon free. Ministers are compromising the truth in many ways and there is a breed of lawless and disorderly Christians filling the pews; demonised people taking charge over departments in the church. It is no wonder that we are not seeing the manifested glory of God that brings about the miraculous.

I once met a Pastor and we began to chat. I was expressing my concern about the state of the churches in the UK especially in London and the so-called Charismatic churches in particular. I told him I have a great difficulty in taking my eyes of sin in the church I lead. Whenever I address it, the people get offended and leave.

He then said to me that the Bible says there is a sin not unto death. Some people might need to be left alone to continue in their sin after they have received one rebuke; simply because they are needed to sustain the church through their tithes. This really disturbed my spirit so I went and read the Scripture over and over again and I decided for myself that I could not operate like him, even though I could see his point.

Bearing in mind that even Jesus had Judas among the disciples, demonstrating that you cannot turn people away because they have one struggle or the other. One thing I know is, someday I will give account unto God concerning the flock over which He has made me a steward. I will apply what *Jude 17-23 says, "But beloved, remember ye the words which were spoken before of the Apostles of our Lord Jesus Christ; How that they told you there should be mockers in the last time, who should walk after their own ungodly lusts. These be they who separate themselves, sensual, having not the Spirit. But ye beloved, building up yourself in the most holy faith, praying in the Holy Ghost, keep yourselves in the love of God, looking for the mercy of our Lord Jesus Christ unto eternal life. And of some have compassion, making a difference: and others save with fear, pulling them out of the fire; hating even the garment spotted by the flesh."*

## Christian Parenting

I have a charge to keep and a God to glorify in all that I do, as a Christian first and then as a minister. Should I condone sin and send people to hell? Definitely not! I will correct in love and I will also rebuke sharply when called for as recommended in the Scriptures. The devil fears the truth because it exposes him, so for the church to be what it should be, the truth should never depart from the pulpit.

Let us wake up and pray for more sensitivity to the Holy Spirit and also to discern the evil spirits sent to the church universal to annul the power and authority of the Holy Spirit. We need the fire back in the church. No demon should be able to hide and wreak havoc in the church any more.

Parents should be sharp in the spirit watching over their children. God has entrusted our children unto us. They are special gifts from God. Psalm 127:3, *"Lo, children are a heritage of the Lord: and the fruit of the womb is His reward."* (KJV) We are responsible for the godly upbringing of our children until they reach the age of accountability.

Do you know the enemy is chasing after our children at an earlier age than ever before? What a four to six-year old knows today was, in my days, what a fifteen-year old would have known. Information is everywhere; it is on the Internet, iPad, Android phones and on the Television. Literally everywhere you turn there is some image to corrupt our children.

The moment governments began to interfere with child discipline in our homes, the devil also seized the opportunity to destroy them. You cannot smack your own children lest you face prosecution and in some cases the child is taken from the parents with the threat of going to jail hanging on their heads.

The Bible says in Proverbs. 22:15, *"Foolishness is bound in the heart of a child; but the rod of correction shall drive it far from him.* Proverbs 23:13, *"Withhold not correction from the child: for if you beat him with the rod, he shall not die. [14]You shall beat him with the rod, and shall deliver his soul from hell."*

The Bible clearly has provided us with guidelines to discipline our children in Proverbs 22:6, &15, *"Train up a child in the way he should go: and when he is old, he will not depart from it." This is God's* mandate for parents. The reason is given in verse 15, *"Foolishness is bound in the heart of a child; but the rod of correction shall drive it far from him."* Proverbs 23:13 says, *"Withhold not correction from the child:* (Here is God's recipe for correction) *for if thou beat him with the rod, he shall not die. [14]thou shall beat him with the rod and shall deliver his soul from hell."* This is how I was brought up but now society says  not to spank children, it is an abuse; I know some parents are cruel and abusive but has this changed the few wicked ones? No, rather it has changed society for the worst.

I took the Godly way and I thank God I did.

Again, it comes back to the Scripture, *"Train up a child in the way he should go: and when he is old, he will not depart from it." (Proverbs 22:6)* I have taught my children what is what, to the best of my knowledge and ability as the Lord had taught me and is still teaching me.

Does this mean they have not watched anything demonic? I would not be that sure since human beings are very curious, and children are even more inquisitive. But what I can make my boast in the Lord about is, my God is the God who watches over His Word to perform it. His Word says in Isaiah 49:24-25, *"Shall the prey be taken from the mighty, or the lawful captive delivered? But thus, says the Lord, even the captives of the mighty shall be taken away, and the prey of the terrible shall be delivered: for I will contend with him that contends with thee, and I will save thy children."*

Even if our children, out of curiosity, touch the untouchable, our covenant with God will bring deliverance as we daily cry out to God on their behalf. God is faithful like that; yes, He is faithful. Ours is to teach them the ways of God and He will do the rest. I trained them not to watch certain movies, not to listen to certain music or partake in certain activities like Halloween. We never bought them any demonic toys or games. Once again, I am not saying they observed all these to the letter, I cannot guarantee that, but I know I built some awareness in them and now, decades later, I can see the fruits of those teachings.

This does not mean I brought up perfect kids. Oh no, but God has been merciful and faithful to me. I made mistakes because I neglected certain areas in my parenthood due to the fact that I did not balance my work and home properly. I worked too hard and neglected certain of my children's needs. God in His mercy has shown me kindness and He who begun the good work in my family, will be faithful to complete it. I can boldly say, by faith that all is well in Jesus name.

God is not an abusive God; no, not at all. He is a loving God who also rebukes, chastises and corrects us as His children, because He wants us to do well and excel in life. God wants us to do the same with our children. Everything must be done in moderation as Proverbs 11:1 says, *"A false balance is abomination unto God but a just weight is His delight."*

Love goes with correction. You cannot correct a child that is unloved by you and you cannot say you love your child too much, and not correct him, there has to be a healthy balance.

As believers in Christ Jesus, we do not have to depend on anyone to train our children for us, not even the Sunday school teacher. Society must not be permitted to dictate to us how to bring up our children because when they fail, it is the fault and responsibility of the parent. This is the verdict over parents when a young adult offends. Meanwhile this is the same system, which criminalizes any parent who tries to discipline their child. These are the same voices that have forbidden parents to correct children the same way they were corrected by their parents.

I know of friends whose children were taken from them by social services as a result of the parents spanking them. The parents neither burnt them with hot irons, cigarettes nor fed them salt and there were no marks from any previous 'abuse'. The child was upset and mentioned an incident to the teachers who kept on probing and encouraging the child to talk about 'abuses'. Action was quickly taken; Police and social services were called. What about those children who were insanely abused with bite marks, broken ribs and even skulls but were let down by social services?

Let us go God's way to bring up our children in the fear of the Lord that they would not fall prey to the evil one. Always explain to them why they are to be punished for whatever they have done wrong.

## Spoken Words: Negative or Indirect Curses:

These are utterances made by men in anger, hatred or out of sheer resentment or dislike. These come out in the form of bad, bitter or evil words. They include, invoking curses, enchantments, and negative pronouncements.

There are many of us who have suffered verbal abuse in our lifetime, and I accept that there are degrees of verbal abuse. The abuses I am talking about are those that affect the person's self-esteem and confidence. Parents curse their own children by saying hurtful things to them. Some even go to the extent of telling them they will amount to nothing; they are a failure and so forth and so on.

All these negative comments and insults empower demons to afflict the victims. If they are not in a position to pray to nullify them, they grow up battling one issue after another; all because the poison from man's tongue has been released into their system. The Bible states in Proverbs 18:21 that, *"Death and life are in the power of the tongue: and they that love it shall eat the fruit thereof."*

What we say to each other, even in anger, has to be weighed carefully before discharged because words are like arrows with the ability to stick into the heart and destroy or wound the recipient. We have the choice to speak life into a situation or poison it with our choice of words. Psalm 64 talks about arrows and likens them to words. Psalm 64:2-3, *"Hide me from the secret counsel of the wicked; from the insurrection of the workers of iniquity: who whet (sharpen) their tongue like a sword, and bend their bows to shoot their arrows, even bitter words."*

The Psalmist is referring to the demonic activities against us as a result of words or curses intended to destroy us. Many lives have been destroyed by words from an evil tongue. These spoken words stick into the very soul of the person over whom they are declared and the enemy confirms these lies making you believe that is exactly who you are or will become. Once the person believes this, he resigns himself to it and lives subconsciously according to the declarations.

Please, do not let anybody try to redefine who God says you are. It does not matter how far you have fallen; God is able to make you rise again to fulfill His designed destiny for your life. Arise; shine for your light is come!

Please note that there are two realms in the world we live in, the Physical realm and the Spiritual realm, the seen and the unseen. The realm where God dwells and where Satan and his demons dwell is the unseen realm. Everything that happens on the earth is controlled by one of these realms.

The seen realm is where we dwell as human beings. Where everything we know, is visible to the human eye. Even though we live in the visible world, there are spiritual entities operating and influencing in our world. The Holy Spirit and the evil spirits of Satan are the unseen forces that operate within human beings to establish their rule on earth.

Both realms operate with and through words. God created the world with words. *"And God said, let there be light, and there was light."* God operates with spoken words, what we say to Him in prayer is what He works with. The Bible says in Isaiah 1:18, *"Come now, and let us reason together, says the Lord."* God is always seeking to have interaction with man and this is done through words (communication). God seeks to hear His people on the earth say good things concerning other people so He can work on their behalf.

Satan also works with words. Since he is everything anti-God, he works with bad and bitter words. The moment a bitter word is released against somebody, demons pick them up and take it to their world and use it to harm that person. Ask yourself this question, why should someone's words affect another person? It is what is in the person's tongue that made those words effective in the other person's life; it is either the power of life or death.

The Bible describes the tongue as a weapon and our words are the ammunition. Whenever the weapon is discharged, the ammunition (words) are sent to specific targets to destroy, kill or wreak havoc. It is the power of the spirit behind those words that does the work. Jesus said the words that I speak, they are spirit and they are life; but when the devil speaks, they are spirit and they are death because they can destroy and kill the person against whom those words were released. The words from Jesus give or produce life whereas the one from Satan produce death and destruction.

If you have suffered emotional abuse or any form of abuse, which has affected you, know that there is a balm in Gilead. Jeremiah 8:22, *"Is there no balm in Gilead; is there no physician there? Why then is not the health of the daughter of my people recovered?"*

The house of God is supposed to be among other things a surgery for sick people to be delivered and healed. Deliverance is for us today as it was when Jesus walked the earth.

The Bible declares in *Isaiah 55:11 "So shall my word be that goes forth out of my mouth: it shall not return unto me void, but it shall accomplish that which I please, and it shall prosper in the thing whereto I sent it."*

It can be deduced from this Scripture, that when words are released, they are released for a purpose and there is power behind these words to perform that specific task and to fulfill that specific purpose. These words do not return void, they have to return with an accomplishment of the purpose for which they were released.

As it is with the Lord God Almighty, so it is with the devil. Everything that is done in the spiritual world is done based on words declared in the visible world. There are numerous Scriptures confirming this, Isaiah 54:17, *"No weapon that is formed against you shall prosper; and every tongue that shall rise up against you in judgment you shall condemn."*

The tongue is referred to as a weapon; a weapon of destruction. You and I know that words are released from the mouth via the tongue. Look at another Scripture in *Psalm 64:3, "Who whet (sharpen) their tongue like a sword, and bend their bows to shoot their arrows, even bitter words: that they may shoot in secret at the perfect: suddenly do they shoot at him, and fear not."*

This is to emphasize that everything is done primarily through words; blessings and curses are all products of the fruits of the tongue. Words are spirit, Jesus said, and therefore, when a bad or a negative word is released, it carries a mission and this mission will have to be accomplished. Many a life has been destroyed by words that were released against them. You can be delivered through the power of the Holy Spirit and the power of the Blood of Jesus. Remember, *"He sent his word, and healed them and delivered them from their destructions."* (Psalm 107:20)

As destruction comes through the words of evil men and women, demons quickly pick on such words and work with them in order to bring it to pass, so does God Almighty bring deliverance by the words from anointed lips of men and women of God empowered by the Holy Spirit.

It was the word breathed out from God that brought creation into being and therefore, every created thing is subject to the power of the same word that authored its existence. Rise and be healed and be delivered in the name of Jesus, for it was for this cause that He was made manifest, that He will destroy the works of the enemy. Deliverance is ours as children of the Light. Darkness has to flee when the Light shows up. Do not just sit and be swallowed up by the wicked one, seek help and it shall be well with you, in the name of Jesus Christ of Nazareth.

There is power in the name of Jesus to bring deliverance to the downcast and the downtrodden. Through counseling and deliverance, we can deal with the root cause and expel the demons responsible for the person's predicament. The Holy Spirit is more than capable of doing that which is uncommon to man. He can bring the captive out of captivity through deliverance as taught by Jesus Christ Himself. He came to set the captive free! There is help in the Lord so please do not suffer in ignorance. Seek help from the Lord and His servants whom he has anointed to bring deliverance to His people. This is boldly spelt out in Isaiah 61:3, *"To appoint unto them that mourn in Zion, to give them beauty for ashes, the oil of joy for mourning, the garment of praise for the spirit of heaviness; that they might be called the trees of righteousness, the planting of the Lord, that He might be glorified."* This is repeated by Jesus Himself, in Luke 4:18.

Dearly beloved, provision has been made for you and I to walk in total liberty and enjoy our walk with the Lord here on earth before we go to glory. I recommend you seize every moment and every opportunity to be totally free to fulfill your purpose and destiny. Know that the Lord will help you if you desire it, for nobody has the right to redefine who you are.

You have been predestined to be who you are created to be by your Creator. The only person who can stop you from fulfilling your purpose and destiny is you. The devil cannot stop you if you do not cooperate with him and he can only overpower you if he has a legal doorway into your life. I pray that this book will point you in the right direction to obtain help from the Lord.

 Know that the two worlds are governed by words. By this I mean the kingdom of Light and the kingdom of Darkness. In the beginning, at creation, God spoke everything into being except for man whom He formed from the dust and gave the breath of life. Man became a living soul. Whatever God does, is through words. In our relationship with the Lord, we all know that it is based on communication: from Spirit to spirit.

We are empowered or ensnared by our words. This is the reason why Jesus taught us to bless and not to curse. He came to give life and we, as His disciples, are supposed to do likewise. Speak life into every situation regardless of what you see, and you will see the power of words in action. We either empower heaven with our words for our good or empower hell for our destruction.

We have a choice, but I recommend we choose life through Jesus Christ by speaking the Word of God into every situation no matter what. Let God be true and every man a liar!

# CHAPTER 25

# The Power of The Mind

The mind according to the dictionary is the element of a person that enables them to be aware of the world and their experiences, to think and to feel; the faculty of consciousness and thought.

Imagination is an aspect of the mind. It is a thought pattern based on images. The eye sees something and feeds it to the mind. The mind now begins to process the information and based on that, a decision is made either for good or for evil.

There are both good and bad imaginations. Not all imaginations are bad. Good imagination, I believe, can be likened to hope. A good imagination, which is meditated upon and prayed through, can be like having faith, which the Bible says is the substance of things hoped for and the evidence not seen. (Hebrews 11:1) In the story of the Tower of Babel, the Bible says they imagined... Genesis 11:6, *"And the Lord said, behold, the people is one, and they have all one language; and this they begin to do: and now nothing will be restrained from them, which they have imagined to do."*

The Lord saw this kind of imagination as an act of rebellion and stopped it. We can also liken imagination to a dream or a vision. One can have a dream of being, for instance, a pilot and begin to chase this dream until it becomes a reality. And so, for this reason, we know there are both good and bad imaginations. The Word of God is very clear about this. *In* 2 Corinthians 10:4-5, *"for the weapons of our warfare are not carnal, but mighty through God to the pulling down of strongholds. Casting down imaginations and every high thing that exalts itself against the knowledge of God and bringing into captivity every thought to the obedience of Christ."*

This Scripture leads me to understand that there are imaginations that ought to be cast down and that is the imaginations that makes us argue about the things of God, His power and His might. These are imaginations that can make us to question the Word of God; not in a wholesome way but rather in an argumentative manner, which can open us up for demonic attacks on our minds. Doubt, fear, confusion, wavering and others are all the result of evil imaginations, with which the demons infest and pollute our thoughts.

These imaginations magnify our situations and circumstances above the nature, the attributes, and the divine abilities of the Most High God. These and many other thoughts, can lead to demons invading our minds and entrenching themselves in our lives. All thoughts of hopelessness and worthlessness are ways the enemy employs to hold us in bondage to remain where we are, so we will accuse God. Such thoughts give us the wrong impression about who God really is. They make the enemy rejoice that he has tricked another of God's people into his grip.

The Lord Jesus laments over us when we permit the enemy's lies to penetrate into our soul. Remember, He came to set the captives free, so permit Him to deliver you so you can enjoy the Lord and all that He has for you both as a person and as an individual. Yes, He has much for you; His promises are Yea and Amen.

Good imaginations are, I believe, the foundation of our faith in the Lord. Good imagination can also be described as hope. The Bible says in the book of Hebrews 11:1, *"Now faith is the substance of things hoped for, the evidence of things not seen."*

Faith, I personally believe, is a good imagination as is praying and chasing a dream until you see it become a reality. In this case, visualize the things you hope for in the light of the Word of God and believe with all your heart that God will do that which He said He will do. He is not a man that He should lie; He has said it, He will also perform it.

The devil will do everything in his power to stop us from dreaming, and dreaming big. He throws his arrows of lies at us. It is for the individual to choose to believe what is written in the Bible about who he or she is in Christ Jesus, and the benefits of His horrible death on Cavalry's cross.

The Bible says the expectation of the righteous will not be cut off. Expectations are the byproducts of good imaginations that are in line with the Word of God. I am who the Word of God says I am. I believe that His plans for me will never fail as long as I believe and trust in Him. This should cause you and I to have good imagination; to dream big and expect fulfillment from the Lord. Without faith it is impossible to please God so let us seek to please Him and discard the enemy's suggestions which will only lead us to destruction.

We need to renew our mind in the Word of God continually in order to remind ourselves who God is, and who we are as His children whom He loves so much. Romans 12:1-2, *"I beseech you therefore, brethren, by the mercies of God, that you present your bodies a living sacrifice, holy, acceptable unto God, which is your reasonable service. [2]And be not conform to this world: but be you transformed by the renewing of your mind, that you may prove what is that good, and acceptable, and perfect, will of God."*

The mind plays such a major role in our life as Christian and even non-Christians that I want us to look at it a little further

## What is The Mind

The mind is the seat of consciousness, thoughts, the intellect; and intellectual power. I have decided to stay with these few definitions since there are so many, many more.

The brain is part of our physical body, whereas the mind is part of the soul, but they both need each other to operate. The brain is a very powerful faculty in the entire human body. It controls our very existence. This is why a person is rendered useless if they become brain-dead after an accident. The brain controls every activity of the human body.

The mind and the human brain are somewhat intertwined. The brain is like the hardware and the mind is like the software. Every movement of the human body depends on the brain and every decision we make takes place in the mind having being processed by the brain. The brain is in the human body (physical) and the mind is in the soul (spiritual).

One operates from the unseen realm and the other the seen realm. Remember, we are spirit, soul and body. The brain captures an image or hears spoken words, processes it and the mind takes over to decide what to do with that information.

In Genesis 11:1-4 we see the power the mind has in influencing the day to day decisions we make. This can affect our lives for better or for worse. It can affect our children and it can affect a whole generation. Here, we see the power of agreement, but I want to show you something else there; the power of the mind and the power of imagination.

*"Now the whole world had one language and a common speech. [2]As people moved eastward, they found a plain in Shinarb and settled there. [3]They said to each other, "Come, let us make bricks and bake them thoroughly." They used brick instead of stone, and taro for mortar. [4]Then they said, "Come, let us build ourselves a city, with a tower that reaches to the heavens, so that we may make a name for ourselves; otherwise we will be scattered over the face of the whole earth."*

The people had a mental picture of what they intended to do. They talked about it and decided to go for it. It was the thought first; discussion was made and a decision took place before the agreement of implementation.

Whatever we do as human beings first begins with a thought based of some kind of imagination. Proverbs 23:7 says, *"As a man thinks so is he."* In other words, you are what you think, or better still, you become what you think. The devil knows this truth and that is why he races for our minds. In the case of bad thoughts, there is nothing that can stop someone whose mind is made up except for God's intervention. If a person's mind is seized by demons, he or she is not able to think straight, let alone make proper decisions.

The demons are the ones who dictate their agenda to manipulate and control the way they want you to go; which is the path of destruction. I want us to consider why the devil does not target any part of the human body other than the brain and mind? This is because he knows that once he captures the mind, the rest of the person's life falls easily under his control. The hand or any other part of the body cannot make decisions. Every part of the body responds to the brain and mind. This is why it is so important that we feed on the Word of God and other good literature written by proven men and women of God. The Christian who knows the Word cannot easily be deceived. Psalm 119:130 says. *"The entrance of your word gives light; it gives understanding to the simple."*

We can only resist the devil with the word that is inside of us. Even our Lord Jesus, when the devil tried to tempt Him, resisted him with the Word, quoting, *"it is written"* three times. James 4:7 says, *"Resist the devil and he will flee from you."*

How do you resist the devil seeing he is not a physical being but a spiritual being? 2 Corinthians 10:3-4, *"For though we walk in the flesh, we do not war after the flesh. And for this reason, the weapons are not carnal (physical) either but they are mighty through God to the pulling down of strongholds."*

So, you see, it is a spiritual being we are dealing with and we have to use spiritual weapons to fight him off, and that is the Word of God, our prayers and our attitude and behaviors as children of God. According to Ephesians, the Word of God as a sword and other protective armor with which we need to protect ourselves before we engage the enemy of our soul in warfare. Ephesians 6:12-17 *"For we wrestle not against flesh and blood, but against principalities, and against powers, against rulers of the darkness of this world, against spiritual wickedness in high places. [13]Wherefore take unto you the whole armor of God, that you will be able to withstand (resist) in the evil day, and having done all, to stand. [14]Stand therefore, having your loins girt about with truth, and having on the breastplate of righteousness; [15]And your feet shod with the gospel of peace. [16]And above all, taking the shield of faith, wherewith you shall be able to quench all the fiery darts of the wicked. [17]And take the helmet of salvation, and the sword of the Spirit, and watching thereunto with all perseverance and supplication for all saints."*

In Genesis 11, we see the people decided to put into action what they had imagined in their hearts. Verse 6, *"And the Lord said behold the people is one, and they have all one language; and this they begin to do: and now nothing will be restrained from them, which they have imagined to do."*

God who made man knows and understand the power of the mind and the power of imagination. That is why He wants us to think on things that are pure and are of good report. In order words, things that will not contaminate our soul but keep us clean from within so that the wicked one cannot get anything to feed on or gain access into our life.

In most cases, rapists do not just set out to find a victim. Before they decide to look for prey, they may have thought about it for days; before setting off to put their thoughts in action. Some might have been feeding themselves with hardcore pornographic films or magazines. Others are purely evil and seriously possessed by the devil, and kill their victims afterwards.

In a recent case in the UK, a rapist killed the victim before raping her; sickening! You see the evil spirit of lust and perverseness enters in through the eyes and into the mind. Immediately the spirit enters in and sets the person on a mission to go and destroy someone's life without even considering the consequences. No normal human being can willfully kill another human like that; you have to be under the influence of an evil spirit.

Sometimes we argue they were under the influence of alcohol or drugs. I would disagree with this as, if that were the case, then we would expect to see all alcoholics or drug addicts to be killing or raping people. Instead it is an evil spirit that gains access into these rapists and murderers through them watching distasteful materials for their enterprise. They only use drugs and alcohol to become desensitized to the crime they intend to commit.

Evander Holyfield, at over forty years of age, sat down and thought, "I have to have a shot at the heavyweight title once again." At the time, Mike Tyson, a far younger man, was the reigning champion. The age difference between the two is well over ten years, but that did not deter Holyfield at all, As a believer, he told himself that "*I can do all things through Christ who strengthens me*" and on the night of the fight that was the inscription on the robe that he wore into the ring.

He had a mental picture of himself being able to beat "Iron Mike" as he was called, to take the title, and he surely did. He defied all the odds against him and won the bout.

As believers, we ought to think highly of our God and his Word. We have heard that we are soldiers of the cross. That is true, but have we been properly told and taught in the kind of battle or warfare we are to engage? I believe many a believer does not know this in its proper context. Why should coming to Christ be likened to the enlistment in the army? Is it not supposed to be a transition to peace in life? Why then is it all about warfare?

I suspect many soldiers would have reconsidered their enlistment into the Armed Forces had they known of the imminent possibility of war. I also believe the same is true with believers. "Oh, all was well with me when I was in the world, I did not see all these problems, I had money, I was never short of lovers... but now look."

Come on, let us be honest. How many of us have not thought things like this? "Oh, since I came to the Lord things have become hard, unbearable…" Ecclesiastes 7:9-10, *"Be not hasty in thy spirit to be angry: for anger rests in the bosom of fools. Say not you, what is the cause that the former days were better than these?"*

Whoever puts his hand to the plough and looks back is not worthy of Him. It is an insult to our salvation and the price Jesus paid to redeem us if we even think this way. Surely the old days are not better that these. The devil wants you to believe this so you will not see that God has called you into His marvelous Light with even better plans in store.

This is the battle we face each and every day as the devil intensifies his attacks against our minds, and that is why the mind of man has become the battlefield. The war or the battle in which we are engaged is an unseen, yet a real one. The fact that things look a bit tough does not present the full picture of the plans that God has for us; rather the process. Just as the coat given to Jacob as proof of Joseph's death was one that had been drenched in goat's blood, I want to encourage you that the image you have now about your situation is not the truth, and definitely not as real as it might seem. Please allow the Holy Spirit to guide you into the truth about yourself so you can find peace in the midst of chaos.

The devil attacks us through our minds by dropping thoughts of torment, discouragement, doubt, fear, disappointment, failure, and snippets of mistakes we have made in the past just so he can keep us in bondage in order that we do not experience the full benefit of the Cross of Calvary. Remember, we have a redeemer and His name is Jesus. He will deliver you from the demonic invasion that torments you. Only cry out and seek for help and you shall be set free, in Jesus name.

Let us look at what the Bible says about this "soldier thing". The Bible says we wrestle not…, the weapons of our warfare…, God is a God of war, fight the good fight of faith, the armor of God… etc. etc. All these are military allegories. In the Old Testament, the people of God literally had to go to war to fight the enemies of God and his people, to take lands and possess territories. Many wars were fought to bring victory to God's people and to bring glory to His name. Ask yourself why God made them fight to possess the land and occupy territories. The answer is, God wants His children to rule and reign over the earth, but there are squatters who have taken up residency in the land that He has promised His people.

An example is found in Deuteronomy 2:1 *"And the Lord said unto me, behold, I have begun to give Sihon and his land before thee: begin to possess,* that *mayest inherit his land."*

Before God made this statement, He had already instructed Moses, His servant, to rise up, in other words: get ready for your assignment. Verse 24, *the Lord told Moses "Rise ye up, take your journey and pass over the river Arnon: behold I have given into thine hand Sihon the Amorite, the king of Heshbon, and his land: begin to possess it, and contend with him in battle."*

In the New Testament, the battle becomes spiritual instead of physical. It began with Jesus coming down to establish the heavenly Kingdom on earth, which is also a spiritual kingdom. In fact, the Lord Himself declared this by saying *"My Kingdom is not of this world"* John 18:36. This is not seen through physical eyes. For this reason, the enemies of this unseen kingdom are spiritual, invisible to the physical eye. Nobody sees the air we breathe but it is real and we feel it.

I watched a debate on YouTube where an atheist explained his reason for not believing in the existence of God as not being able to believe in something that he could not see. The host went on to ask if he had a brain. His answered, yes. The next question was, "do you see your brain?"

"No", he said.

"Does that mean you do not have a brain simply because you cannot see it?

The supernatural is real, as real as the natural only it is unseen. Believing its existence is the beginning of freedom and I pray to God to bring this truth to every church and into every Christian so we can also help the world to come to Christ.

Hence Ephesians 6:12, *"for we wrestle not against flesh and blood, but against principalities, against powers, against rulers of the darkness of this world, against spiritual wickedness in high places."* These are all unseen forces of evil, which the Bible warns us about. *2* Corinthians 10:3 -4, *"for though we walk in the flesh, we war not after the flesh, for the weapons of our warfare are not carnal, but are mighty through God to the pulling down of strongholds."*

There are many other Scriptures, warning us that there is a war raging. The question is where is this battle taking place? The answer is, in the mind. Every decision is made in and by the mind. The Bible says *"let this mind be in you"* in other words, do not depart from this decision concerning the truth. There is a race between the Holy Spirit and evil spirits for the human mind. There is also a struggle in our mind between these two forces. The mind has become the spiritual battle ground, and we believers are admonished to renew our minds continuously with the Word of God. (Romans 12:2)

Everything we do begins with a decision made, based on information received and processed by the mind. Someone witnessed to me and I decided to accept Jesus as my Lord and Savior. This decision was based on the information I received and how my mind processed that information. The mind therefore, is an important part of the human body that is to be closely monitored and guarded with all diligence, both for emotional or spiritual reasons.

In fact, in all that we do, we have to observe this fact critically, as one bad decision can cost us dearly for the rest of our life unless God intervenes. When we are dealing with knowledge or understanding, the mind plays a major role in these areas as well. There is no life without the mind, no life at all.

Remember, we were once held in the devil's camp as prisoners, according to *Psalm 142:7, "Bring my soul out of prison that I [may] will praise your name."* Jesus came to the rescue. The devil has decided to fight for what he believes is his right to possess and to have his revenge for deserting him. How he does this, is to fill our minds with distorted images, twisted truths, and many other strategies.

Satan comes in through our ear-gate, our eye-gate or the doors of our mouths. These are the three main doors of entry for the devil and his demons. He began this in the Garden of Eden with Eve, then in the wilderness with Jesus, then in the garden of Gethsemane with Jesus again. The first Adam and the last Adam were both targeted and we, the descendants of Adam, will forever be a target. Even after death, Satan was still contending for the bodies of Moses and Joshua, but Jesus left us a legacy as to how to overcome and remain victorious like He did. On several occasions, Jesus taught us how to live and walk in His peace.

In John16:33 Jesus says, *"These things I have spoken unto you, that you might have peace. In the world, you shall have tribulation: but be of good cheer; I have overcome the world."*

Another one Scripture in *1John 2:13 says, "I write unto you fathers, because you have known Him that is from the beginning. I write unto you, young men, because you are strong, and you have overcome the wicked one."*

All we need to do is to walk in obedience to His Word and love the Lord with all our hearts, and not the world, so we can be recipients of His peace of mind. The mind that is at peace is difficult for the enemy to penetrate. The Bible says God will keep in perfect peace whose mind is stayed (focused and trusting) on Him. (Isa.26:3)

In these instances, that is, taking you back into the two Gardens, we can see clearly how destiny can be affected if the devil wins this battle of the mind. In the Garden of Eden, notice how the devil spoke to Eve, appealing to her imagination and subtly through her mind. Genesis 3:4, "*...and the serpent said unto the woman, ye shall not surely die. For God doth know that in the day that ye eat thereof, then your eyes shall be opened, and ye shall be as gods, knowing good and evil.*"

At this point Satan had gained access into Eve's mind; through her ears first, then her eyes. He then gave her something to consider by speaking to her concerning the object of contention, the forbidden fruit. Remember, he battles for our minds. His twisted truth concerning the fruit became an image before her very eyes. She fed on this imagination and decided in verse 6, "*and when the woman saw that the tree was good for food, and that it was pleasant to the eyes and a tree to be desired to make one wise...*"

Eve then took a bite of the fruit, which is through the door of her mouth, and immediately sin was birthed and separation from God and spiritual death became consequential. A decision was made followed by an action. Sin was birthed and this affected the whole of mankind. The destiny of mankind was affected for the worst.

I often ask myself, did Eve not see this tree and its fruit all this time before the serpent came to her? If she did, which I believe she did, then why did not she consider it as something to be desired before the serpent suggested it to her in the garden? Why was it not pleasant to her eyes before the appearance of the serpent? You see, the devil will make anything that God forbids us to do, look attractive to us in order to lure us to rebel against God's authority.

That which God has created for us to enjoy, is not sinful in itself but can be corrupted by the devil to cause us to rebel and sin against the giver of these good things, our God. I was admonishing a young woman and what she said made me think and I almost agreed with her. She said, "Sin is sweet." Walking on the broad path feels better than the narrow way that leads to God; but we know that the broad way leads us to destruction and death.

In the wilderness, Satan showed up again in confidence, knowing that the rule of the earth realm had been handed over to him by Adam and Eve through his strategy of using God's own words in a twisted form to illegally gain control in the earth. He knew who Jesus was but that did not deter him because he had convinced himself he would win again. He knew who the first Adam was, and he was able to deceive him. He thought it was worth trying again with the second Adam, the Son of God.

Matthew 4:3, "*And when the tempter came to him, he said, if thou be the Son of God, command these stones to be made bread. Vv. 6 and he said unto him, if thou be the Son of God, cast thyself down: for it is written, he shall give his angels charge concerning thee: and in their hands they shall bear thee up, lest thou dash thy foot against a stone.*"

Notice how the devil frantically tries to gain access into the mind of Christ by using the Word of God in negative and twisted ways.

When he realized that he was not making any headway with Jesus, he being a thief, tried to break in by force. Look at how he did it in verse 8-9, *"Again, the devil takes him up into an exceeding high mountain, and showed him all the kingdoms of the world and the glory of them; and he said to him, all these things will I give thee, if thou will fall down and worship me."*

When his steady and slow approach did not work, he resorted to push his ultimate goal through anyway and by any means; and approach through a vivid imagery. This he did by setting Jesus on an exceedingly high mountain. From this place, the beauty and the glory of creation could be clearly seen. What the devil was doing here was trying to get Jesus to fall into sin in order to be disqualified from His mission to save mankind.

Please remember, that is how the first Adam fell, through twisted truth and imagery and, finally, a suggestion. With Eve, he only had to try once, but he soon realized that was not going to be the case with Jesus. Satan decided to fire three times and on all three occasions, the Lord defeated him with the whole truth as He, Himself, is the Word. Satan failed! He failed and was not happy so then he continued to lie in wait until the final showdown.

The final showdown took place in the Garden of Gethsemane. Here we see the devil intensifying his attack on the Master; to such a degree that Jesus came very close to giving up. In Matthew 26:39, *"And He went a little further, and fell on His face, and prayed, saying, O my Father, if it be possible, let this cup pass from me: nevertheless, not as I will, but as thou wilt."*

If not for the divine intervention of heaven, the devil would have won because he had wearied the Master with images of the torture, abuse and the ultimate humiliation that He was going to endure. Jesus was tormented by the images of nails being driven through His hands and feet, a spear driven through His side and everything one can imagine was running through His mind. Being all human at the time, with the sins of the whole world upon Him, he was wearied by the taunting of Satan.

Images are the number one weapon of the enemy and this is what we have to be mindful of at all times and guard our minds with pure things. Philippians 4:8, *"Finally, my brethren, whatsoever things are true, whatsoever things are honest, whatsoever things are just, whatsoever things are pure, whatsoever things are lovely, whatsoever things are of a good report; if there be any virtue, and if there be any praise, think on these things."*

The devil will stop at nothing to win the minds of human beings in order to cripple us, to hinder us and to stop us from fulfilling our purpose and destiny The Lord has won the battle for us and we are supposed to lift up high the banner of victory wherever we go, any time, any place. The world will know that we are the children of the Light and we are overcomers, as we have inherited the victory He won over two thousand years ago.

The devil knows this, but that does not stop him from trying to see if we know our rights, the power and the authority we have over him through Christ Jesus. Beloved, let us walk in the Light, for light always dispels darkness. John 1:5, *"And the light shines in darkness;*

Jesus is the Light and the devil is the prince of darkness and we are in the Light. The devil cannot touch us as long as we remain in the Light.

I believe we have established the way the enemy attacks us through our minds. According to the Scriptures, he starts by sowing seeds in our minds that include words of fear, doubt, worry, anxiety and many more. These are based on things happening to or around us at any particular time. The devil is not a fool; he pounces at the right time; the time of our vulnerability, the time of crisis, and when we hit our lowest ebb.

Look when the devil went to Jesus, at the end of forty days of fasting, and in His agonizing moment in the Garden of Gethsemane. Satan cleverly picks his moments for his attacks. He is very calculating in his orchestrations. When he sows the words, and does not succeed, he then moves on to show you images. If those also fail, he becomes demanding and forceful. When that also fails, he then turns up the heat. This is when our faith is put to test. The song writer put it beautifully, "Will *your anchor hold in the storms of life?"*

It is only the Word of God in us that can resist the devil and sustain us. Do not ever think he will strike once or twice and leave you alone. Satan is very persistent, tenacious, relentless and heartless in his attacks against us. The most dangerous thing is when he uses the Word of God in a twisted way to confuse us if we are not grounded in the Word. Remember, he is not the originator of anything; he is a counterfeiter of all things. He uses the original things of God, twists, perverts and uses them against God's people. He does this in an attempt to gain advantage over the weak and the vulnerable and ultimately destroy them.

Our Lord Jesus is our example. We, too, can overcome as He did, if only we will let Him in and surrender all to Him. It happened in the Old Testament garden, it happened in the wilderness, and in the Garden of Gethsemane. The Bible says the servant is not above the master. If the enemy attacked the Lord Himself, then we better believe that we will face attacks in the same way He did. The Master therefore, being all-knowing, knows that we will be tried as He was.

Jesus went through his temptations to show us how to handle it His way. There is no other way except for His way, and it is only through His way that we can defeat the enemy's evil attacks against us. Jesus overcame by the Word and we can only overcome by the Word and the Blood and in His Name. Revelation 12:*11 says, "And they overcame him (Satan) by the blood of the Lamb, and by the word of their testimony."*

This is how we overcome, by the Word and the Blood as the Master himself did. We need to guard our hearts with all seriousness, knowing that the enemy's words, as arrows, will have to be processed in our hearts before decisions will be finally made to adhere to or discard them.

James put it all together nicely to help us understand this. James 1:13-15, *"Let no man say when he is tempted, I am tempted of God:*

*for God cannot be tempted with evil, neither tempts He any man: [14]But every man is tempted when he is drawn away of his own lust, and enticed. [15]Then when lust is conceived, it brings forth sin: and sin when it is finished, brings forth death."*

This is exactly what happened in the Garden of Eden and it is still happening to mankind today. We are surrounded by images everywhere we go. On billboards, television, computers, tablets and mobile phones, buses, walls and in fact, everywhere we turn there are images to provoke our thoughts.

The undisciplined mind is at risk of being caught by this demonic bait of Satan. Do not pay attention to words spoken to you or about you, especially in anger and from people you know do not wish you well. Reject words that are not good, using the Name of Jesus and His blood. What about those that are declared in private and in your absence, one may ask? I will only say that it is for our sake that the Scriptures were written, so use it in your daily prayers.

The Lord has promised us in Isaiah 54:17 that no weapon formed against us shall prosper and every tongue that rises up against us in judgment, we shall condemn. You do not have to wait to hear the words spoken before you counteract with prayer. Every day, the enemy is working overtime to pull us down or destroy us. We have to be armed with the Word of God.

# CHAPTER 26

# False Religion and Doctrine

In addressing ways in which the devil captures the minds of men, one area well worth addressing is false doctrine. Any practice outside the Kingdom of God is false religion. It does not require a rocket scientist to know this to be true although those deceived will not accept this and may even be offended by it. There is no other way to put it other than being blunt about it. That, however, is not what I am going to talk about here but rather about the false doctrines that have invaded the Kingdom of our God; any doctrine contradictory to the wholesome Gospel of Jesus Christ.

Any doctrine that challenges any aspect of the full Gospel and causes confusion is a false doctrine and the Bible warns us that such will become rampant in the last days. False doctrines have been prevalent since the days of Jesus and the Apostles. Jesus confronted the Pharisees and the Scribes, not forgetting the Sadducees, when they tried to challenge His teachings.

A typical example is found in Matthew 12, when the Pharisees challenged Jesus about permitting His disciples to pluck and eat corn on the Sabbath. The Lord responded in Matthew 12:3, *"But He said to them, have you not read what David did, when he was hungry and they that were with him; how he entered into the house of God and did eat the showbread, which was not lawful for him to eat neither for them which were with him, but only for the Priests? [5]Or have you not read in the law how that on the Sabbath days the priests in the temple profane the Sabbath and are blameless? [6]But I say to you that in this place there is One greater than the temple. But if you had known what this means, I will have mercy and not sacrifice, you would not have condemned the guiltless. For the Son of Man is Lord, even of the Sabbath day."*

Apostle Paul also encountered the Pharisees in some of the churches in his days, even in the church in Galatia. In Galatians 3:1 he says, *"O foolish Galatians, who has bewitched you that you should not obey the truth, before whose eyes Jesus Christ has been evidently set forth (clearly portrayed) crucified among you? [3]Are you so foolish? Having begun in the Spirit, are you now made perfect by the flesh?"*

Clearly the Apostle was upset by what he came to see after handing over the reins of the church he planted to men that he had trusted. He had hoped that they would continue to build upon the foundation he had established, that is the Truth. The church had reverted to preaching and teaching the law, which none can fulfill.

False doctrine takes the finished work of the Cross back to legalism. This has brewed confusion and division in the body of Christ.

The Apostle echoes this in the book of Colossians 2:14, *"Blotting out the handwriting of ordinances against us, which was contrary to us, and took it out of the way, nailing it to His cross. [15]And having spoiled principalities and powers, He made a show of them openly, triumphing over them in it. [16]therefore let no man therefore judge you in meat, or in drink, or in respect of a holyday, or of the new moon, or of the Sabbath days. [17]Which are a shadow of things to come. But the body is of Christ. [18]let no man beguile (deceive) you……vainly puffed up by his fleshly mind."*

I like to link this to his epistle to Timothy. 1 Timothy 4:1, *"Now the Spirit speaks expressly, that in the latter days some shall depart from the faith, giving heed to seductive spirits, and doctrines of devils; [2]Speaking lies in hypocrisy, having their conscience seared with hot iron. [3]Forbidding to marry and commanding to abstain from meat, which God has created to be received with thanksgiving of them which believe and know the truth."*

Here, the Apostle is warning the church of the great deception that was to hit the body of Christ. Men will deviate from the truth and cause others to stumble and fall because of the release of the false doctrines that men will begin to propagate. He made mention of few of these in 2 Timothy 2:16, *"But shun profane and vain babblings: for they will increase to more ungodliness. [17]And their word will eat as does a canker: of whom is Hymanaeus and Philetus; [18]Who concerning the truth have erred, saying that the resurrection is past already; and overthrow the faith of some."*

Another vivid example is found in Titus 1:10, *"For there are many unruly and vain talkers and deceivers, especially they of the circumcision (Christians): [11]Whose mouths must be stopped, who subvert whole houses, teaching things they ought not, for filthy lucre's sake. (Dishonest gain) [12]One of themselves, even a prophet of their own, said, the Cretians, are always liars, evil beasts, slow bellies. [13]This witness is true. Wherefore rebuke them sharply, that they may be sound in the faith; [14]Not giving heed to Jewish fables, and commandment of men, that turns from the truth. [15]To the pure all things are pure: but to them that are defiled and unbelieving, is nothing pure; but even their mind and conscience is defiled. [16]They profess that they know God; but in works they deny Him, being abominable and disobedient, and to every good work reprobate."*

I believe the Apostle could not have put it in any other way but to be blunt about the issue and has left us with this word of truth that is dominating our world as believers today. We need the truth and nothing but the whole truth, which is the full Gospel of Jesus Christ, and not doctrines of demons being preached from many pulpits across the world today.

There are multiple Scriptures to confirm this but I will leave them for now. False doctrine is on the increase and this is bringing confusion and leading us astray. These false doctrines are originally propagated by demons who then impart the ideas to men and women in charge of God's people to be preached and taught. I see that the days when the Lord Jesus drove the moneychangers, oxen, sheep, goats and even doves out of the temple, are here again.

The Holy Spirit will cleanse His temples once again. I believe with my whole heart that there is going to be a complete overhauling to purify the church one more time before the Lord returns. Remember, He said He is coming for a glorious church, without spot or wrinkles, and without blemish. We do spring cleaning when we want freshness in our home, do we not? Yes. So, the Lord will undertake a spiritual spring-cleaning in His church before He returns

# CHAPTER 27

# Guard the Door to Your Heart

The heart of man is the also the main place where our life flows. If the heart does not pump the blood and circulate it to the brain, we would be dead. As it is in the physical so it is in the spiritual. The Word of God is our lifeline and without it we are but dead. This is the reason why we need to guard our hearts as closely as you protect yourself physically. With the heart we believe then with our mouth, we confess our Lord as our personal Savior.

We need to watch out and guard our hearts diligently as the Bible teaches us against opening doors for demons to enter in to torment us. Nobody is saying that being offended by an attack on your emotion is easy to deal with. Betrayal or any form of abuse, disappointments, from ourselves or from friends and family (the list goes on and on), are real and inflict deep emotional wounds on us.

How you deal with these things is what will make or destroy you. Proverbs 4:23, *"Keep your hearts with all diligence: for out of it are the issues of life."* This is vital to us as human beings. Peace of mind is very essential for our very existence. We have to make sure we have clear minds as Christians, so the Holy Spirit can minster His grace to make us both spiritually and physically healthy for the sake of the Kingdom and also for the world outside.  This serves as a good witness of our faith.

Who wants to get close to a miserable person? The devil knows that a wounded heart or spirit does not function properly, and is vulnerable. In fact, if you harbor hurts and pains in your hearts for too long, the Holy Spirit, after trying several times to heal you without success, leaves you. He will not force you to do anything you do not want to do. When this happens, the devil quickly sends his demons to invade your wounded heart with his poison. You soon become bitter and resentful.

I worked with a woman who was very quarrelsome. She would fight with everything that moved, and if it moved again, she would fight with it again. I mean this literally. All it took was some little thing, done by accident, and all hell would break loose. She fought with almost everybody in the work place including myself. I believe it stopped with me.

It took me three years of restraining myself before I finally lost it with her. I do not want to go into details, suffice it to say I dealt with her in my 'old man' way. I am not proud of this but at least it changed the dynamic for everyone in the office. I sat and pondered about her behavior and came to the conclusion that she was not a happy person at all. She may well be harboring some deep pains in her heart because her behavior was frankly, abnormal

It was not long before I stumbled on some information, overhearing some locker-room gossip as I was relaxing during my break. Some friends of hers confirmed my suspicions. I have come to know that hurting people tend to hurt others. This is because their wounds from previous hurts have not been healed and are now being used by the enemy to hurt others. We do not know if underneath these "horrible people" is very nice person who is bound by the enemy. All they need is love, counseling and, most probably deliverance.

I have had my fair share of all the abuses one can think of. I have experienced false accusations that led to severe beatings, sexual abuse by family members who were supposed to look out for me and extreme physical and verbal abuse. I will not go into details here, but all these happened to me in my childhood and teen years.

Talk about betrayal? People I went out of my way to help later turned on me as if they did not recall what I had done for them. The Lord God Almighty whom I serve has been gracious to me. He was my present help in my hour of need for comfort, healing and restoration and He will be there for you if you let Him.

# CHAPTER 28

# Offence

This is a wounding of your feelings. This is inevitable; it is part of living amongst other people whether we like it or not. There are times when it is our fault and, sometimes, it is not.

Jesus in Luke 17:1, said, *"Then said He unto the disciples, it is impossible but that offences will come."* There is no one person who ever lived and died and went to his grave without being offended by something or by someone. No one can say that he or she has never offended someone, it is impossible. We will all be offended by someone or by something at some point in our life, and we will also offend people.

It is how we handle this that determines whether it destroys or strengthens us. In life, I believe there are lessons to be learnt with every experience we go through. As believers, we have the Holy Spirit in us, and He is our helper in every situation and He will surely help us if we ask Him. I have learned by the Spirit that I have to surrender my will, and my sensitivity to Him. It is my choice alone if I surrender to Him or let my flesh have the better side of me.

The moment we allow our flesh to tip and dominate the greater part of the scale for too long, we are opening ourselves up to demons. The Bible says to guard our hearts with all diligence for out of it, are the issues of life. (Proverbs. 4:23) Please do just that, and do not give any opportunity to the devil through dwelling on the offence and seeking vengeance.

Sometimes the enemy will cause you to rehearse the whole thing over and over again or replay it like a video in your mind. The more you do this, the fresher the pain becomes, and the more your level of bitterness increases. Please, if you are at this point or getting there, find someone you can trust who can counsel you and pray with you to stop you from opening up yourself to demons.

Choose to forgive, I know there are levels of offence and sometimes it is difficult to let it go, but please hear me; give it all to the Lord and sincerely ask Him to heal your wounded heart. He will do it for you. Ask the Lord for the grace to forgive. It is the work of the Holy Spirit and if you will call on Him to help you, He surely will. Even medical science has linked unforgiveness and bitterness to some kinds of cancer? Selah!

Let me tell you of some of my personal experiences before and after I became a Christian. I have mentioned before that I was seriously abused in every way one can think of. Physically, verbally emotionally and sexually, up until my late teens. This hardened me as there was no one to come to my defense.

My mother was living in one part of town and I was living with my paternal grandmother on the other side. What was not clear to me until today was whether it was my mother who gave me up at that tender age of four, or if I was taken from her as is sometimes the case with many African children. I remember vaguely some of the things that took place at that time.

I remember the brown Gola shoes that I had on were yanked off my feet and I never saw them again. I remember other things like the day I slipped into a pot of porridge on the coal stove and sustained serious burns on my buttocks: I still bear the scars. My story would fill a whole book but I want to highlight what I have become despite my painful and abusive childhood.

I was the 'Cinderella' of the house and was never allowed to visit my mother, never allowed to go on vacations with my cousins. I was just an object and not a human being. From the age of five, I was doing most of the household chores and running errands for everyone.

I became highly rebellious when I reached my teens. On the outside was this sweet little girl but, on the inside, was such anger, hurt and pain. I used to ask myself why I was born into this world only to suffer in this way. Why was I singled out and treated differently from my other cousins? I had loads of questions in my mind and yet, I could not find any answers.

My grandmother would say to me that, whatever others obtained with ease, always proved difficult when it came to my turn. I honestly believed there was something not quite right with me. I look back now and see the grace of God has been with me all along. It would have been easy for demons to befriend me as I isolated and cried myself to sleep most nights.

I loved a song I learnt in Primary school, "Nearer my God to thee." This was my favorite song and I would it sing most days after I had been severely beaten, and red-hot pepper pushed into my front and back passage all at the age of six, seven or eight. I was an angry girl and I would attack anyone who offended me, and I mean I would attack and fight both male and female. I did not know where the strength came from.

I would verbally attack anyone as well, both young and old; anyone who tried to say anything bad to me. To cut a long story short, there was this feeling inside of me like a volcano ready to erupt any time I was provoked. My mother begged me to let it go when people offended me, but I felt I had to fight to defend myself. This was the result of years of abuse. I was hardened and very much toughened.

I never realized that the pain I suffered had been stored in my heart and had hardened me. I was an inwardly angry girl with a cool demeanor on the outside, even long after I became born again and would give prophetic words in church and in my private devotions. It was the teaching of one of the great 'Generals' of God, Derek Prince, of blessed memory, that brought deliverance to me.

I knew there was a change in my temperament after hearing the Word from him and praying consistently about it. The Lord in His mercy delivered me and I knew it. This is why I can sincerely talk about it. Listen, my dear reader and friend, the Lord will do it for you too. All it takes is for you to desire to be free. Yes, desire freedom and you shall surely receive it from the Lord.

Pain is real and pain can destroy you if you permit it. Please deal with it and let the Lord Jesus, the Healer, touch you and make you whole. Do not let the devil continue to afflict you, knowing you have already suffered enough. Give it all to Jesus. Give Him all your tears and sadness and the pain that you have suffered and He will heal and deliver you today.

We often categorize every expression of anger as a problem but this is not true. Even the Bible gives us permission to exercise this emotional act. Yes, it is an emotional response to a provocation or offence.

The Bible says to be angry and sin not, and do not let the sun go down on your anger. What this means is, since you cannot stop someone from expressing his or her emotions, neither can you stop yourself. You cry when you are sad, you laugh when something is funny, you sigh, you mourn, you moan - the list goes on and on. These are mere expressions of our emotions and are involuntary. They are part of our emotional expressions in our soul.

Anger is the same but unlike the others, anger can be held on to for a long time. When anger is incubated for a long time, it turns into rage and rage is a spirit. Rage can cause one to do horrible things or even kill when provoked. So, what we are dealing with now is extreme anger, which is rage. The Bible is clear about this. The moment you allow the sun to go down on anger, you have moved from expressing your displeasure of a thing or a person's behavior to the level of the incubating mode, and it is being nursed into a full-blown thing ready to explode any moment you are provoked. That is why we have anger management in the secular world. It is to teach how to handle anger, but in Christendom we know one needs to be counseled and delivered if possible, because it is gone beyond the normal expression of emotions.

Proverbs 18:14b, *"…but a wounded spirit who can bear?"* Surrender everything to the Lord. The devil loves it when we become offended and carry these offences in our hearts. The heart then becomes a breeding ground for his demons to throw more arrows into our already wounded heart. If we do not deal with it as the Bible states, we will be plunged into bitterness and resentment. One demon spirit will give birth open the door to another and then another.

Offence breeds pain, pain gives birth to bitterness, bitterness produces hatred, and hatred turns to resentment and vengeful thoughts. What is happening is that the demons are making sure that there is no way for you to be free, they are lying to you. There is always a way out through our Lord and Savior, Christ Jesus. Still, if at this stage you do not seek counseling and prayer support, you will end up in your self-made prison.

I was watching two of my granddaughters playing, and I do not know what kept me watching, but I did. Playing turned into something else as I observed the younger one willingly presenting herself to be 'attacked' in a certain way by her sibling. When it hurt her, she cried out and her sister would stop and the whole scenario would start again.

Their mum stepped in and, not knowing what was actually happening, wanted to discipline the older one. What came out of my mouth surprised me, and my daughter and I both laughed about my statement. Nevertheless, it is a statement that I believe is true and the Holy Spirit wanted me to acknowledge this truth. I said to my daughter, "Do not smack E because A is a willing captive; she presented herself to be abused."

A 'willing captive'. It was only when I started repeating it that the Holy Spirit began to minister to me how; indeed, some of us are willing captives. We do not resist the enemy but rather permit him to come in to mess us up and eventually take over our life. We have the power, by the grace bestowed upon us by God, to overcome every situation through the Blood of Jesus. We need to use this for our benefit and the benefit of others too. Let us use the power of the Word and the Blood to resist the enemy of our soul, not yield to him to poison our hearts.

The Lord has promised us in Isaiah 49:24 *"Shall the prey be taken from the mighty, or the lawful captive delivered?* [25] *But thus says the LORD, even the captives of the mighty shall be taken away, and the prey of the terrible shall be delivered."*

# CHAPTER 29

# Unforgiveness

Unforgiveness is one of the tools the devil uses to destroy Christians and non-Christians alike. It is one of the top issues that contaminate our soul. In fact, to put it bluntly, it is a sin in the eyes of God. It is hard, I know, and believe me I know, how hard it can be sometimes to let go. But as Christians there is no choice at all.

We need to and have to forgive. God requires it and we have to do it. All we need to do is, to ask for God's grace to forgive. In our Lord's Prayer, it says *"forgive us our debts, (sins) as we forgive our debtors."* (Matthew 6:12) This means, if we do not forgive, we do not receive forgiveness from the Father and whosoever is not forgiven by the Father is none of His. If you are 'none' of His, the devil has the legal right to touch and attack you in whatever way he wants to.

This also destroys our fellowship with the Lord. In Matthew 18, the subject is discussed extensively and the consequences are clearly stated. We have received forgiveness from God through Jesus and we are required to extend the same to others, no matter how deep the hurt is.

I remember a friend who felt betrayed by a woman she thought was spiritually matured but had relayed confidential information at a home cell meeting. She spoke to me and expressed her disappointment and vowed never to speak to the woman again. I initially counseled her and left her to go through it; not to come down too strong on her.

A week later I called to enquire about how she was feeling and I soon realized that she still had not dealt with it as the Lord would want her to. I then took my time to expound what the Scripture says about forgiving those who offend us. She finally got it. You see, the one who has been offended has every right to be offended and angry, and act out their anger, but the Bible is very clear on this subject

Matthew 6:14-15, *"For if you forgive men their trespasses, your heavenly Father will also forgive you. But if you forgive not men their trespasses, neither will your Father forgive your trespasses."*

The word 'if' brings home the fact that we have a choice and yet, we do not have a choice in this matter. You can choose to hold on to an offence against your brother or sister or anyone else, but the bottom line is that, in making that choice, you have also chosen not to receive God's forgiveness for the sins we commit against Him. I do not see how one could live with that.

There was a time in my early walk with the Lord, that a very close friend, or so I thought, really hurt me, I mean, she really hurt me. The wound inflicted was deep. I believe the Lord knew that if he did not intervene, it would have destroyed me, so He did.

Do you know how the Lord delivered me? The Holy Spirit told me to go and make peace with this person. I said, "Lord, she is the one who offended me so she should be apologising to me, not me to her."
He repeated the same statement, saying, "Go and make peace with her." I felt the Lord was not being fair with me. This was my

immature mind speaking to me at the time. I was reluctant to obey the Lord and I spent three days in torment. Throughout those three days, I did not have peace.

Eventually I said, "Ok Lord, you win." I set off to this person's apartment and climbed up the flights of steps to her apartment on the fourth floor. It was difficult for my flesh, to see her face to face after the incident, but I knew I would not win unless I did as the Lord had said. I reluctantly spoke peaceably to her and she was all smiles and chatting away as if nothing had happened. This was hurting me the more knowing that it should have been her in my house doing what I was doing but I kept my feelings under control.

Do you know that I actually felt better afterwards? It took the sting out of my pain and within hours I felt some weight lifted off me.

This happened three times on different occasions, and each time, it became easier for me to do as the Lord instructed me. I have now learned to let go without expecting the person in the wrong to apologise before I forgive. During this process, one lesson the Lord taught me is, and He actually said to me, "Learn to give up your right of being right for peace sake."

You have the right of being offended and holding on to it by not forgiving the offender I repeat the same to you. Hopefully it will help you as it did me. Choose to give up your right of being right and let God vindicate you. It is rewarding. You have favour with God and the enemy has nothing on you, neither is there any doorway for him to enter in to torment you.

Another instance I can share is, after a senior brother had held a discussion with me. I happened to be talking to my niece, his daughter, later and mentioned the subject to her. I did not think anything of it and certainly did not expect her to call her father immediately after our conversation. My phone went off soon afterwards and it was my brother fuming on the phone, hurling insults at me.

My former self would have given him back just the same but I kept quiet and, when he was done, he hung up on me. This was Sunday afternoon after I had returned from church and was having a rest. You can imagine how that old devil was telling me to call my niece and confront her about the issue but I had to exercise self-control. Let me tell you, I was hurting badly inside because I did not see what the fuss was all about.

I carried the hurt until the next day and the Holy Spirit said to call my brother and apologise. This time He explained to me the reason I needed to apologise. He said, "Your brother discussed an issue with you as his sister and you had no right to tell your niece. Although it was a commonly known issue, the decision to tackle it was his business; and had confidentially discussed that with you."

I immediately called him and apologised and he also apologised. Telling me he lost his peace after he insulted me and went and knelt down and asked the Lord to forgive him. Listen, my brother was not a practicing Christian but the Holy Spirit convicted him as He did with me at the same time.

What came out of his mouth was what made me believe the more that, when we surrender every pain or hurt to the Lord, He works on our behalf. These are the exact words that came out of my brother's mouth, "I know you are my younger sister and I can insult you and tell you whatever, but I also felt convicted because you are a woman of God, I was present at your ordination and I know it. So please forgive me." Can you imagine how that felt like?

Our God has His way of healing us from every pain or affliction we go through. Give it all to Him and do not allow the devil and his demons to use this to hurt you the more; for there is a balm in Gilead. Jesus, the Great Physician, will heal and strengthen you. I have numerous testimonies on the subject of dealing with hurt and pain God's way; I am a living witness so I can talk about it with empathy.

Jesus said in Matthew 5:23-24 *"Therefore, if you bring your gift to the altar, and there remember that your brother has anything against you: leave there your gift before the altar and go your way; first be reconciled to your brother, and then come and offer your gift."*

God does not take it lightly when we refuse to forgive those who offend us. Unresolved issues have to be thoroughly dealt with His way and His way alone. That is, through forgiveness and release in exchange for your own freedom. I say, for your own freedom, because the moment you surrender it all to the Lord, He gives you His peace and you feel the heavy burden of carrying the hurt and pain rolled away. The weight is replaced with a blanket of peace and there is nothing like it. You feel light and liberated from carrying the pain.

In short, unforgiveness will make the chambers of your heart the breeding ground for Satan to cause his spiritual vagabonds, his demons, to produce poison to infest and destroy you. Pease do yourself a favor and seek help from your Pastor or any elder that you believe you can trust. There are certain things that you can overcome by just talking about it to someone you have known to be spiritually matured. James put it clearly in his book. James. 5:16, *"Confess your faults one to another, and pray for one*

*another, that you may be healed. The effectual fervent prayer of
the righteous man avails much."*

*In verse 13 the question is asked, "Is any among you afflicted? Let
him pray...* [14]*Is any sick among you? Let him call for the elders of the
church; and let them pray over him, anointing him with oil in the
name of the Lord. And the prayer of faith shall save the sick, and
the Lord shall raise him up; and if he has committed any sins, they
shall be forgiven him."*

Dear friend, I want you to take a little time to read this Scripture
over and over and get the understanding of what it really means to
us as Christians. There are two different questions asked here; is
any among you afflicted, and is any among you sick. Do you know
you can be sick in your soul? I believe this Scripture cuts across the
board. It is not just talking about being sick in your body alone. We
can be afflicted in our minds as well as in our body. Seek healing for
your soul and do not let anybody convince you that all is well and
you do not need help.

The world knows there are different kinds of ailments and we have
different hospitals and specialist doctors that have specialised in
their fields. I am no medical doctor, but I know that, in medical
school, the students are taught about the human anatomy and the
various diseases that afflict various parts of the body, and how
they can be treated. I also know that qualified doctors can choose
to specialise in a particular area of their profession such as
cardiology, neurology, gynecology and the like.

So, it is with us as Christians that God Almighty has called us to be
His servants in the Kingdom of God. Every Pastor should be able to
pray over the sick for healing but God has also anointed some
specifically for the healing ministry that wherever they go, this

anointing follows them. They are "specialist." If the world refers you to a specialist for some medical conditions, why can Christians not do the same.

After all, everything established on earth is derived from the principles of the Bible. Seek help if you need it and seek it from the right person and the right place. The reason I say that is, we have different ministries and diversity of gifts and operations. As in the natural you would not go to an optometrist with a heart problem, so it is also, concerning spiritual things. You cannot just go to anyone to deal with demonic activities and possession. If they do not believe in deliverance, or they are unwilling to do it, it is obvious they cannot help you. If they do believe in deliverance, then the prayer of faith shall save the sick.

The Bible goes on to say that if they (the sick) have committed any sin, they shall be forgiven. Ask yourself this question, why should I be forgiven for being sick? This is referring to the sin of harbouring offence in your heart against your brother that can literally cause one to be physically sick. Medical science has proven this to be true.

Please do not be deceived, unforgiveness is a sin in the eyes of our God and, until you deal with it, you are walking in sin and the devil has a legal right to afflict you. (Matthew 18:29-35) Our God is merciful and He will help you if you cry out for help. The Holy Spirit is our Helper, call on Him and He will come to your aid. I often use this illustration when talking about forgiveness. If you choose not to forgive someone who has offended you, you lock him or her in the prison of your heart and you become the prison warden.

In the natural sense who does the hard work, the prisoner or the warden? Who paces up and down to see if the prisoner is ok? Who carries the weight of dozens of keys, running up and down the long prison corridors making sure that everything is ok? Meanwhile the prisoner is fast asleep. The warden has no rest until his or her shift is over.

If you have been offended and you have not fully dealt with it the Bible way, the enemy will use it to torment you. The one who offended you may be fast asleep not thinking about you let alone the pain he or she has caused you, yet you have sleepless nights. Please choose to forgive with or without an apology.

Think about this and release the offender for your own sake and you will enjoy God's peace. Give place to God's wrath as vengeance belongs to the Lord and He will repay. (Romans 12:19) The devil can use offence to emotionally put you in captivity and harass you. Please deal with it before it destroys you. The enemy gains legal access to torment the believer who refuses to let the Lord work with you and on you. Let the Lord walk you through your pain.

Some of us are still carrying the hurt and pain from the past and we still have not found solutions or sought help. I recommend you seek help in the Word of God or from your Pastor or a trusted Elder in the church. You need help, do not suffer in silence and do not give the devil a foothold in your life. Remember the prayer of faith shall heal the sick.

I want to tell you a true story that happened in my family. My uncle fell out with his wife of many years and, though they were living under the same roof; they were not talking to each other at all. This feud went on for several years and during those years, I would usually visit my uncle when I was on vacation.

On one particular occasion, as I was preparing for the trip, packing the stuff I was taking with me, the Holy Spirit spoke and asked me, "So how do you feel as a Minister of my Gospel, visiting your uncle year by year and knowing that he and his wife are not on talking terms and you have done nothing to bring reconciliation?"
You see, God knew my heart and the fact that I was not in the least interested in the situation. I had a personal vendetta against my uncle's wife going back decades to when I lived with them. To cut a long story short, I repented of my own sin of unforgiveness and prayed for their reconciliation before I set of to see them.

After we had a meal and talked and had family discussions, I went in to have a word with my uncle separately. He called me by my name and said, if his wife would apologise, then he would forgive her. I said to him, "Uncle, in this world there are certain people who never apologise even if they know they are wrong. I want you to do yourself a favour and choose to forgive her with or without apology." I went on to ask him, "What would you do if you wake up tomorrow and she is no more? Have you considered the guilt you would be carrying for the rest of your life?"

My eighty-five-year-old uncle burst into tears like a child and said to me, "Let's go." So, we went to find my aunt and after I was done speaking to her, she was not going to let go without telling her side of the story. I would not permit this and pushed the need to forgive one another irrespective of whatever had happened. By the grace of God, His favour brought peace so that, following my return to the United Kingdom, every time I called home to enquire of their well-being, they were still talking to one another. Praise God!

Sadly, my aunt died about six months after their reconciliation. When I called my uncle to express my sympathy and condolences, as soon as he came on the phone, he burst out crying like a child, calling me by name saying, this is what I had said and warned him about. I was able to comfort and remind him of God's love for him and the fact that he forgave her and they were happy together again before her passing.

My dear friends, God cares about us and He does not want us to carry unnecessary burdens. Let us learn to forgive. Will you do that today? Choose to forgive. Let me tell you the truth, forgiveness is all about you and not about the person who offended you. Forgiveness frees you from the enemy's plan to hurt you and it brings pleasure to God when we choose to forgive. It also draws us closer to God. That which the devil thought he could use to destroy you will be used to draw you closer to God.

Surrender all to the Lord Jesus who paid the ultimate price with His death on the cross. He will see you through every pain and every hurtful situation you may face. Remember, the Lord Jesus knows what it feels like to be betrayed by the people you have healed, delivered and, in some cases fed. Did He not feel the pain of rejection? He did but He even asked for forgiveness from the Father on our behalf whilst hanging on the cross.

# CHAPTER 30

# Bitterness

Bitterness and resentment are similar. Both are the result of a pain suffered justly or unjustly. Bitterness breeds resentment towards the offender.

I have heard people say they can never forgive. Indeed, you can never do it in your own strength but God will help you to forgive. Another one will say they will never forgive a certain person. This is a serious matter because God will not go against your will so please choose your words carefully so the Lord God Almighty can help you and heal you.

This feeling is mental torture for anyone who allows it to fester for a long time in his heart. This is a serious doorway that the enemy uses to torment you if you do not handle it properly through God's Word and, sometimes, through proper counseling. Bitterness erodes your joy and peace and makes you vulnerable to demonic invasion. Guard your heart with all diligence the Bible tells us. Yes, it is very important to adhere to this word of wisdom.

The Bible continues to say; out of it are the issues of life. Proverbs 17:22, "A *merry heart does good like medicine; but a broken spirit dries the bones.*" Bitterness is poison to the soul so please deal with it and, if you find it difficult to handle, then seek help before it seizes you and opens up your soul to the enemy for destruction. Whenever you find yourself in a situation that causes a surge of anger to rise within you or a name of someone who had offended you is mentioned in conversation and you find this awful resentful feeling rising up within you, then, please know that you have not dealt with it completely. Do not let the devil deceive you that you have but rather run to the Lord and pour out all your pain unto Him.

Sometimes you hear people say, I can never forgive this person or that person. My dear one, you cannot afford not to, as this can cause severe pain which can result in serious sickness. Yes, people literally get sick because of not letting go. They end up with diseases like high blood pressure, cancer and others. Medical science has proven this to be true and has published their findings.

There are times when the wrongdoer who has caused you such pain and driven you to the point of bitterness, has moved on with his or her own life. They most likely may not even think about you, let alone remember the pain they caused. It is a cruel and a vicious world in which we live.

As long as we have this adversary who will use people to conduct his evil business, to attack us, we need to draw closer each day to the Lord Jesus and depend on His Word to guide us. In so doing, we will learn how to deal with such issues as they arise. Jesus warns us in Luke 17 that it is impossible to live in this world without offences.

Know also that the more you harbour bitterness in your heart, the farther away from the Lord you become. This is sad because you are the one that has been wronged and you deserve to be angry; but the Bible says to be angry and sin not. Do not be consumed by this feeling for it will lead to self- destruction. You do not have to hold a pity party either because this will only lead to depression.

Depression will prepare a habitation for demons in your soul and before you know it, the devil has taken over your life. In some cases, the devil will use his gained territory to harass you and tell you that life is not worth living; so why do not you end it all. Know that nothing is more important to God than your life. God gave His Son for you to have and enjoy life according to John 10:10, *"I am come that you may have life and that you may have it more abundantly."*

Life is for living and I pray you will not allow the devil to have any say in your life. Deny him access and give the Holy Spirit the permission to put things right for you. Yes, cooperate with Him to lead you out of any path of destruction.

Remind yourself that the Holy Spirit is our Comforter and our Helper. Confess it aloud and the moment you cry out to the Lord, the demons that are lurking around you to destroy you, will flee

## Betrayal

Betrayal is: 1. an act of deliberate disloyalty, 2. to abuse trust or stab one in the back, 3. when one discloses something shared in confidence, this is a violation of confidence. An example is when a friend tells others your secrets

This is one of the major causes of pain and bitterness that I know so well. What do you do when you have been brutally betrayed? First of all, prayerfully pour out your complaints to the Lord after you have done your own soul searching to find out if you have contributed to this action or not.

You see, one thing the believer has to do at all times in situations like this, which come as a result of people not acting appropriately in the event of disagreement, is to honestly search your own conscience to see if you did something wrong to trigger this act of betrayal. Please do this sincerely with the help of the Holy Spirit who will convict you of any wrongdoing.

If you find that you did something wrong or these people felt offended by something you did or said, then please take a bold step to first of all seek forgiveness with a heartfelt apology. Seriously? Yes, seriously. The Holy Spirit will help you to do this.

You may then add afterwards that, "I know I offended you unintentionally, but you could have cautioned me instead of betraying my confidence; however, I have chosen to forgive you."

If the person is a true friend who acted on his or her feelings, there will be an exchange of apologies and then you can move on from there. The harm is already done so now you can choose to walk in wisdom and keep the brotherly love alive. This is a soothing balm in the healing process and it will free you from opening any door for the enemy to come and inflict you with even more pain.

I have suffered a number of betrayals in my life, but the most painful ones are those from within the church. My challenge was the fact that I thought we were all Christians and the love of God was in us, to love one another and to trust one another. So, I let down my guard in my early walk with the Lord and I suffered, oh I suffered.

That was when I learned many of the lessons I have discussed and shared in this book. I learned to run to the Lord, to pour out my complaints and pains before Him. On one occasion He told me,

"Know that not all that are in Israel are of Israel." In other words, my assumption that everyone in church is a Christian, was wrong.

That was my mistake, as I would welcome into my world everyone who professed to be a Christian without holding back. You see, I love the people of God and in my naivety never thought that someone could be in church and remain in the flesh, be wicked at heart or not be born again. The Lord taught me through my pain how to deal with offences and walk uprightly before Him with a clean heart; not to give any foothold to the devil.

These were painful lessons. I am not saying it is going to be easy to practice but I am saying, trust Jesus to walk you through your pain and you will come out victorious, in His glorious Name.

What happens when a cheating husband tells his mistress everything that is going on in your home? Sometimes he stretches the truth to make him feel justified in his sinful venture? What happens if this mistress becomes emboldened enough to confront you and tell you how bad a wife you are, and that you need to release your husband as he does not want to be with you anymore?

This has led to some real-life murder incidents, simply because the women involved, the wives, could not take it. They did not seek any help but became consumed in their pain to an extent that the enemy just convinced them that killing the husband or his mistress was the only option to alleviate the pain. Will killing alleviate the pain? Maybe, but I doubt it. You will pay the price of murder in the court of justice and also in the eyes of God. If there are children in the midst of all this, they will suffer too. All this for what, one may ask?

Betrayal is a very painful experience and I will not even try to downplay it at all. What I am saying is, pray about it and seek help if necessary, by talking to a friend you trust or an Elder for counseling and prayer.

If the above proves too difficult for you, then seek counsel from your Pastor; that is if he or she is not the one who has betrayed you. I believe your Pastor should be able to walk you through your pain and teach you how to deal with it God's way. If the Pastor is the one who has caused you the pain, then pour out your complaints unto the Lord as if He did not know it. I know of many incidents that people have left the church because of the Pastor's betrayal. Things that were told in confidence, were later either used in preaching or were repeated to someone else.

Talk it over with Jesus as you would to your loving earthly father. As a matter of fact, the Lord should be your first point of call, for the Bible says there is a friend that sticks closer than a brother and that is Jesus. Tell it all to Him and ask Him to heal you, and surely, He will.

He has done it for me many, many times when I have suffered at the hands of those I thought were friends. I learnt from my earlier walk with Jesus that I can talk to Him and He will hear me and heal me and cover me with His blanket of peace, which is His perfect Peace. So, my dear friend, do not allow the devil to steal your joy or peace. He will only torment you with thoughts that will make you vulnerable to him and his demons.

Remember the song,
> *What a friend we have in Jesus,*
> *All our sins and grieves to bear.*
> *What a privilege to carry*
> *Everything to God in prayer.*

Is it not wonderful to know that you can run to the Lord to find peace and love? Do not suffer it alone and do not suffer in silence either.

# CHAPTER 31

# Doubt

Doubt is a sin in the eyes of God. It means you think He is not who He says He is. It means He cannot do what He said He would do. In other words, He is not trustworthy.

As it was in the Garden of Eden, so it is today. Satan tested and won the mind of Eve by suggesting that God had an agenda and that is why He did not tell them the real reason they should not eat of the tree of knowledge and good and evil.

This was to confuse Eve and make her doubt God's integrity. When the enemy is attacking you because of one thing or another, or due to an opened door you have created for him, he will slowly cause you to lose faith in the Lord. Then he comes in to harass or torment you.

The enemy can use doubt to deprive you of the good things that God has in store for you. When this happens, some of us become bitter towards God, and we murmur and complain about Him. The sad thing is, Satan and his demons do not let it seem like bitterness in your mind, but it is and the Lord who knows our thoughts, knows it and is grieved.

It grieves Him because we have allowed the devil to deceive us out of our blessings. Sometimes we do not perceive ourselves as being doubtful, but do you know that certain statements we make are actually a reflection of our thoughts? The Bible says God knows our thoughts from afar. Your confession reflects your thoughts and your thoughts reflect your perception of God. Giving up on yourself is telling the God who made you that, He is not able to help you.

Some of us have been in certain situations for a very long time and have prayed, fasted and done all we know to do, but still there seems to be no breakthrough. Even though we might not say it aloud, we are inwardly angry with God. Especially when we see people who we think do not deserve certain blessings, prosper before our eyes. We have been praying for the same and yet, nothing seems to happen for us. After being in this situation for a long time, you tend to switch off.

At this point, all that is left for us is to go through the motions of being a Christian with no joy, no relationship and no intimacy with the Lord. Where there is no trust there cannot be a true relationship. Trust is always needed in order to build a healthy relationship. Proverbs 3:5 says *"Trust in the Lord with all your heart and lean not to your own understanding, but in all your ways acknowledge Him and He shall direct your path."*

Doubting God means He is a liar, or incapable to do what He has said He will do. Doubting God means He is not all that He said He is, that is, our all-powerful, all-knowing and ever-present help in all that we go through or have to deal with. Doubting God is an insult to His sovereignty as possessor of everything in heaven and earth. He is not only the possessor but also the Creator of all things who has all power over His creation.

The Bible teaches us that anything that is not done in faith is a sin as far as God is concerned. The lord who doubted the prophetic Word of God, angered God to declare his doom. In 2 Kings 7:1, *"then Elisha said, hear ye the words of the Lord: Thus, says the Lord, tomorrow about this time shall a measure of fine flour be sold for a shekel and two measures of barley for a shekel, in the gate of Samaria."*

This was God's hour of deliverance for His people. He made known to His people His plans for deliverance by telling them, through His Prophet, how it would be accomplished. After all, the Bible says in Amos 3:7, *"Surely the Lord God will do nothing, but He reveals His secrets to His servants the Prophets."* He also declares in 2 Chronicles. 20:20 to, *"Believe in the Lord your God and you shall be established; believe His prophets, so shall you prosper."*

My question then is, why would someone so close to the king make such doubtful remarks as in verse 2 of 2 Kings 7, *"Then a lord on whose arms the king leaned answered the man of God and said, Behold if the Lord will make windows in heaven, might this thing be? And he (the prophet) said, Behold, you shall see it with your eyes, but shall not eat thereof."*

Look at this picture well and I pray that you see that God does not take lightly any move of ours that casts doubt on His very being or takes His Word lightly. Take the Word of God seriously whether it is written or 'thus says the Lord', which is a spoken Word from the Lord. He is His Word and His Word is Him. Trust God to do what He says He will do and it shall be well with you.

From this account, we know that doubt is a consequential sin because the lord suffered dearly for his words of doubt, which could have foiled God's plan of deliverance for the people of Israel. The Bible says in verse 17, *"And the king appointed the lord on whose hand he leaned to have the charge of the gate: and the people trod upon him in the gate and he died, as the man of God had said, who spoke when the king came down to him."*

Do not doubt God, for He is faithful and all His promises are, Yea and Amen. Satan moves in on us when we are confused, troubled, fearful and doubtful. Know that he is the one who is behind all that and, if we believe his lies, he quickly moves in to destroy us. Have faith in God.

James. 1:6 says, *"But let him ask in faith, nothing wavering (doubting). For he that wavers (doubts) is like a wave of the sea driven with the wind and tossed. For let not that man think he shall receive any thing of the Lord. A double minded man is unstable in all his ways."*

Jesus rebuked Simon Peter when he took his eyes off Him and began to sink. Our God takes it seriously when we doubt him and expects us to trust Him even when the odds are stacked against us. He is more than able to do beyond our expectations. As He brought deliverance over and over again to the children of Israel so will He do it for you and me.

Remember, God is the same yesterday, today and forever. All we have to do is let Him know that we need His help and He will swiftly respond.

# CHAPTER 32

# Anger

Anger is extreme or passionate displeasure. We have every right to express our emotions as this is natural, but emotions out of control will be a tool for the devil. The Bible did not say we should not be angry, but it recommended for us not to sin when we are angry. Ephesians 4:26, *"Be ye angry, and sin not: Let not the sun go down upon your wrath. Neither give place to the devil."*

This is clear enough. If you allow anger to linger on for a long time, it will lead to other stuff that is not godly. When anger is allowed to fester for a long time, it proceeds into rage. Rage is allowing anger to escalate to a point of losing control of one's self. It is also from keeping anger harboured in one's heart for any length of time. Such anger only grows over time into an intense rage within the heart.

What the enemy does, is to bombard our minds with thoughts of vengeance. As believers, we are to give the place of vengeance to the Lord. Anger, if not properly dealt with is like volcano that can erupt at any time with devastating consequences. Anger can cause people to do things they will live to regret for the rest of their life.

People have killed as a result of anger. Proverbs 18:19 says, *"A brother offended is harder to be won than a strong city: and their contentions are like the bars of a castle."*

The Bible tells us to resist the devil and he will flee from us. (James 4:7) Take hold of the Word of God and it will work for you if you apply it. Pray for the *fruits of the spirit,* one of which is long suffering, which can be seen as self-control. An angry man is easily manipulated by the devil. Guard your heart with all diligence the Bible says, for out of it are the issues of life.

Finally, let me leave you with these words from Proverbs 16:32, *"He that is slow to anger is better than the mighty; and he that rules his spirit than he that takes a city."* Prov. 22:24-25, *"Make no friendship with an angry man; and with a furious man thou shall not go: Lest you learn his ways, and get a snare to your soul."*

Extreme anger is a spirit that will contaminate your soul and this particular verse in Proverbs tells us how the spirit of anger, if not properly dealt with, can affect your soul and the people around you for the worse. Know that demons can project their thoughts through people into others. That is why one lie about someone can spread like wildfire. Demons are using human beings to do the work of Satan, the accuser of the brethren.

Did you know that if you hang around an angry person for too long, it will not be long before you start getting easily angered yourself. This is projection of demons. Projection means the unconscious reception of transfer of one's own impression or feeling to an external object or persons. This is a very common means whereby demons are transferred from one person to another. You become like the person you constantly hang out with. James 3:16, *"For where envying and strife is, there is confusion and every evil works."*

Demonic spirits infest people who then pollute their surroundings. When you enter into that domain, you will be infested as well, if you do not guard your heart. Have you ever heard the saying "show me your friend and I will show you your character?" That is a true presentation of how people's behavior can influence others. This does not mean we should not associate with people like that, no, but only with the purpose of winning them to Christ or by you being a good influence in their life. During your time of hanging around them keep your spiritual antennae plugged into the frequency of heaven so you will receive warning signs about wrong moves or demonic traps.

Extreme anger or rage can often be a trait of an abused person. People who have suffered through abuse  always carry this trait. Most have years of unresolved issues and accumulated pain that have never been properly dealt with, simply because the subject has not been talked or spoken about let alone been taught. Some do not even think or know there is a problem and yet they cannot explain why they get angry and fly into rage at the smallest provocation.

We are also in the church, I say we, because I was once like that and I was in church and I have seen many like that, including people in positions of authority. Jesus said in John 8:32 that, *"You shall know the truth and the truth shall make you free."*

The Son of God came to set the captives free but we, like the Jews, think that when we are born again, there is no need for any form of deliverance. In verse 33, *"They answered Him, we be Abraham's seed, and were never in bondage to any man: how sayest thou Ye shall be made free?"*

The people of God need to know the truth and be set free. It is not acceptable for the church to walk in deception or pretense anymore; we need the full Gospel of Jesus Christ. There is a need to teach and enlighten people about demonisation and deliverance. Some even say, we must not talk about the devil; but Jesus talked about him; and the Apostle Paul also talked about him and his devices.

Therefore, if we do not talk about the devil, how can we teach young and vulnerable Christians how to identify his ways of deception and destruction so they might resist him? A Minister friend of mine said there is nothing like deliverance and demonisation because it is a 'mind thing', that is to say, it is all in the mind. I asked him later on, if that was the case, then the teaching in Ephesians 6 is also all in the mind. He said yes!

At that point I realised that we have serious issues in the body of Christ. How can it be in my mind when the Apostle was teaching the church about the hierarchy in the in the satanic kingdom? How can it be a 'mind thing' when I have seen demons manifesting, throwing people about and threatening me with things that are not known to the person?

So, when Jesus cast the devil out of the people who were possessed, was it in His imagination or that of the people he delivered? What about the Apostle Paul, in Acts 16:16? Was it the mental state of the woman or was there a real demon involved?

As we are living in dangerous times now, my prayer is for us all to draw closer to the Lord. The Lord and the Holy Spirit, and not our intellect, can interpret His Word so we can be a people prepared for the Lord's coming. Psalm 11:3 says, *"If the foundations be destroyed what can the righteous do?"* In other words, if the basic truth is tampered with or misinterpreted what can the righteous do?

The devil is a liar! The Lord will build His church upon Himself, and the revelation of Truth and the gates of hell shall not prevail against it. The Truth shall and will always prevail.

A young woman once attended our Bible study class and, when the subject of forgiveness arose, she asked one challenging question after the other, which were all answered according to the Scriptures After all that, she was still adamant that she could not forgive her father for the things he had put the family through.

I seized the opportunity to minister to her through the Word of God and word of wisdom. As she poured out her heart, I realised that her bitter mother who had not forgiven her ex-husband for abandoning them had unfairly put her into this position. There had been transference of the spirit of bitterness. By the end of the meeting, we all saw the change in her and her gratitude to God for allowing her to be at the Bible study that evening. She confessed she had not wanted to come but was called by one of the ministers.

You see, people are hurting and the enemy is using their silence to destroy them. It is about time the church dealt with the lies and deception of the enemy concerning deliverance and free the people of God, to live a *more abundant* life.

This is an excerpt from a teaching that I came across. It caught my attention because of the title.

Manna for the day@ Monday 16th October, 2019
<u>The New Creation Needs No Deliverance</u>

*Who hath delivered us from the power of darkness, and hath translated us into the Kingdom of his dear Son* (Colossians 1:13)

Our opening verse is a present truth. A verse like this makes one wonder at folks who though born again, are still seeking deliverance. The Word of God says God has delivered us from the power of darkness, and has transferred us into the Kingdom of His Love-Son. He has done it already. You do not need deliverance. Even the non-Christians have been delivered, because the death of Jesus Christ brought redemption, deliverance to all men, not just those who become Christians.

Understand who the Christian is: He is a new creation, a brand-new man; he was never set free from sin or from Satan, because he was never in servitude to sin or Satan. 2 Corinthians 5:17 says if any man is in Christ, he is a new species of being that never existed. Everything about your life from that moment you received Christ, is brand new. You have a brand-new life that is not subject to the devil, sin and its consequences. It just does not add up to think God would give birth to a new creation that is subject to Satan!

James 1:18 says, *"Of His own will begat He us with the word of truth, that we should become the first fruits of His creatures."* We are literally born of God; we are His legal and vital offspring, with power and authority to cast out devils. We are one with God; we have His very life, and are in His class of being! This is who the Christian really is! He has been raised together with, and made to sit together in heavenly places in Christ Jesus, far above all principalities and powers.

If at any time, Satan or any of his demons shows up around you, cast him out. You have the power and authority in the Name of Jesus to that effect. Irrespective of the experiences that you may have had, what you might be going through now or what you think, God's Word remains true: you're superior to Satan; keep him where he belongs - under your feet."

You see, the interpretation of the above Scriptures to prove we do not need deliverance is greatly flawed and this is exactly what I have been talking about all along.

The writer has even contradicted himself by saying even the non-believer does not need deliverance and yet he is quoting the Bible as *"if anyone be in Christ Jesus"*. How do you now explain this contradiction? If the death of Christ brought redemption to all men, then the Lord Jesus, on the Cross, would have told both men crucified with Him that they would be with him in paradise, but He only made this statement to the one who acknowledged his sins and asked for the Lord to remember him.

Luke 23 40-42, *"And one of the malefactors which were hanged railed on Him, saying, if thou be Christ, save thyself and us. But the other answering rebuked him saying, dost not thou fear God, seeing thou art in the same condemnation? And we indeed justly; for we receive the due reward of our deeds: but this man has done nothing amiss. [42]And he said unto Jesus, Lord, remember me when thou come into thy Kingdom. [43]and Jesus said to him, verily I say unto you, today shall you be with me in paradise."*

Check this out as it explains the Scripture that says, *"As many as received Him, to them gave He the power to become sons of God, even to them that believe on His name. Which were born, of neither blood nor the will of the flesh, but of God? (That is to be born of the Spirit)"* John 1:12-13.

So, how can this statement be made by anyone who "teaches" the Bible, that even unbelievers have been delivered, in order words, saved? How can a non-believer be delivered from something that he does not believe in? I can comment on this piece of "teaching" forever with supporting Scriptures, but I leave the readers with this brief explanation to disprove the notion that Christians do not need deliverance. That is a false doctrine from the pit of hell. The enemy does not want you to be free

Another case is a young woman who was raped by someone in the church. She went and told the Pastor and he arranged for private counseling sessions for her only for this Pastor also to rape her. She left the church feeling hopeless and filthy.

With nowhere to go and no one else to turn to, she ended up becoming a lesbian. All my efforts to help her did not work and she blocked contact with me. You see, people are really hurting, not getting proper help and are needlessly suffering. We have been given the power to destroy the works of the devil, so let us rise up and begin to set the church back on the ancient landmarks, which the Bible commands us not to destroy.

Let us do it as Jesus did, and only then will we see the change and the transformation that the Lord is expecting from us. Let us clean up the temple of the Lord, in order to create a holy habitation for the Lord. Our Lord Jesus is coming soon, and He is coming for a glorious church without spot or wrinkles. Let us make the crooked paths straight in order to receive the end time harvest.

Extreme anger or rage that seeks revenge is not godly and has to be looked at properly in order for the right solution to be applied. It can put one in trouble with the law as in some cases, people have maimed or killed because they could not control their temper.

You hear about people killing people in road rage, is this normal? Patience makes room for other people's mistakes. I get angry when other drivers do the unthinkable right under my nose, but I will not go out of my way to chase them down or engage with them in any form of altercation. There is nothing wrong with expressing your anger in any provocative situation. The Bible clearly states in Ephesians 4:26, *"Be angry, and sin not: let not the sun go down upon your wrath. [27]Neither give place to the devil."*

It cannot get any clearer than this. If you permit the sun to go down on your anger, you have given the devil the chance to come in and take over your emotions, and to dictate to you how to handle things. We know the devil's way leads only to destruction.

In verse 27 we are made aware that in our anger, no permission must be given to the devil to step in to instigate you to react in rage. Seek help if you are struggling with your temper and the prayer of faith shall heal and restore you.

# CHAPTER 33

# Lying

Lying is: 1. being deceptive. 2. Imposture; or false belief. Not giving a true picture of a situation or a thing. Being evasive can also be avoiding the truth which then becomes a lie or an attempt to deceive. We can also say that lying is the opposite of telling the truth.

I believe that in every one of us there is the tendency to lie in order to avoid confrontation, losing a loved one or an opportunity, to escape a penalty for an offence and many other personal reasons. An example might be when someone offends you and you cannot hide your feeling; however, when the person asks, "what's wrong with you?" Your answer is, "nothing." There is something wrong but you do not want a confrontation with this person, so you lie. I do not believe there is any person on earth that can boldly say they have never lied in their lifetime.

That is not what I am talking about here. The above are what are termed as white lies, because they are not hurting anyone, even though a lie is a lie. I am talking about lying consistently without cause.

There are some people who will lie for no reason at all; in fact, lying is their second nature. Such a person started with one lie and did not see anything wrong with it and, therefore, there was no repentance. I have known some compulsive liars who simply lie about everything. Even things that need not prompt a lie. Their life is a life of lies and they have come to believe their own lies as the truth. A demonic spirit has possessed this individual. Jesus said in John 8:44, *"You are of your father the devil, and the lust of your father you will do. He was a murderer from the beginning, and abode not in the truth, because there is no truth in him, when he speaks a lie, he speaks of his own: for he is a liar and the father of it."*

Here Jesus is pointing to the fact that when a person lies and believes their own lie to be true, then they are of the devil; that is to say, the demonic spirit of lying is in control over this person's life. It is as simple as that, and only deliverance that will expel this spirit from this person.

I have heard people describing such people as professional liars, pathological liars, or as being economical with the truth. Once you are labeled like that, it means that you have not been caught lying just once or twice, but rather habitually. You live and breathe lies. You need help. It is embarrassing for your family. Seek help as any other addict needs to seek help because it is demonic.

Of all the demonised conditions of man, this is one of the most hated by God. Proverbs 6:16, *"These six things doth the Lord hate: yea, seven are an abomination unto Him: 17. A proud look, a lying tongue."*

Jesus describes the devil as the father of lies. I believe this is an ancient spirit, which started its operation in the Garden Eden when the devil possessed the body of the serpent to deceive Eve.

I recommend that one tries not lie at all and if, at any point, you need to get out of a situation which calls for you to lie, quickly repent before the Lord so the enemy will not use it as a starting point to get you to be a liar. Proverbs 16:6, *"By mercy and truth iniquity is purged: and by the fear of the Lord men depart from evil."* Proverbs 12:22, *"lying lips are abomination to the Lord but they that deal truly, are His delight."*

Lying is the true nature of the devil. Jesus said he is a liar and the father of lies. Practice telling the truth and it shall be perfected by God. Present things before God truthfully and He shall deliver you from the wicked one. Tell Him you need His deliverance from the father of lies and surely, He will deliver you.

Lies can cost you your dignity and respect. Your integrity will be lost when this ugly demon shows up in your life. Seek help in the form of counseling or deliverance before you humiliate yourself. Know that extreme lying will lead to further sins and the devil will destroy you through these.

There is a lying spirit according to the Scriptures, which is sent to deceive people. Lying and deception are a couple. If you find yourself trying to deceive people or change their opinion about people or certain things, then know that you are being used by the devil to do his bidding. In 1 Timothy 4, the Holy Spirit warns the church of the spirits that the enemy will unleash in the latter days, and we are now in the latter days. 1Timothy 4:1, *"Now the Spirit expressly says that in the latter times some will depart from the faith, giving heed to deceiving spirits and doctrines of devils. [2]speaking lies in hypocrisy and having their own conscience seared with a hot iron."*

Let us be watchful and vigilant as the end draws near. The enemy, our adversary, is seeking whom he may devour. Jesus has warned us. My prayer for Ministers is: now is the time to be on high alert as the shepherds of God's flock. We need to warn the people of the intensity of the onslaught of the devil against humanity, and more so the people of God. We need to teach them how to deal with any attack of the devil. Now is the time to equip the saints through the Word of God. Let us do our best to curb the epidemic of spiritual illiteracy in the Kingdom, for the Bible declares in Hosea 4:6 that, *"My people are destroyed for lack of knowledge."*

I also urge the believer to make every effort to attend Bible studies and stop queuing for prophetic words. Prophecy without knowledge will profit us nothing. You have to prove the word of prophecy with the Word of God and war with it. If you lack knowledge then you believe anything whether it is from God, the flesh or from the devil.

All the works of the flesh named in Galatians 5:19 are doorways to be avoided as these lead to demonisation if left to fester in one's soul. When that happens, your soul will be contaminated. Let us seek to please God always, and constantly hand over those areas in which we are struggling, for Him to deliver us.

# CHAPTER 34

# Pride

Pride is a high or overbearing opinion of one's worth or importance. It is one of the things that God hates most according to Proverbs 6:16-19. *"These six things doth the Lord hate: yea, seven are an abomination to Him. A proud look, and a lying tongue, and hands that shed innocent blood. A heart that devises evil imagination, feet that be swift in running to mischief. A false witness that speaks lies and he that sows discord among brethren."*

Remember, it was pride that caused Satan to rebel against God and the same brought about his downfall. We, as children of God should always check ourselves to see if there is any element of pride in us, as this will separate us from God. He is working on us daily, and if we allow Him, He will walk us through the process of change and, if necessary, deliverance.

I strongly believe that there is a measure of pride in every human being, but it takes our submission to the Lord Jesus Christ to make us 'die' to our flesh. Pride and lies work together as these can be described as believing and thinking more highly of one's self. It is an exaggerated or an inflated self-esteem or elevation of how one sees his or her person or achievement. This is done to get praises or win the accolades of men. *Romans 12:3a, "For I say, through*

Pride, if not dealt with God's way, soon develops into a spiritual problem; where the demon spirit of pride takes over and from thereon, begins to exhibit itself through this person. Some of the characteristics of a person under the influence of this spirit include, the attitude of knowing it all, being beyond correction, refusal to admit when they do something wrong or offend someone, let alone making an apology.

Pride tells you that you are perfect in every way. Pride makes you to exalt, praise and commend yourself in everything you do. Pride finds fault with other people and not yourself, not even when you are blatantly at fault. Pride says, I am perfect and wiser than everyone I know. Pride says no one can do it better than I can. These traits can be picked up by people close to this person but are often too intimidated by what the response might be, were they to point it out. Instead, they keep quiet.

Exaggeration is another characteristics of someone under the influence of this spirit. He or she wants people to know that they are 'somebody', and they have it all, when in reality, they know nothing, and the little that they do know is blown out of proportion. They are self-promoters, always talking about their achievements, and have a strong desire to be the center of attention wherever they go.

Remember I said earlier on, that the spirit of lies and the spirit of pride work hand in hand? In 1 Kings 18, a lying spirit was released to come upon the tongues of the prophets. The purpose was to deceive King Ahab to go to war and die. I reference this story just to illustrate how the lying spirit and a spirit of pride work to hand-in-hand. The gift of humility is the antidote to pride given by the Bible so let us begin to practice it and it shall be well with us all, in Jesus name.

Sometimes a prideful spirit of can hide itself well from being detected by the victim. It takes those closest to them to notice and boldly point It out. It takes pride to utterly dismiss it without taking a good look at one's self and your motivation for doing and saying certain things. I am not saying you need to admit to anything negative that just anyone mentions. However, one thing I have come to know is, next to God, I know myself better than anyone else if I am honest with myself. That being the case, you should know certain truths about yourself.

If in doubt of what is being said to you, take it to God in prayer in all sincerity of heart and God Almighty will help you acknowledge the truth. Seek help from your Pastor who should be able to counsel you and deliver you from the claws of this wicked spirit.

On one occasion, the Holy Spirit spoke to me as I was thinking about a certain person that I know who has most of the above traits. I had tried in a gentle and loving way to talk to him, but to no avail. He (the Holy Spirit) said, "Do you know that when Wisdom speaks, it is only pride that does not listen?" The Holy Spirit personified Wisdom and Pride. Why? My answer is simple. They are both spirits. One is given by The Holy Spirit (Spirit of wisdom) and one is given by the devil (spirit of pride) I thought about it, repeated it to myself over and over again and realised the truth in it.

There is help in the sanctuary of the Lord so do not permit the devil to live his life through you. Seek help and be delivered. The Word of God says we should work out our own (personal) salvation with fear and trembling. (Philippians 2:12) The Holy Spirit, our Helper, is always at hand to help us overcome our weaknesses and areas in which the enemy seems to have the upper hand.

Please do not forget that pride is what brought Lucifer down from his high position as an Archangel. He is the embodiment of pride and he wants man to be filled with this spirit so man will be rejected by God. Do not let pride destroy the relationship between you and your God, deal with it sooner rather than later.

# CHAPTER 35

# Rejection and Abandonment

This means, among other things, non-acceptance, refusal to accept or believe in one's self after experiencing abandonment or feeling unloved by people closest to you. Rejection has different dimensions in its effect. Parents, teachers, friends and even some Pastors can reject you.

I know first-hand what it means to feel you are the odd one out or the 'black sheep' of the family. It goes deeper than even that; with both parents still alive, I had to be raised by a grandmother, surrounded by aunts and uncles, who made me felt that I was a reject of the family. I was physically, verbally, and emotionally abused. Considering that both of my parents were alive and I had to go through this was a constant pain I had to deal with growing up. I was the "Cinderella" of the house.

Every child was allowed to go on holidays during school vacation except me. I had to stay behind and work, work and work, until school reopened. I felt abandoned by my parents especially my mother who lived not far from where I was living with my grandmother. I was constantly asking her to at least come and confront my abusers but all she kept saying was to "give it to the Lord."

What does this mean to a six-year-old who was constantly beaten and told she would amount to nothing? Absolutely nothing but more pain. As for my father, I dreaded his occasional visits because, whenever he came to visit, there would be bad reports about me to him, half of which were fabricated stories anyway, and yet he would beat me until I bled from the caning. As a child, I used to question myself through most of my early years. Why was I born into this world at all if I had to come and suffer like this?

As soon as I was able to defend myself, I took control of my life and in my mid-teens I became highly rebellious and aggressive. Thank God for Jesus who came to set me free from all the mess I was in. Yes, He touched me and made me whole. Know that He will do the same for you if you let Him. You will experience the love of The Father and you will never be the same again.

Rejection and Abandonment are similar. I know of a case where someone, who looked very much like his father, was rejected by him from his conception. He grew up, graduated and yet his father never accepted him until on his deathbed. This young man grew up to become a prominent member of society, to be precise, a medical doctor. However, even with all the intellectual achievements there were signs of demonisation.

Nobody helped him or supported him to deal with this as no one understood his plight. The most painful of all for him was growing up looking exactly like the person who disowned and rejected him. He came into the world through these two people; whether a one-night stand or a long term relationship, yet he suffered the most. Both parents moved on to live their own lives, leaving the past behind them.

I saw the devil seizing the opportunity to slowly destroy this precious soul through self-destruction, alcoholism, womanizing and lies. How do you deal with such a painful life growing up in an environment where you are constantly reminded of who you are? The enemy targeted him right from the womb and did not spare anything at all to destroy him. It is a very sad story and I believe there are many more stories similar to his.

I tried counseling him but I realised that the wounds were deep and, because of that, he had resigned himself into serious drinking that opened him to other demons. He was not ready to let the Lord in to rescue him. Look, one demonic door that is not dealt with, can open other doors for several other demons to enter and, once they entrench themselves in your soul, it is very difficult to be free except by the Blood of The Lamb of God, Jesus Christ.

Do not let the devil destroy you and take you to hell with him. There is help in the Lord Jesus Christ. Do not suffer in silence; know that your case is not new to your Creator. He will deliver you and beautify you and you will live for Him both here and in eternity. He loves you. Oh yes! He truly loves you and wants to deliver you. Please let Him in and let Him free you from the guilt and shame that you do not deserve to carry. He did all that for you on the Cross.

Rejection is a very painful thing to suffer or go through. It feels like there is something wrong with you causing you to be rejected. Let me tell you, it is very easy to believe this lie of the enemy. I have seen some teachers behaving in this same manner, rejecting the downtrodden.

If you were a child of the elite, you were treated differently to those from poorer backgrounds who were rejected unless they were exceptionally brainy. I have seen some Pastors doing the same thing to people who are not in a position to bless them personally with material things. In fact, this is the most disgusting of all because the church is supposed to be a place of healing and deliverance, not a house of humiliation and victimisation.

Such rejection can lead to serious wounding of an individual's emotions, thus opening the person up for demons to harass him or her, if not properly handled. Rejection causes the enemy to whisper in the ears of the victim that there is something horribly wrong with them and that is why people reject them wherever they go, even in the church. What this does is cause the victim to begin to believe this lie and sink into isolation.

Have you ever had colleagues at work or even in the church that are recluse? You try to go into their world and you will find it is a no-go area. God wants to use you to bring a change into their lives. Some are on the opposite side. They are very aggressive to keep everyone at arms-length and, anyone who tries to cross that boundary is met with hostility. More often than not, people around such afflicted people misunderstand them and begin to shun or resent them. I have found that when such a person tries to stop me from getting closer to them, I subtly push even more towards them until it works. Believe me, underneath all the hostility, these can be very nice and loyal people.

People used to ask, "How did you manage to befriend this horrible person?" and I would explain to them that I honestly did not know how I did it, but I believe it was the grace of God. I also tell them that the person in question is a very nice person when you get to know him or her. Sometimes, all they need, is for someone to show them love, and to give them a little bit of attention just to get to know them. Many do not know how to open that door for fear of further rejection; but if you persist, slowly edging forward into their world until they feel they can trust you with their emotions, they will let you in.

In today's society, some of our sons and daughters join gangs and other groups simply because there is a void in their lives that a gang fills with promises of brotherhood and love. This we all know is a lie from the devil; it is just to lure them into the dark world of death and destruction. My prayer is that we would rise up wherever we are, in our working places and in the churches, to fish out these hurting ones and bring them to the healing waters.

Do you know some parents do not even know what their children are involved in late at night? Is it their fault? No, I do not accuse or blame anyone. Some are single parents and have to work to put food on the table and meet other needs in the home. What I recommend is to be a praying parent first, and then befriend your own child. Do not leave them to their own devices for it is very dangerous.

I had a very dear friend who was also a single parent. She would leave her son alone to go to work at night. This situation took place from when the boy was under ten years old. Now, the son in his mid-twenties has become used to being alone. The good news for my friend was that her son never went out or brought any friends home. In her own words, whenever he tried to chat with her, she would send him away claiming she was tired.

Years rolled by and now, when she wants to have a conversation with him, he does not even acknowledge her. She bought him everything he ever needed and yet he did not budge. In his twenties, she was diagnosed with a brain tumor and still he would not talk to her. After surgery to remove the tumor, and in recovery at home, her son was living with her like a stranger.
Friends including myself, would help her with cooking and household chores. Her son was very cold-hearted, in fact, the coldest heart I have ever encountered in my life and ministry. Every friend of his mother was very concerned. I assessed the situation and realised that there were signs of demonisation.

He showed no regard for anyone. You would be talking to him and he would not even look at you, let alone respond. In short, he kept himself to himself and during one of my several visits, during which I would spend hours in cleaning and cooking, this young man would not even pop out of his room to see who was there or what was happening in the flat.

Some of the things that I cannot relate were indicative of what the years of isolation had done to him. I believe he felt rejected by the father who was not there for him at all and also neglected by his mother. Let us befriend our own children besides been parents so they will feel the sense of belonging; providing material things alone is not enough.

Demonisation can be as a result of isolation from neglect. Whom was he playing with in the absence of his mother? Someone had to fill that vacuum, and trust the devil to do just that.

The young man in this story was playing games in his room most of his time. His room was his sanctuary, he ate there and only came out to use the bathroom. Do you know that most of these games are highly demonic so, I believe; he became infested and grew very cold towards his own dying mother. He had no friends and he only went out for shopping and back.

He was abandoned by his father who did not want to know or have anything to do with him, and his mother who thought working long hours to buy him everything he wanted would make him happy, yet failed miserably to balance things. My prayer for parents is: let us spend quality time with our children especially in their formative years. A good and healthy foundation is very necessary so we do not expose our young ones to the ways of the enemy which creep up on young and vulnerable minds if left to their own devices.

Prayer is the answer to deal with all these issues. Counseling and deliverance might also be necessary for anyone who sees himself or herself in this situation.

# CHAPTER 36

# Strongholds

A stronghold is: 1. a fortified place. 2. Centre of support for a cause. This word, when separated, gives you two different words and meanings; strong and hold.

Strong means something capable of exerting or resisting great power. Hold is to keep in one's possession or control. It is a means of exerting influence

A stronghold, biblically speaking, is an entrenchment of the enemy in a believer's life. This happens when the devil pushes his lies on the individual until the person believes. He does this by convincing the victim that, whatever he (Satan) is selling, is truth.

The devil then seals this in the person's mind and, from that moment on, he sends more demons to harass and torment. The devil takes the truth, twists it and confuses us. This he does by causing the believer to use his mind to reason out the instructions of the Lord. This ultimately leads to sin against God as we see from Adam and Eve.

As the story goes, we know that Satan took what God had told Adam and twisted it. He then overpowered them and took away their right to rule over the earthly realm. Their sin also broke their relationship with God. This strategy of Satan has not changed. He is still operating the same pattern. He always attacks us in the area of our vulnerability. The enemy pounces where there is lack of knowledge or ignorance.

A demonic stronghold is nothing but an attack of the wicked one on the way we perceive things of God and things about us. He whispers his lies and contaminates the Word of God in our minds. I say in our minds, because if the truth is in our hearts, it is difficult for the enemy to reach it. When we believe the lies of the devil and begin to live accordingly, that is, accepting what the devil is saying to you or about you to be true, then he gains access into our hearts through our minds. From there, he takes control over our life.

A typical example of this, is the eating disorders, anorexia and bulimia. All who suffer this bad ailment will tell you when they look at a mirror, they see themselves as fat people. These lies and distorted images about themselves did not happen overnight, it took days, weeks or months of believing and living that lie from the enemy. Satan has deceived them and also led them to deceive their parents by hiding away to eat and then throw up. He teaches them how to cover it well by wearing baggy clothes so they can go undetected until it is too late for some of his victims.

All this starts with a seed. Someone might have commented on these victims' weight, which put them on the path of destruction. We have to understand that God works with words, and so does the devil. Once the truth settles in a believer's heart, it is settled, even though in our challenging moments we tend to shake a little bit, but our faith in the Lord kicks in and we stand strong upon His Word to defeat the enemy.

Sometimes challenges can make us fearful or doubtful but the true believer quickly adjusts himself in the Word with the help of the Holy Spirit, and bounces back again. The Bible says that David *"encouraged himself in the Lord."* He did this because he was facing some tough times in his life, and was going under, but he quickly made the adjustment to use the truth that he knew, to strengthen himself.

The enemy is always hovering around us just to see if we will drop our guard so he can attack us. Be assured that the Lord is your strength in times of trouble and the Holy Spirit is your helper and your Comforter. All you need to do is cry out for His help and He will send it, just like that.

There have been times in my life when I have been under serious demonic attack and could not even utter prayers. All I had the strength to do was to cry out for help. For days all I could say was, help! Yes, just send me help Lord.

He heard me and delivered me. Look, He is not a God from afar, He hears even the weakest and faintest cry of His children, and moves swiftly to rescue us. So do not waste time and do not waste the little strength you think is left in you; instead just shout, HELP!
The devil cleverly picked the moment of John the Baptist's vulnerability to attack him. This led to his ultimate beheading. Before John got to the point of questioning who Jesus is, I believe the enemy had bombarded him with doubts and negativity, and these thoughts became a stronghold in his mind. He totally forgot

the revelation he had received about the Man he baptised and introduced to the world. The Lamb of God!

We should be mindful of how we process things in our mind and be careful of our thoughts. If you yield to demonic thoughts, it will not be long before you lose control and allow Satan to take the steering wheel of your life instead of the Holy Spirit. Take control of your thoughts and do not let any opinion of men, or any other thing, derail your good and holy thoughts onto a path of destruction.

Think about the goodness of the Lord and all He has done for you, and is still doing for you. Let every adverse situation be a challenge, driving you to your goal in Christ Jesus. James writes in 4:7, *"submit yourselves therefore to God. Resist the devil, and he will flee from you."*

Let God be in control of your thoughts; by this I mean, let the Word of God guide you and your thoughts through every situation. This will deny the demons access to hijack your mind. Remember, you cannot stop the arrows of the wicked one from flying around your head, but you can block them from penetrating into your heart, if you resist.

The devil indeed takes us captive through our thoughts. Once Satan is able to break in, he breaks in to steal our peace, our joy, and our sanity. There is no other way for him because he knows our hearts are for the Lord.

John the Baptist did not renounce Christ, he doubted if He is the one or there is another one to come. This was purely the doing of the devil, simply because John was in a situation which made him vulnerable. He lost his boldness, and fear took over. Once fear took over Satan shot his arrow of doubt into John's mind and entrenched himself through the spirit of fear and, behold, that which John feared (death) came upon him.

The Bible has the antidote for dealing with every negative thought that the enemy uses to attack us. We need to cast them down and tear down these strongholds as stated in 2 Corinthians 10:3-5. Our weapons are only mighty through God, and it is only then can we pull down these strongholds.

Our strength and our resistance can only be effective if we depend on God. Surrender your thoughts to the Lord, meditate on the Word of God as Joshua recommended in Joshua 1:8, "This *book of the law shall not depart out of your mouth but you shall meditate therein day and night, that you may observe to do according to all that is written therein: for then you shall make your ways prosperous, and then you shall have good success.*"

# CHAPTER 37

# Fear, Failure and Disappointment

## Fear

This is an unpleasant emotion caused by exposure to danger or an expectation of pain. Fear is one of the normal expressions of our emotions. There is absolutely nothing wrong with being afraid of a thing or a situation. I believe if you have never expressed this emotion, then you are abnormal.

The fear I am talking about is the spirit of fear that literally torments you. It is a spirit from the devil. The Bible says in 1 Timothy 1:7, *"For God has not given us the spirit of fear; but of power, and of love and of a sound mind."*

When emotional pain is not properly dealt with, the enemy seizes on it and turns it into a dreadful thing whereby the person becomes totally afraid of whatever he was fearful of before. Some women are terrified of their husbands due to the abuse they are suffering at their hands. This started gradually and the victims did nothing to resist or stop it but allowed this to go on, some for years, without confronting their abusers or seeking help.

This results in the victim developing low self-esteem. Worthlessness and hopelessness cripple such people and they believe nobody else will want them so they better endure this bad behavior. You do not have to suffer in silence. Cry out to God and seek counseling.

We need to confront our fears by taking authority over this feeling by confessing and believing the Word of God for what it is, what it stands for and what God meant for it to do for us. The fact that you failed in something does not mean you are a failure. You cannot live your life being afraid of failure anytime you face a challenge.

Do not listen to the devil's lies, you are not a failure. Yes, you failed, but use it as a learning process and trust the Lord to see you through the next time. God never promises plain sailing. Even Jesus did not have plain sailing, honestly, He had the fiercest opposition from the Pharisees and the Sadducees and all who felt He had come to destroy their traditions.

Jesus is our example. He came to show us the way to do things and handle the affairs of the Kingdom life. Is the servant above the master? He went through the process so we may learn from Him that there will be similar scenarios in our lifetime as well. We should remind ourselves that we are overcomers through Him.

Fear can cripple you and reduce you to nothing. People have panic attacks and phobias. God has delivered me from the fear of being in a place all by myself. Now my children are grown and have left home and I live by myself, I have no fear whatsoever. This would have been impossible before I came to Christ. I did not like being left alone and I was extremely scared. I was aware of evil spirits even at a very young age. There were times I felt an evil presence around me, and I did not like to sleep on my own. I had to cover my entire body with sheets from my head down to my feet. I would be sweating and yet, would not uncover my head. It was that serious, but The Lord has delivered me from this spirit of fear and He will do the same for you. Only believe and trust in Him to do it for you.

I was so afraid to be left alone because I felt there was some unseen entity hanging around me, to harm me. I had it in my head that the departed were always hanging around the house. To a degree, I felt justified in my belief as, at night, I could often hear movement and other noises. I remember my grandmother used to tell us to make sure we filled the cooler with drinking water so when the departed come, there will be water for them to drink.

I grew up knowing that we had these spirits visiting us. Now I know they were all demonic. My grandmother believed that these departed souls come home to visit and, basically, we have to welcome them by making water available for them. I fully believed this and was trapped in that fear until I became born again.

Information is very important, the Bible says in Hosea 4:6, "*My people are destroyed for lack of knowledge.*" Seek knowledge, and do not just accept anything as the norm. The world says 'what you do not know, won't kill you, but the opposite is true to the believer. That which you do not know can still and often will destroy or kill you. Study the Word of God and be properly equipped. Get understanding in the knowledge of the truth and seek help if necessary.

The Apostle Paul says in Philippians 4:8, *"Finally, my brethren, whatsoever things are true, whatsoever things are honest, whatsoever things are just, whatsoever things are pure, whatsoever things are lovely, whatsoever things are of good report; if there be any virtue, if there be any praise, think on these things."*

The Apostle Paul knew that the enemy can and will attack our minds, so he gave us this antidote. Let us apply it to defeat the wicked one.

The devil plants a seed in our minds in order to isolate and attack us by invading our thoughts with more demons. Seek help if you find that it is becoming difficult to shift this feeling. Resist him with the Word before your thoughts become a tormenting tool in the devil's hands. The Bible says fear is a torment and, let me tell you, it is very true.

Some people are so fearful they do not want to venture out of their rooms or homes. This is very serious demonic oppression and help is needed for this person before the demon spirit of suicide kills him or her. Always remember that God has not given you the spirit of fear. This oppression is definitely not sent by God, but from the devil.

Resist him with every fiber of your being, with prayer and the Word of God. If all these fail, then seek Godly counseling, and deliverance in the case of acute oppression. Finally, I want to encourage you with this scripture in 1John 4:18a "There is no fear in love; but perfect love casts out fear." Always think on how much Christ loves you and gave His life for you and be encouraged.

## Failure and Disappointment

These are some of the areas in our life that the enemy can use to gain advantage over us if not dealt with according to the knowledge of the truth in Christ Jesus.

Who has never failed before? Who is perfect in all their ways save the man, Jesus Christ? From Genesis to Revelation, do we not see man failing over and over again? I was lamenting a serious mistake I had made which landed me in an uncomfortable position because I did not seek the will of God. The Lord in His mercy, came to my rescue before the enemy got to my confidence. He said to me *"I never told you, you will not make mistakes, and know that your mistakes are not recorded in heaven if you continue to walk with me as your Lord and saviour."*

The Lord reminded me further, *"The Bible says Abraham did not stagger at the promise but I tell you, he did. However, under the New Testament, my Blood has erased every handwritten ordinance against him so his mistakes were not found in the books of records. If Abraham did not make any mistake, where is Ishmael coming from?"* *Colossians 2:14, "Blotting out the handwriting of ordinances that was against us, which was contrary to us, and took it out of the way, nailing it to his cross."*

Indeed, if Abraham did not stagger, where is Ishmael coming from? From his mistake, of course! Remember in Isaac was the promise. The Lord went on to say, *"Your dependency on me becomes stronger if you realise and acknowledge your inadequacies."*

Please take serious note from this and it will bless you. This loving statement from the Lord has set me free from fear of making mistakes and failing, and has released me from dwelling on past errors. It has helped me to trust God that, even if I do make mistakes in assumptions, He, God, will look to my motives and show me mercy.

Peter failed as a disciple, in that he betrayed Jesus, and so did Judas Iscariot. Judas killed himself because he felt disappointed in himself and did not repent, but Simon Peter, when he realised what he had done, went out to weep, and that was a sign of repentance.

Surrender all to the Lord and He will deliver you. Do not give an inch to the devil in any area of your life lest he will quickly entrench himself in your sub conscious and harass you. Remember that Jesus took upon Himself all of our guilt and condemnation and, for that reason, we do not have to suffer as His blood finished the work for us. Jesus did not come to condemn us but to reconcile us to God. In Romams 8:1, the Bible says, *"There is therefore now no condemnation to them which are in Christ Jesus, who walk not after the flesh but after the Spirit."*

This means, as long as we have accepted Christ and are seeking Him concerning our growth and maturity, with the Spirit bearing witness in our spirit that we are the sons and daughters of God, there should not be any feeling of guilt or condemnation. Such a feeling comes from the devil who wants you to doubt your salvation and the power of God to make things right for us.

Perfect love cast out fear and doubt. (1 John 4:18) God's love for us is evident in that whilst we were yet sinners Christ died for us, He did not wait for us to be perfect before taking our place on the Cross. Have faith in God for deliverance and He will never let you down. He is with us every inch of the way as He has promised to never to leave us nor forsake us. He is Faithful.

Disappointment is part of life and so we have to learn to deal with it properly before the enemy pounces on us, to trap and destroy us. Not everything that we hope for becomes reality for us and not everything we desire comes to pass in our life. These are facts of life and they are for reasons best known to God. Ours is to pray and seek the will of God in every situation, learning to be at peace with ourselves in the knowledge that God is in control.

There is bound to be disappointments here and there, but the one I want to zero in on is the recurrence of painful experiences. As I have already pointed out, life is full of disappointments, and that is normal, but when you keep on suffering disappointment in one area of your life, for example, in your love life, career, friendships or other areas, then you need to seek counseling, prayers and probably deliverance. God never intended for us to suffer such horrible pain all of our life. *"Weeping may endure for a night but joy cometh in the morning."* Psalm 30:5. Verse 11 says, *"You have turned my mourning into dancing: you have put off my sackcloth, and girded me with gladness."* Praise God!

We serve a God who cares about everything that concerns us because He loves us too much to give up on us. That is why He says in Isaiah 43:2. *"When thou pass through the waters, I will be with you; and through the rivers, they shall not overflow you: when you walk through the fire, you shall not be burned; neither shall the flame kindle upon you."*

You are never alone and the Good Shepherd is always with you, guarding you. And let me assure you, it does not matter whether you know Him or not. Remember, whilst we were yet sinners, Christ died for us. In my life, I can say first hand that when I was a child, and growing into adolescence, my Lord was with me, even though I did not know Him and moreover, I was living a life of sin. Yet, He delivered me from many traps of the enemy. My testimonies are many; oh, they are many. That is why I love Him so very much.

Look! He did it for me and He will do it for you for He loves you! Do not ever believe the devil's lie that God is punishing you for this sin or for that sin, and that is why you are going through horrible pains. The God I know does not work like that. He is merciful to all men and more so to those who believe in Him.

I remember, few months into my being born again, I asked one of the deacons in the church during one of our numerous retreats, if God will punish me for my sins, and he said, yes. My immediate response was, that is ok if I would only make it to heaven. I sincerely meant it and there was no fear in me at all whatsoever. This, I eventually learnt, was completely false and I praise the Lord that this statement did not derail my walk with Him as a baby Christian. Always remember that His perfect love casts away every fear and do not entertain this spirit of blame at all.

The songwriter said, "Turn *your eyes upon Jesus; and look full in His wonderful face and the things of earth will grow strangely dim. In the light of His glory and Grace.*" Everything in this world is temporal but even so, God really cares about how we enjoy our sojourning here. Do not allow the enemy to rob you of your godly right to rule and reign in the earthly realm. It is your right; your God-given right, so do not give that power to the thief. You are the rightful owner of all that God Almighty has made.

We were created by God to have dominion over the earth. Pick yourself up and seek help. If you keep going through a vicious cycle of disappointments, seek deliverance to be totally set free from the satanic plan to destroy you.

Know that Jesus came to set the captive free!

# CHAPTER 38

# Low Self-Esteem

Low self-esteem is not just not having good opinion of one's self; it is also lack of confidence in one's self. This happens, in most cases, when people who have been abused and told negative things, have accepted them as true, and have begun to live a life in accordance with these words of abuse.

Such people believe that they are bad or God does not love them, and that is why they are like that. This sometimes makes them doubt God's love for them. As far as they are concerned, He loves certain people, not everyone, and certainly not them. Such people tend to ask many questions about themselves and finally conclude that it is just the way they are destined to be. This is another lie from the devil.

A young woman once said to me, "I feel like the black sheep of my family and among my own siblings, all because I am the only one that seems to experience failure, and my life is filled with hopelessness. Everyone is celebrated for his or her achievements except me because I am not academically strong like my sister. When I won merits in physical training no one celebrated me, not even my parents. I am only noticed for the bad things that I do, and sometimes I feel like a ghost in the house."

This woman was battling with low self-esteem and, whether she has a legitimate reason to feel like that or not, is not for me to judge, but one thing I know, is Jesus loves her. Only He can change things for her through godly counseling and prayers of restoration. God loves us all equally and says in His Word that He wishes above all else that we might prosper and be in good health, even as our soul prospers. (3 John:2)

God cares about all men but takes obedience to eat the fruit of His mercy and grace. Get to know what He thinks and says about you. Walk according to His principles and it shall be well with you and your confidence in Him will grow stronger. As a child of God, your confidence must first be in the Lord and then yourself. The Bible says in Hebrews 10:35, *"Cast not away therefore your confidence which has great recompense of reward."*

Do you know that once you have suffered bouts of disappointments, you risk the possibility of suffering from low self-esteem? The devil is a liar and God has not given up on you so do not dare give up on yourself.

As a child, I was raised by my paternal grandmother from the age of four, following the breakdown of my parents' marriage. I was physically, sexually, emotionally and verbally abused, so much so, that I began to question why God brought me into the world only to suffer all this abuse. I was told repeatedly and on a regular basis that I am a girl with bad luck following me everywhere and  that which was easy for others to obtain or achieve was always difficult for me. I was repeatedly told I was hopeless, useless and many more horrible things.

I remember, at the age of eight, I would wait until everyone went to sleep so I could just sit outside and weep. I would sing this song I was taught in primary school, "Nearer my God to thee." I did not know why I sang that song at that age because I did not even know the Lord then. The answer is simple, God knew me and He was with me through all my pain and suffering. He sustained me. He kept me by His power, mercy and grace.

I recall vividly, incidents that could have claimed my life but for God, oh yes, but for God! One thing that the Lord used in preserving my confidence was the academic blessing with which He endowed me. I was always an academically gifted child . This helped me to be confident and never doubt myself in that area. This confidence then permeated the other areas of my life as well. My teachers were proud of me, but not my abusers. This was all right because all I needed was for someone to believe in me.

Your story may not be the same as mine but still know that you can be delivered. There is no mountain too high for the Lord to come and get you, neither is there any valley too low for Him to reach you, only let Him in to deliver you. There is a balm in Gilead. He did it for many others and me; know that He will deliver you too. Trust Him with your life and He will lead you to the Healer, Jesus Christ, our Lord, Saviour and Friend. Trust in the One who made you and called you His own and remember, He created you in His own image and likeness and, therefore, everything that concerns you concerns Him.

God loves you and wants the best for you. Do not forget He died for you so you will live, He was made poor so you and I could be rich in every area of our life.

Do not permit any human being, not even your own parents, to redefine who you are. You were born with a purpose and for a purpose. Some spouses will reduce you to nothing in order to keep you in an abusive relationship. They will literally tell their partner; and it is most often the women, that they are too fat, too ugly, and too messed up for anyone to like, let alone to love. Unfortunately, vulnerable women believe these wicked words and remain in the abusive relationship. Please seek help before your life is destroyed, for your life is too precious to be wasted.

The same goes for men as well, do not let any woman control you, all in the name of love. Please know that anyone who tries to control another is themself being controlled by the devil; and that is the truth. God Almighty who created us does not control us, He has given us the freedom to make decisions according to our own choices. It is only the devil who forces man to do his biddings, and he does this through other human beings.

Where you see controlling and manipulation of the highest level, you can be sure that the devil is the one calling the shots from behind the scenes. Deal with this by seeking counseling and deliverance if necessary. The Bible says in Proverbs 24:6, *"For by wise counsel you shall make your war: and in the multitude of counselors there is safety."*

You can only survive and be rescued through fighting back by obtaining a proper method of dealing with demonic oppression. This proper way is through Godly counseling and prayers of deliverance. You may think there are some brilliant counselors outside Christendom. Yes, I am not disputing that at all, but as a servant of God, I can and will only recommend Godly counseling The Bible declares in 1 Corinthians 6:1, *"Dare any of you, having a matter against another, go to law before the unjust, and not before the saints?... [5]I speak to your shame. Is it so, that there is not a wise man among you? No, not one that shall be able to judge between his brethren"*

After all, the anointing to effectively complete the job is in the hands of the Lord and He has also delegated that authority to His servants for the benefit of His people; hence my recommendation.

Ministers must pay heed not to be too quick to administer deliverance without first taking time to counsel the victim. It makes the process easier and more fruitful as the victim is taught through counseling how to be demon free.

I attended a prayer and fasting retreat in a friend's house with other prayerful women. One had a word of knowledge that we should pray for the host's daughter. We asked her to fast as well, so she did. During our night vigil, we called her to be prayed for and one of the women started immediately casting out spirits. The girl just stood and looked bemused, like, "what is going on here?". She knew nothing about demons or deliverance but it was clear that the family was under attack from the enemy.

I then took over and explained to her what we intended to do for her and explained a few things to her. Once she understood, we had her full cooperation. It was awesome how the Good Lord delivered this young woman and her parents, and turned their lives around, as Christ became the Lord of their home.

It is purely the mercies of God to deliver His people and transform their lives, so please do not suffer in silence. Seek help. Counseling brings understanding and realisation of what is and what is not to be tolerated or permitted. The church needs overhauling in order to be able to bring salvation, deliverance and healing to the dying and the needy world; for this is our great commission!

Did you know there are women who abuse their husbands? Yes, and they are also in the church. Their victims are the men who hold on to the Word of God and say, God hates divorce and so, no matter what happens, they try to make it work. The more they accept, the more these women become bold in their abusive ways. This is a higher level of demonisation and witchcraft.

By nature, a woman is supposed to be gentle and loving to her husband and children, but when you see an extremely domineering woman, begin to observe her critically, and you will notice a problem somewhere. No matter how strong-willed a woman is, there ought to be a balance and a measure of humility in her as a wife. Proverbs 14:1 says, *"Every wise woman builds her house: but the foolish plucks it down with her hands."*

No matter how strong a woman is, she is not to use it against her husband but rather use her strength to support the husband in private, and let the man praise her in public. Woman! Do not use you strength to manipulate and control your husband, be the helpmate God intended you to be. Proverbs 21:9 says, *"It is better to dwell in the corner of the housetop, than with a brawling woman in a wide house;… [19]it is better to dwell in the wilderness, than with a contentious and an angry woman."*

I have known of women who sexually starve their husband to a degree that the man will have to beg on their knees and even then, he is met with a tirade of insults. This is serious and will inevitably affect any man's self- esteem, as well as his calling and ministry. I know one man in the Kingdom of our God whose wife calls the shots in the home. I believe she is not alone as there are many like her in the Kingdom.

She goes to work while he does the household chores. I mean everything in the house from looking after the children, feeding, bathing, cleaning, school runs and all, but there is no appreciation from his wife. In fact, the abuse from this woman towards her husband is beyond imagination, yet the man still held on to the notion that God hates divorce. She shouts at him; she hurls insults at him even in the presence of their young children, from the moment she walks in from work until bedtime. As for sex, well, he has to beg in tears only for his wife to insult him; calling him a fool among other things. This is a true story!

This is witchcraft. She has literally turned her husband into a slave and that is witchcraft. Slave masters have no regard for their slaves; they treat them with disrespect and degradation. The likes of this  woman need deliverance, that is, if they will accept or acknowledge that such behavior towards their husband is unnatural. I am talking about women in the church not outside.

I know the man in this story is an illiterate and the woman knew this before she married him. He did everything to support his wife to better herself academically as he took over the running the home. Such a man ought to be highly appreciated but rather, he was greatly abused and disrespected.

Some women do not openly abuse their husbands but wittingly 'ride' them like horses. They use what I call the Delilah spirit to coerce their husband to do whatever they say. This becomes a strong spiritual issue if the man finds himself unable to say no, because his wife says so. The end result can only be similar to Samson's as the man and all he stands for or has built will eventually be destroyed.

This is manipulation and a subtle way that some women use to control things from behind the scenes. This is common with women whose husbands are in key positions in the church of Jesus Christ. If you find yourself in any of the above categories, please do not take offence, but rather seek God repentantly and He will deliver you, peradventure it has not reached the demonised stage yet. Even if it has, God has the power to deliver if only you give Him your consent

## Panic Attacks

A panic attack is also one of the ways in which the devil makes you a prisoner or a captive? A panic attack is a by-product of low self-esteem and fear. It is one of the ways the enemy really shows his covert way of destruction.

People become so afraid of life such that some will not even dare venture out of their homes. They have in their mind that something bad will happen to them if they step out of their safe haven. It is an extreme form of fear, and a very crippling one too. This is truly the spirit of fear in operation. These victims are afraid of something that probably does not even exist. Remember fear is false evidence appearing real, and is an imagination that comes from the devil.

Some victims of this horrible demon sometimes feel they are too ugly or too messed up to be seen in public. This lie has been received and believed by the victims such that they have permitted the devil to imprison them. The Lord says, fear not, He will deliver you from this prison and you will be set free by the power of the Blood of Jesus Christ of Nazareth. He indeed came to set the captives free!

You have to know and believe the Scripture that says perfect love casts out fear, because fear brings torment. When the everyday emotional fear, which is normal, is not dealt with properly, the evil spirit of fear takes over and begins its reign of torment in one's life.

One of my siblings is such a fearful person. I noticed this from when she was about five or six years old until now, in her fifties. Ordinary fear has given birth to full blown torment such that she needs someone to help her to cross even a quiet street; as for busier roads, forget it. She would have to call a taxi right to her doorstep before traveling from point A to point B. She told how she feels like fainting and would be grabbing unto people when she attempted to cross any road. It was that serious and I realised we were dealing with a spirit that had entrenched itself into her life to torment her.

There are times she became short of breath as a result of these attacks. The devil is a liar! The Lord has delivered her from this. What we call a panic attack is actually a demonic attack and has to be dealt with the Biblical way, which is through deliverance.

## Hopelessness

Hopelessness is the feeling of despair, inadequacy or incompetence. Why would someone feel this way except some people around him or her have repeatedly made certain remarks about him or her to him or her. Demons use these words to constantly harass a person into believing that, indeed, he is or she is hopeless.

This is one of the most serious doorways through which the enemy can enter into our sub-consciousness and afflict us. I want to announce to you, dear friend, that there is always hope in Christ Jesus.

Give Him all your worries and pains and He will take care of you. Pray and praise through your pain and do not give the enemy a single moments thought. It may be difficult, I know, but it works if you practice it.

David was a man who went through a lot, but he trusted the Lord. In Psalm 42:5, he said, *"Why are you cast down, O my soul? And why are you disquieted in me? Hope thou in God: for I shall yet praise Him for the help of His countenance."*

Lamentations 3:26 says, *"It is good that a man should both hope and quietly wait for the salvation of the Lord."* This tells us that if we put our trust in the Lord, and have patience, He will deliver us from every plan of the enemy. Please do not give up on yourself and, certainly do not give up on God. He is faithful in all His ways. All you need to do is cry out for help and He will surely send you help.

What is it that you are going through? Is our God not bigger than your issues? He is well able to deliver and give you double for your trouble. He is more than able to do exceedingly abundantly above all that we ask or think, according to the power that works in us. (Ephesians 3:20)

No matter who we are, we go through seasons when we feel a sense of hopelessness and, if they are not properly handled, these can expose us to demonic attack. Remember Job was a righteous man, and the Bible described him as a man who feared God and hated evil, nevertheless, he was ruthlessly attacked by Satan and went through a period of hopelessness. In the end God came through for him and He will do the same for you.

In some extreme cases, the people involved have literally heard voices saying, just kill yourself and free yourself from these troubles. Many have yielded and died through overdose, shooting themselves, hanging, jumping from bridges and the list goes on and on. Many who had miraculously survived told of the voices and the intense feeling of the need to check out from this life. These are demonic forces that are after human life either to destroy or kill and if you are experiencing something like that you need to get help quickly before you even get to the point of suicide. Deliverance is as relevant today as it was in the days of Jesus. Do not let anyone deceive you that you do not need deliverance; every one of us needs it. The Apostle Paul dealt with the woman in Acts 16:16 who was a diviner so what are we wasting our time on, debating the subject when souls are suffering?

A Woman of God, a very dear friend of mine, once asked me "Where did all the demons that Jesus cast out go?"
Hmm… I had never thought about it but I answered, "Nowhere."
She then said, "Indeed, they are still here with us." I continued to ponder over it for some time until I came to realise that we are dealing with medieval spirits that have reproduced and multiplied themselves and assigned themselves to harass, destroy and kill as many people as possible.

Arise, God's people, and receive all that the Father has for you and all that gave His Only Son for. *For this purpose, the Son of God was manifested, that He might destroy the works of the devil.* 1 John 3:8. Let God be true and every man a liar, let the Son of God deliver you because that is why He came.

## Worry and Anxiety

Anxiety is the state of being anxious. It is also a state of excessive uneasiness concerning a thing or a situation. I believe that there is a point in every person's life that you worry about something, and that is quite normal, but if you allow it to go on for too long, it gives the enemy an open door to enter in and attack you. There are people who are worriers; all they do is worry about everything and anything. They do not even give themselves the chance to calm down and wait upon the Lord for His intervention. Jesus said that we should cast <u>all</u> our cares upon Him for He cares about everything that concerns us. So, learn and practice just that; trust Him to do that for you, for He is faithful.

Worry and anxiety are intertwined. You have to have something you are worried about to become anxious. Worrying is allowing your mind to dwell on your troubles or to pay too much attention to the problem. It can make you lose sleep or your appetite. This can eventually rob you of your sanity in some cases.

Some of us worry too much about what people think about us, about our looks and other irrelevant things. Remember, the Bible says not to make any room for the devil. This is because the moment he sets his foot into a place he does not want to leave. Instead he entrenches himself in the soul. Make a conscious effort to keep worrying out of your life, so you can enjoy the life that Christ has given to us freely.

Anxiety, like worrying, is another doorway to avoid. Do not allow any situation to eat you up. Jesus told us not to worry about anything since we have no power to do or change anything but to cast all our cares unto Him. (Matthew 6:27) Jesus said, *"Which of you by taking thoughts can add on cubit unto his stature?"*

If there is something we can humanly possibly do about any situation in our life, I believe we will make every effort to do so. We must learn to surrender to the Lord those situations beyond our control, and trust Him to fix it. 1 Peter 5:7, *"casting all your care upon Him for He cares for you."* When we do this, we invite the Lord to take over our case and when our Great Advocate, Himself, is dealing with our case, rest assured that no demon from hell will be able to defeat you, in Jesus powerful name.

# CHAPTER 39

# Ways to Overcome the Attacks of the Enemy

## Arm yourself with the Sword of the Spirit.

The Bible clearly teaches us about spiritual warfare and how it is conducted. It also teaches us about the enemy, dealing with, his tactics and how we are to deal with him, with which methods and weapons. Ephesians 6:17, *"And take the helmet of salvation, and the sword of the Spirit, which is the Word of God."*

It is impossible to confront your adversary without the Word of God. The devil fights from a point of knowledge because he knows the Word of God, even better than some believers and when he realises the lack of information in the believer, he wastes no time at all to pounce on his victim.

Jesus is our example and we can only overcome as He did, by doing what He did and saying what He said in any given circumstance. The Word makes you aware of whom you are in Christ Jesus, and the power available to you through Him. It teaches you how to overcome adverse situations, how to please God and much more. In short, the Word of God helps us to live the Christian life. The Word of God is quick and powerful, and sharper than any two-edged sword. (Hebrews 4:12)

It deals with our spirit, soul and body. Everything we need to know of how to live a victorious life in Christ Jesus and much more is to be found in the Word. It is our weapon of warfare and must be known for our own benefits. It is sad to know that these days not many Christians are willing to learn or study the Word.

Romans 12:2, *"And be not conform to this world, but be ye transformed by the renewing of your mind."* The renewing of the mind is done through the Word of God. Since the devil attacks our mind, the Word of God is our best weapon to counteract any demonic advances. The only way to defeat the wicked one is by knowing and living the Word of God and prayer.

He will keep in perfect peace all those whose mind is stayed (focused) on Him. Jesus defeated the enemy with the Word, to show us how to do it. He is the Living Word. In the wilderness, when Satan came to tempt Him, He used the Word of God on all three occasions; it is written...it is written...it is written. (Luke 4 & Matthew 4) This is how Jesus overcame and this is how we will overcome.

The Word of God is our training manual. And like everything else, you follow the manufacturer's guide in order to ensure the proper functioning of a product. The Word of God is our mirror that gives a true reflection of life. It is food for our soul and spirit. As we feed on it, we are changed into the very image of the Word, Jesus Christ. *Psalm 19:7 says, "The law of the Lord is perfect converting the soul; the testimony of the Lord is sure making wise the simple. The statutes of the Lord are right, rejoicing the heart; the commandment of the Lord is pure, enlightening the eyes. The fear of the Lord is clean, enduring forever: the judgment of the Lord is true and righteous altogether."*

This is how the Psalmist elaborated on the Word and how it

functions. As we walk in this revelation, it will do exactly what it stands for and what it says it will do. The Word of God heals, delivers, corrects, reproofs, rebukes and builds us up as believers. Today many of us are not reading let alone studying the Bible, but if we are to live a victorious life and be who God says we are, then we have to fall in love with His Word, and let it be part of our daily life. Living according to the Word of God is what makes one a believer in Christ Jesus. We can only overcome with knowledge and understanding of the Word. If you understand the Word, then you can use it effectively to combat the evil forces of darkness. Jesus did it and we can do it too, through Him and the power of the Holy Spirit.

## The Blood of Jesus

Do you know the purpose of the shed Blood? Do you know the importance of the Blood? Do you know the power in the Blood? Do you know the wealth and the worth of the Blood?

If you have answers to the above, then you can wage successful warfare in the Lord and be assured that the victory is already yours. The purpose is in the book of Isaiah 53:6, *"All we like sheep have gone astray: we have turned everyone to his own way: and the Lord have laid on Him the iniquity of us all."*

In other words, the wages, the punishment or the consequences of all our sins were laid on Jesus and He paid the penalty for us all with His very life. He shed His royal and precious Blood to pay for our sins. This was necessary because no other blood was enough or qualified to secure our freedom from the devil. The Blood of Jesus is the only blood that both worlds recognise. The blood of goats, sheep and oxen, bulls and cows are not enough; it does not suffice for the redemption of man. (Hebrews 9:12-14)

In the sight of God, all of the above had been offered but still man was not totally liberated from the bondage of sin. God had a plan to free man once and for all, and that is *"For God so love the world that He gave His only begotten Son that whosoever believes in Him should not perish, but have everlasting life"* John 3:16.

The Blood of Jesus is priceless. Its value is unimaginable; nothing can be compared to it and it is a universal currency recognised and spiritually accepted in the realms of the spirit. No matter where you are in the world, demons know and recognise the power, value, purpose and the power of the Blood. When the Blood is invoked from the tongue of a true believer, hell itself, dives for cover. There is power in the Blood of Jesus!

Apply the Blood of Jesus on your mind daily. Revelation 12:11, *"And they overcame him (Satan) by the Blood of the Lamb, and by the word of their testimony; and they loved not their lives to the death."* Know that every step of the way to the Cross spelt defeat for the enemy of our soul, Satan.

Have you ever considered why the devil showed up in the Garden of Gethsemane? His sole aim was to stop Jesus from taking the walk to Calvary to be crucified. Every drop of blood that Jesus shed defeated the devil in one area of our lives or the other.

What is it that you are troubled about? What is it that you are allowing the devil to torment you with? Is it about your health? His blood took care of it. The Bible declares that by His stripes we are healed. All we need to do is to know what the Word of God says about a particular situation we are facing, then correctly apply the Word, releasing our faith in the power of the Blood, in the Name of Jesus, and the power of the Holy Ghost.

I cannot emphasise this more. We need to let the devil know that we are armed with the Truth. The enemy we are fighting knows what we have, and is afraid, but he tries us to see if we ourselves are aware of the power we have in the Word or if it just head-knowledge. Some of us do not even have the knowledge; all we have is nothing really, just emptiness. We can possibly lose what we have when Satan begins to deal with us by bringing adversities our way.

How does this happen? It is when we allow him to release the spirit of fear into us. We do not see the way out and begin to talk negatively into our already adverse situations. Folks! There is power in the Blood, there is power in the Name of Jesus, and there is power in the Word. The Holy Ghost is with us and in us to enforce these to bring glory to the Lord God Almighty.

Jesus paid for our peace of mind in full. Remember, the chastisement of our peace was upon Him (Isaiah 53:5b) and that is why He declared it boldly to us in John 14:27, *"Peace I leave with you, <u>my peace </u>I give unto you: not as the world gives, give I unto you. Let not your heart be troubled neither let it be afraid."*

Please note that I have underlined the phrase 'my peace'. The Lord was laying emphasis on the kind of peace He was talking about. As a matter of fact, He even said it was not an ordinary peace. He made us doubly aware that He paid for this peace. How? He paid with His own royal Blood.

Wow! We are talking about the Blood of God Almighty, Himself. This is cause for celebration. This is the unconditional and unfeigned love of God for us. Satan knows this, but does modern-day believer fully know and understand this? We need to get closer to God through His Word and let Him breathe fresh breath on His Word to bring us understanding. Understanding, believing and acting upon the truth make us overcomers indeed.

We need to have revelation as well as knowledge about the power of the Blood of Jesus; it is not just a mystery but also a profound truth. All we need is to believe and have a child-like faith that the Blood works. Oh, it works! It might sound crazy to the doubtful and the fearful, but the Blood applied to every area of our lives, works.

Let me share this testimony about a co-worker. This woman told me she was always scared of intimacy with her husband. She explained that her private parts would be sore for days whenever she had been intimate with her husband. I knew straight away that something was not right, so I suggested we pray over a tiny drop of oil, asking God to turn it into the Blood of Jesus and for her to apply it to her private parts whenever she was ready to be intimate with her husband.

She did this the very first night I had counseled her and the result was unbelievable even to me. She reported back saying, "You would not believe what has happened! My husband's manhood was on fire this morning and when we checked, there were cuts, blisters and discharged fluids oozing from his penis. He could not wait for the children to go to school so he could walk around the house naked because of the burning sensation that he was experiencing."

I knew as soon as she told me, that it was a demonic case and it was only the power of the Blood that could expose and deal with it. It later on turned out that her husband was under the influence of demonic powers. You see, when the devil is exposed and dealt with by the Blood of Jesus, he loses and flees. Hallelujah, Jesus is alive!

His Blood is forever powerful and effective. Amen!

Apply the Blood on your car, yes, your car, your bed, pillows and everything, and I mean, everything. Do you know the song that says *"It reaches to the highest mountain, and it flows to the lowest valley, the Blood that gives me strength from day to day, it will never lose its power."* There is nowhere higher than the blood can reach; neither is there anywhere lower than it can go. It is all in all powerful. Yes, the Blood of Jesus is exceptionally, supernaturally powerful.

As powerful as the Blood is, so is the Name of Jesus. Call upon Him in all situations and you will see demons trembling and pleading for their lives. Oh yes, I have witnessed it. A demon once asked me, "You! Are you a male or a female?" He could not comprehend the sheer power and strength that oozed from me, I mean spiritually and physically.

When the spirit was arrested by the Holy Ghost as I was ministering, the individual fell under the power of the Holy Ghost and became violent, as I went ahead to cast it out. The physical strength with which I was able to keep him under control before the men rushed in to restrain him, was supernatural. The sheer strength of this demon was unbelievable and it eventually took four men to restrain it.

He asked me the question about my gender before the men came to help me. Later on, the demon identified himself as 'strong', by name. What am I saying here? It is not by any man's power or strength but by the power of the Holy Spirit and in the Name of Jesus. There is no might in me at all; except I surrender to God to use me to do His will.

God wants to set us free from the oppressor, Satan. He wants us to have faith in Him as He is all-powerful and all power belongs to Him. Any other power is false and evil, designed to destroy mankind and ultimately lead man to hell. Remember this always; Jesus loves you and me so much that He died for us to have abundant life. So let us put our trust in Him to fulfil His plans for us in this life and hereafter.

One time I was praying and the Holy Spirit asked me a question, "my daughter, what cannot I do?"
I said, "You cannot lie."
He said to me, "I know, that is my nature, but what can I not do for you?"
I said, "Lord, you can do all things.
He said, "Yes, that is my Word, and that is the truth but there is something I cannot do for you."

That started me thinking hard and fast but I still could not get the answer. Then the Lord told me, "my daughter, know that I cannot do what you do not allow me to do for you?" I was shocked at this because that had never occurred to me. The more I pondered over this; the more it made sense to me. He says: *"call on me and I will answer you"* Jeremiah 33:3 *"Delight yourself in the Lord and He shall grant you the desire of your heart. (Psalm 37)*

All this calls for you and me to do something before He responds in His nature concerning that thing. If you do not call, you do not receive answers. Throughout the Bible, God tells us, if you would do this or that, I will do this or that for you. It calls for action from man, then God responds on our behalf.

## Prayer

Everything boils down to prayer, our lifestyle and how we receive and live the Kingdom way. As you know, prayer is the lifeline of the believer. Prayer is the fuel that keeps our spirit-man running. It is our spiritual enabler as the Holy Spirit not only teaches us to pray, but also operates through our prayers. Our spiritual growth depends on our prayers, fasting and the Word of God.

Prayer plays a major role in our lives and in the area of warfare as clearly stated in Ephesians 6:12-17. It first of all talks about what we are up against in the realms of the spirit. Verse 18 declares, *"Praying always with all prayer and supplication in the Spirit and watching thereunto with all perseverance and supplication for all saints."* You have to be dressed for battle and this dress code is not a physical one but a spiritual one that can only be put on by prayer.

We are required to put on the whole armour of God, as stated in Ephesians 6:11-18; and to be always praying in the spirit. We are taught to guard ourselves with the armour of God. This is done through prayer and the Word of God. We are first of all to be built up in the most holy faith, then, as we grow, we become established and rooted in Him. This is when we start to know who He is and who we are in Him.

We cannot know this without spending time with God in His Word and in prayer. As we do this, God reveals Himself unto us in ways that we did not know before. He becomes our shield and defense. Psalm 91 sums it all up perfectly in verse 9 *"Because thou hast made the Lord, which is my refuge, even the Most High, thy habitation; there shall no evil befall thee, neither shall any plague come nigh thy dwelling. [11] For He shall give His angels charge over thee, to keep thee in all thy ways…. [14] because he has set his love upon me, therefore will I deliver him: I will set him on high because he has known my name. He shall call upon Me and I will answer him, I will be with him in trouble; I will deliver him and honour him."*

This is God's love presented to us here, if we take Him at His word and believe Him for who He is, we will be untouchable as far as the enemy of our soul is concerned. That does not mean we will not go through trials and tribulations, but the Lord knows those who are His and He has promised to come swiftly to our aid. If He has said it, He will surely perform it. He never fails. The Bible says, if we deny Him, He cannot deny Himself, simply because He abides faithful. He is to be trusted because there is no deceit in Him. He is the Way, the Truth and the Life.

## Casting down imaginations

*2 Corinthians 10:5, "Casting down imaginations, and every high thing that exalts itself against the knowledge of God, and bringing into captivity every thought to the obedience of Christ."* Believe what the Word of God says about you and not what the devil suggests to you.

Do not doubt God or His Word. When we walk in unbelief and doubt, we are telling God He is not able to do what He says He will do, or He is not who He says He is. You know the Word of God says in Matthew 12:43, *"When an unclean spirit is gone out of a man, he walks through dry places, seeking rest, and finds none. Then he says, I will return into my house from where I came out; and when he is come, he finds it empty, swept, and garnished. Then goes he, and takes with himself seven other spirits more wicked than himself, and they enter in and dwell there: and the last state of that man is worse than the first."*

The devil is highly deceptive and wants us to believe that a Christian cannot be demonised. However, the Lord Jesus spoke about demons and, not only that, but also taught us how to cast them out and keep them out for good. Jesus, Himself, had to cast out devils during His ministry, and He said all that He did, we will do also, and even greater works will we do in His name. So then, why is a faction of the Body of Christ vehemently anti-deliverance? Should we believe and practice part but discard other parts of the Gospel of Jesus Christ? No! It is either we believe all, or we do not believe at all.

In short, do not believe the words of the devil but rather believe God, for His promises are *"Yea and Amen!"* When we walk in doubt we might as well say to the devil, we believe in you and your lies. When we walk in unbelief and doubt, we open ourselves to the devil to afflict us more with his spirit of fear, manipulation and control. We know that, according to Scripture, fear has a torment.

One thing we should consider is, when the devil gains a foothold, he is never satisfied with just that, so he will push for more ground to fortify his entrenchment in the believer's life. When we do not activate the Word of God in our life, it stays dormant and, after a while, it dies. It then seems as though we never heard it before. The Word of God must be acted upon. The fruits must be visible in our life. Do not allow your mind to become the playground for the devil and his demons. Surrender all to the Lord and remember, the weapons of our warfare are mighty through God and God alone to the pulling down of strongholds. No matter how much you have suffered from the attacks of the enemy, there is help in the Lord.

Anything or any thought that question the validity of the Word of God or the very nature of God has to be quickly dismissed before you begin to doubt God. It is not a bad thing to have imaginations, but know that there are good and bad imaginations.

See the beauty of our Lord in all that you imagine. No matter what is happening around you, do not allow the enemy to fill your mind with negativity. Think about the goodness of our God and all the things He has done for you. Philippians 4:8, *"Finally, brethren, whatsoever things are true, whatsoever things are honest, whatsoever things are just, whatsoever things are pure, whatsoever things are lovely, whatsoever things are of good report; if there be any virtue and if there be any praise, think on these things."*

Discipline your mind. Take aggressive action against Satan's attack against your mind. (2 Corinthians 10:4-5) It involves continually arresting and bringing into captivity every thought that is contrary to the will of God concerning your life. That means any time the enemy attacks you with negative thoughts, reject it out right by speaking the Word of God out aloud to counteract it. When the enemy tries to bombard you with negative thoughts, you have to resist him fiercely.

How you do this is by looking at things through the eye of Scripture. For this, it is important to know the Word of God. You cannot fight the enemy who knows the Word with any other weapon. When he goes to accuse us before God, on what do you think he bases his accusations and arguments? He bases them on the Word and the principles of God. He wins his arguments when he shows how we have violated God's Word.

It is therefore paramount that every believer is well-versed in the Word of God; bearing in mind that a half-truth is as dangerous as the lack of knowledge. We do not only study to show ourselves approved unto God, but also to let the devil know that we know who we are in Christ Jesus.

How can you execute a will if you do not have understanding of the legal terms and conditions of the contents? It has to be explained by a solicitor or attorney. We have the Holy Spirit who will do the same for us if we desire to know and understand the Word of God. Only then only can we inherit and preserve what is ours.

Romans 12 talks about *"renewing our mind in order not to conform but rather to be transformed."* Constantly feeding on the Word for our spiritual growth and refreshing of our minds will help us to achieve this. It also keeps us spiritually alert and healthy. The state of our mind is very important if we are to win the battle and keep demons at bay. Feed your mind with wholesome stuff. Reading, studying and meditating on the Word of God is extremely essential, as it is both our defensive and offensive weapon during an attack of the enemy.

Apart from that you can read Christian literature and other books by known and proven authors for your well-being. Refrain from anything that sows confusion, as this is not from the Lord. Any material that focuses on the self, is a New Age product and must be avoided at all cost as this will not only bring confusion, but can also be destructive.

Some books can be the doctrine of demons, neatly packaged to make you believe that you are your own god. Keep your mind pure as the Bible clearly teaches us. Be mindful of what you watch, in other words, be mindful of what you permit to go through your eye gate. Stay away from horror movies, and other deceptive and demonic materials like certain books magazines and games as these can contaminate your spirit.

Joshua commands us in Joshua 1:8 to meditate in the word day and night so we can have good success. Be wary of things that can defile you such as pornographic movies or magazines or images. If you stumble on these quickly turn it off so you will not get hooked on it.

## Faith

Have a grip on faith. The Bible states in Hebrews 11:1 *"Now faith is the substance of things hoped for, the evidence of things not seen."* It means you believe in something for which there is no evidential proof at the time, even though the natural mind is telling you it is insane to believe. It also means something is real even though the evidence is not yet visible.

Who has seen God before? But we believe with our whole heart that there is a God and, by faith, we accept Jesus Christ as our Lord and Saviour. The Jewish Saul, (Apostle Paul) never had any personal or physical encounter with Jesus nor did he have any knowledge of or belief in Jesus, the Messiah. As a matter of fact, he hated and persecuted Christians until he had a supernatural encounter with the Lord on his way to Damascus to persecute the Christians.

This is the encounter that changed the course of history. This is the man who did not want to have anything to do with the Name, Jesus, yet when he was thrown from off his donkey and the Voice spoke to him, he immediately felt a connection to his spirit and knew immediately that it was the Lord speaking to him. Acts 9:5, *"And he (Paul) said, who art thou, Lord? And the Lord said, I am Jesus whom thou persecute."*

Saul of Tarsus a typical Jew, did not believe in Christ, so what happened on that day and in that instance? What happened was, Spirit met with spirit and the lesser acknowledged the greater. He, who had never seen the Messiah physically, overtook even those who had seen Him, walked and worked with Him, with zeal, knowledge and boldness to propagate the Gospel.

It was all through faith. And by faith we have seen Him too, not with our physical eyes, but with our spiritual eyes. We believe in Him and He has proven to us that He is indeed who He says He is.

Faith can be personified, as the Lord taught me, and faith can also be taught and caught. The Lord once used me powerfully to minister on the subject of Faith. I woke up the next day and the Spirit of the Lord was still hovering over me, replaying the message to me. It reached a point when I said to Him, "Lord teach me faith."

Immediately my mind said to me, "What a stupid thing to ask. How do you teach faith?" The Holy Spirit then quickly said to me, "Yes, faith can be taught, just as anything else. You were taught Mathematics and English, weren't you?"
"Alright teach me faith then", I said, "and give me Faith."
His answer was, "You have Him, and all you have to do is place your hand in His hand, walk hand in hand with Him and you will not lose Him."
I asked, "How do I do that?"
He said, "Place your hand in the hand of Faith and walk side by side with Him, and you will not lose Him."

I immediately understood the message of child-like Faith. It is only children who walk with their hand clutched in the hand of the one they trust for their safety. It sent me straight to the Man of God who led me to Christ and took me under his wings and mentored me. Pastor Collins is a man of faith and would not tolerate any negativity around him at all. He taught me faith and I caught it from him as well.

As a new believer in Christ Jesus, things began to change drastically in my life. My conversion was that drastic that I began to hate those actions of mine that were not pleasing to the Lord. I was working in the accounting department of a big organisation and was co-opted into some fraudulent activities. I was making big money and was living the life that I had never known before; being raised in abject poverty. I was enjoying myself and celebrating my fortune until the Lord caught up with me.

The Lord immediately stopped my involvement in what was the norm in that office. I had no control over this, as it was the Lord who took away my desire. Having said that, my cooperation with the Lord also played a part. Even so, it was the grace of God working in me that enabled me to say no to the malpractice.

The devil immediately went on the attack. I lost everything; I became very poor, as I had to now depend solely on my monthly salary, which was not much. There was never enough left to cater for my sister, my son and I after paying my rent. My faith was put to test but thank God for the Man of God who taught me to take everything to God in prayer to see faith at work. Any time I was moved to complain about my finances, he would say, Gina, go on your knees and as I obeyed, I saw the Lord meeting my needs. I quickly learned that indeed faith in God works.

God expects us, His children, to walk in His grace and totally trust him, even when the circumstances seem gloomy. Christ is the anchor of our soul and He will never fail us. Never! It is important to know that God has not planned any defeat for you in spite of what you may be going through. God's plan for you is to be victorious and prosperous in every area of your life. 3 John 2, *"Beloved I wish above all things that thou may prosper and be in health, even as thy soul prosper."*

This is the Word of truth, and truth cancels fact. Long time ago, long before I became a minister, we were holding discussion in church about how to handle hurts and I said to them, "I refuse to be hurt anytime someone does hurtful things to me, but rather, I choose to

deal with it, forgive and release the person."
"How can I refuse to feel the hurt when it is real?" I was asked.
My answer to that was, we have fact and we have the truth. Jesus said, you shall know the truth and it shall make you free, and whom the Son sets free is free indeed!

In reality we do hurt, we do feel the pain, these are real and cannot be denied, right? It is a fact, but we have Jesus and the Holy Ghost, our helper and comforter. You shall know the truth (Jesus) and the truth (Jesus) will make you free from all your pains and if He sets you free, then you will be free indeed. This means it is only the power of Jesus and the Holy Ghost that can defy nature and make you pain-free.

It is only Jesus who can do this for you. It is a supernatural act of God. This is what I mean by truth cancels fact. God gives us the grace to forgive and release the person. The subject comes up and you are able to laugh about it, joke about it or even talk about it without any ill-feeling. The truth takes away the sting of the hurt and this is done by understanding the Scripture in *Ecclesiastes 7:20-22 "For there is not a just man upon the earth that sins not. [21]Also take no heed unto all the words that are spoken; lest you hear your servant curses you. [22]for oftentimes also your own heart knows that you yourself likewise have cursed others."*

Think about this and also consider Mathew 18, how we who have received forgiveness, must also learn to forgive others. We all have caused someone pain at a point in time and have expected them to forgive us. We cannot forgive if we continue to hold on to our hurts. Pray for the grace to forgive and free yourself from the enemy's entrapment.

Develop and practice purity of mind as the Bible teaches us.

*"Whatsoever things are true---think on these things."* (Philippians 4:8) Fill your mind with the Word of God, hymns and gospel songs. Meditate on the Word of God and seek to walk with the Lord in relationship, not from afar. He is not a God who dwells in Heaven alone, but He is a God who is omnipresent.

God is everywhere at all times. He lives in us and He is with us as long as we remain in Him. Do not dwell on negative things that may happen to you but rather think on good things and the Word of God that comforts, heals and restores your soul As you do this, you leave no room for the devil and his demons to gain access into your mind. This also enables you to build your faith in God.

Take time out for some recreational moments, and also to have fun. It is not a sin to go on vacation to relieve yourself of the day-to-day stress that we face on the job and other areas, even, in Ministry. There are Christian comedians who are wholesome. You can go to such events and have a good laugh. Proverbs 17:22 says, *"A merry heart does good like medicine: but a broken spirit dries the bones."* Enjoy your God-given life in a godly way

God wants us to enjoy life as stated in 3 John 2, *"Beloved, I wish above all that you may prosper and be in health even as your soul prospers."* This encompasses every area of our life, spirit, soul and body.

# CHAPTER 40

# Guilt and Condemnation

Get rid of every feeling of condemnation, guilt and shame, for our Lord Jesus bore it all on the Cross so we will not have to carry it again. The penalty was paid in full. Remember, he took all our guilt and shame. This is done by prayer and believing in the redemptive power of the blood of Jesus Christ.

Hollywood stars walk on a red carpet to show off their prowess and people idolise them. They walk the walk of fame on their famous Red Carpet, but our Jesus took the walk of shame through the market place all the way to Golgotha so we can walk like kings and queens on the earth. It was your shame and mine that He carried to Golgotha.

The Bible says *"There is therefore now no condemnation to them which are in are in Christ Jesus, who walk not after the flesh, but after the spirit."* Child of God, walk with your head up high for He paid the price for you to walk in liberty. He is the lifter of our heads and there is no sin greater and heavier than the weight of the Cross He carried to Golgotha. He did it for you and for me and for the whole of mankind; that whosoever will may come and receive the benefit of His suffering and ultimate death on the Cross.

I happened to be counseling a woman who was about to marry a man who was in a key position in his church. During one of the sessions, she voiced her concern about something that was bothering her. She said, "Pastor, this man wants me to tell him the number of men with whom I have had intimacy but I am not comfortable about doing this."

I told her that under no circumstance should she do that. I said to tell him that all that plus all other sins were taken care *of by the sacrifice Jesus made for us all. If he* insists, tell him that even if he goes past the Blood of Jesus to retrieve his own sins, you, however, will not. The Lord said He will forgive our sins and remember them no more. Why then should we remind ourselves about sins that are wiped away and forgotten?

She gave a sigh of relief, thanked me and left. When she repeated it to the man, it turned out that it was all because she resisted his desire to sleep with her before their marriage. He wanted that information so he can use it to manipulate her. They eventually broke their engagement and cancelled the wedding because of other information she had concerning him. This is a typical example of the devil using people to keep you feeling guilty. This can lead to one being kept in bondage whereas Christ has set you free. This can or may also open the door to demonic harassment. Galatians 5:1, *"Stand fast therefore in the liberty wherewith Christ has made us free, and be not entangled again with the yoke of bondage."*

Always bear in mind that you do not have to go back to your sins by reminding yourself of the things you have done before coming to the Lord and even after, as long as you repent of them and stay under the feet of the Lord. The Gospel artist, Helen Baylor's song, "Into the sea of forgetfulness He placed all of my sins…", ministers to me strongly over this very issue of guilt and condemnation. If you can get hold of it and listen to the lyrics meditatively it will help you too. God Almighty is gracious and will not hold a repented sin against you. No, they are not and will not be found in the book of the records according to Colossians 1:21-23, *"And you, that were sometime alienated and enemies in your mind by wicked works, yet now has He reconciled in the body of His flesh through death, to present you holy and unblameable and unreproveable in His sight: If you continue in the faith grounded and settled, and be not moved away from the hope of the gospel, which you have heard, and which was preached to every creature under heaven… "*

## Beware of the Company you Keep

Remember King Jehoshaphat? His friendship with Ahab nearly cost him his life in 1 Kings 22:30-33. Jehoshaphat did not need to go to war but because he was in friendship with Ahab, he found himself being in the wrong place at the wrong time. It was just the grace of God that saved him from being killed.

Keep company with people who will encourage you in the things of God and keep away from negative people. They will not add to your well-being; physically or spiritually. This is a must do even if you have to lose some "good friends". Good friends are not necessarily godly friends and some will take you back into your former ways. You may be criticised for this, but whom do you want more than anything in this world? Jesus or friends that drag you back into darkness?

Pray for them so they will also come to the knowledge of the saving grace of our Lord Jesus Christ. O taste and see that the Lord is good. In 1 Corinthians 15:33, the Bible clearly states that *"Be not deceived: evil communications corrupt good manners. [34]Awake to righteousness, and sin not; for some have not the knowledge of God: I speak this to your shame."*

This is Paul the Apostle speaking to the Corinthian church and it is sad to say that it is even worse today than then. The church has now become a social club where all sorts come in, not seeking salvation but to infest the people. Their sole purpose is to bring down godly standards in the church, fulfilling Satan's agenda. We, the church, have permitted the world and demons into the church to influence it, instead of the church going into the world as Jesus commissioned us to do. Mark 16:15, *"And He said unto them, go ye into all the world, and preach the gospel to every creature. [16]He that believes and is baptised shall be saved; but he that believes not shall be damned."*

Today's church seems to have embraced the world and all of its practices, all because 'times have changed' and we need to reach the youth and embrace everybody. This may be true, to a degree, because the Light is supposed to overpower and overcome the darkness, but now it is the other way round. The Biblical standard was never compromised to accommodate the *youth* back in Biblical times and even before I was saved.

Timothy was a young man who came from a family of worshippers. He was prayed over and hands were laid on him, and he never looked back. Paul also took him in to nurture him, encouraged him and constantly reminded him of how he came to be a minister; from his grandmother, to his mother and the presbytery who laid hands on him.

There is no indication whatsoever that Paul once said, "Oh Timothy, my son I can understand why you are behaving like this, it is due to the fact that there is peer pressure. Since times have changed, I am going to lower the standard of the Scriptures to accommodate your culture and let you practice it in the church."

Paul was firm in all his admonishing. 1 Timothy 1:18-19, "*This charge I commit unto you, son Timothy, according to the prophecies which went before on you, that you might a good warfare; holding faith, and a good conscience; which some having put away concerning the faith have made shipwreck; of whom is Hymenaeus and Alexander; whom I have delivered unto Satan, that they may learn not to blaspheme.*"

We seldom hear such truth anymore. Paul is literally saying, my son, Timothy, do not do anything that God Almighty has not indicated in the Bible. Keep the ministry pure and without compromise. Always remember the prophetic words that were declared over you and never turn to the left or to the right to please man or yourself. This is so you can effectively wage a good war that has the backing of heaven at all times.

What do we see these days in church? We have permitted demonic dances and dress into the holy sanctuary of the Lord. It is sad, very sad. Let us check other religions to see how they have held on to their beliefs and have not compromised using their youth as an excuse to be "polluted".

Islam and Hinduism are good example. I do not believe in legalism, but I believe in decency within the church of Jesus Christ. Not only in the church but also out of the church for a good witness unto the Lord Jesus Christ, our Saviour.

# CHAPTER 41

# Back to Basis

In order for the church to be a healthy place where souls can be saved and remain saved, it is necessary to go back to doing exactly what the Bible teaches us to do. That is, to preach the pure, unadulterated Gospel of Jesus Christ instead of any watered-down messages.

The Church needs to go back to its original purpose of saving and nurturing souls, and furthering heaven's agenda. There ought to be a difference in people's lives, a total transformation for others to see and when they see that our Jesus is real and alive, they will want to come into the Light too.

I was ministering in a church and I randomly asked who could tell me one of the fruits of the spirit. There was silence so I picked one of the members and she boldly said, fasting. Yes, Fasting! This person, I was told has been in the church for nearly eight years. Do I blame her? No. I do not believe she is alone or she is an isolated case in the Kingdom. The Word of God has to be given its proper place in the church, whether the people like it or not.

We need the power in the church like never before as the end is drawing nearer and nearer. People have to be taught how to live victoriously and be empowered to live and work for Christ, and also to know about the enemy, how he operates and how to resist him. Knowledge is power, they say, and it is true. A soldier, well equipped, is very dangerous and we have to pose a threat to the forces of evil when we are properly armed.

Apostle Paul said in 1 Corinthians 3:5, *"Who then is Paul,* (an Apostle) *and who is Apollos,* (a Pastor I believe) *but ministers by whom you have believed, even as the Lord gave to every man?* (Even as God gave to every man as declared in Ephesians?) *I,* as an Apostle and Apollos, a Pastor. *⁶I have planted, Apollos watered; but God gave the increase. ⁷So then neither is he that plants anything, neither he that waters; but God that gives the increase. ⁸now he that plants and he that waters are one: and every man shall receive his own reward according to his own labor."*

Let me pause here for a moment to point out what Paul is teaching us, which we seem to have lost sight of. The Apostle has clearly clarified the ministerial gifts. One plants and another waters, and neither is greater than the other because it is God who breathes over each work to make it fruitful. The difference is how you labour or work with what has been assigned or apportioned to you. This will determine your reward. This should settle our hearts and stop us competing with each other with envy, strife and contention. This is killing all that the Lord intended His Body to be.

Dear fellow-laborer, if you a 'waterer', keep on watering, and if you are a 'planter', please keep on planting and do not change your course. As you do this, God will increase harmony in His Kingdom. Only when we stay in the lane wherein God has put us, shall we succeed. Have we ever watched an athlete running in his lane and then, in the course of the race, deciding to change lanes? It happens in very few cases. Even though we see it, it is an accident and the athlete is automatically disqualified. Why? This is simply because it is the rule of the sport.

Similarly, we have rules in the Kingdom of God and we have been taught how to walk in obedience and anything outside the rule, is disobedience. I believe similarly, that is what caused Saul to lose his kingship. Saul took upon himself to perform the priestly duties, which was not part of his job specification. (I Samuel. 13:8-14) Even though the athlete completes the course, he is disqualified and does not receive any reward.

1 Corinthians 3:10, *"According to the grace of God which is given unto me, as a wise master builder, I have laid the foundation, and another builds thereon. But let every man take heed how he builds thereupon. [11]For other foundation can no man lay than that is laid, which is Jesus Christ. [12]Now if any man builds upon this foundation gold, silver, precious stones, wood, hay, stubble; [13]Every man's work shall be made manifest: for the day shall declare it, because it shall be revealed by fire; and the fire shall try every man's work of what sort it is. [14]If any man's work abides which he has built thereupon, he shall receive a reward. [15]If any man's work shall be burned, he shall suffer loss: but he himself shall be saved; yet so as by fire…. [20]And again, The Lord knows the thoughts of the wise, that they are vain. [21]Therefore let no man glory in men. For all things are yours; [22]whether Paul, (The* Apostle) *or Apollos,* (The Pastor) *or Cephas* (probably The Evangelist) *or the world, or life, or death, or things present, or things to come; all are yours. [23]And you are Christ's; and Christ is God's."*

This means whether you are called as an Apostle, Pastor, or Evangelist, do not wish or desire another's office. Bear in mind that wherever we are placed by God, we should work and excel therein. Know that we are whom we are through Christ who has given to us all things that pertain to life and godliness. He has given us everything and placed all things under our control, as sons and daughters of God, and as joint heirs of the Kingdom.

Let our walk be worthy of our vocation as prescribed by God in order to alleviate the problems the Church is experiencing today. There is work to be done, let us not forget that the Lord Jesus is depending on us to prepare a people for Him. To present unto Himself a glorious church, not having spot, or wrinkle, or any such thing; but that it should be holy and without blemish. (Ephesians 5:27)

Jesus commissioned Peter to feed his sheep and feed His lambs in John 21:18. How would Peter have done this if he had spent his time focusing on how to gain fame and fortune? There is chaos in the body of Christ as Prophets want to be Pastors, and some Pastors want to be Prophets rather than what the Lord has appointed them to be. They draw large crowds because of our desire to know the unknown and to satisfy our itchy ears, but the prophet, if he has not been anointed to pastor, often shipwrecks people's faith. Please let us keep good lane manners to avoid damaging the flock for which the Lord died, and to ensure we receive a reward for our works.

We have a job to do, people of God. We are in the last days and the Word of God warns us about those things which have to happen before the coming of our Lord. He warns us about the false Prophets and the false teachers, who will invade the body of Christ. That is exactly what is happening now!

Do not be deceived. A false prophet is not the same as a demonic or satanic one. They are different and even the name indicates this. We are not dealing with the satanic minsters now, but the false ones. Balaam was God's prophet who out of greed, went against the voice of God. Numbers 22:32, *"and the angel of the Lord said unto him, wherefore have you smitten your ass these three times? Behold I went out to withstand you because your way is perverse before me."*

Does the story in Numbers sound familiar to what is happening in some of our churches today? Yes. A false prophet says, I will do all that is pleasing to God and yet his motives are impure before God. A little compromise here and there makes a good prophet become a false Prophet. The Scripture that always sends a chill down my spine is from Matthew 7:15. Jesus warns *"Beware of false prophets, which come to you in sheep's clothing, but inwardly they are ravening wolves. [16]You shall know them by their fruits... [21]not everyone that says to me, Lord, Lord, shall enter into the Kingdom of heaven; but he that does the will of my Father in heaven. [22]Many will say to me in that day, Lord, Lord, have we not prophesied in your name, and have cast out devils? And in your name done many wonderful works? [23]And I will profess unto them, I never knew you: depart from me you that work iniquity."*

This is our Lord's definition of a false minister. To the outside world he is a powerful man or woman of God who is moving mightily in the anointing of God, but in the eyes of God, who knows the intents of the heart and sees in secret, they are iniquitous and He knows them not. They are displeasing Him in the way they conduct themselves and His business.

Dear people of God, it a fearful thing to fall into the hands of the living God, so let us cleanse our ways. God is not mocked; whatsoever a man sows, he will reap. Let us see more fruits and fewer pretenses in the Kingdom of God and Christ will shine on us and expel the darkness that has invaded His church. Let us seek to please God in all that we do, by doing His will and His will alone.

2 Peter 2:1 warns us, *"But there were false prophets also among the people, even as there shall be false teachers among you, <u>who shall secretly bring in damnable heresies,</u> even denying the Lord that bought them, and many shall follow their pernicious (destructive) ways; by reason of whom the way of truth shall be evil spoken of. [3a]<u>and through covetousness shall they with feigned words make merchandise of you.</u>"* (Underlining mine)

As it was in the days of Jesus, so it is today. I believe it has grown worse. Jesus had to aggressively enter the temple to drive out those who chose to use the temple to sell their merchandise. Are we going to let the Lord use us to do the same from our pulpits? It is only the pure Word of God, preached and taught, that can do that for us. Let us pray for bold and fearless ministers who will face the devil and defy him as David defied Goliath, to bring deliverance to the people of God.

Jesus will have to be exalted in His temple once again. The church needs to find its feet again in order to stand in the evil days that will soon visit the world. We have to raise a people who will stand in the face of danger and not renounce their faith. The church, as it stands now, will lay down its ammunition and weapons and flee in the face of danger (persecution).

This reminds me of the first Iraqi war when, after the late Saddam Hussein threatened the 'mother of all wars', only to see his troops in their thousands laying down their weapons in surrender. Our name and banner alone will not win any battles for us. It will take the power and authority given by God Almighty to those who are walking according to His Word and principles to defeat the god of this world and his evil army.

Folks, going to church alone does not make one a Christian just as going to the zoo does not make you an animal. Are you truly born again? Are you being properly nurtured? Do not be fooled, the fact that you are marking the register every Sunday does not make you a Christian. Seek God and know Him for yourself.

The church has to wake up from its comatose condition, and be swept clean and well garnished to be ready for the next move of the Spirit before Jesus comes. You may ask what I mean. The Bible says in

1 Pet. 4:17, *"For the time is come that judgment must begin at the house of God: and if it first begins at us, what shall the end be of them that obey not the gospel of God?"*
For the church to become a holy and a sanctified place again, repentance has to precede everything; from the pulpit to the back pew. We need to declare a day of mourning and sackcloth, a day of sincere and genuine repentance.

Jesus went into the temple and drove out the moneychangers, the goats and the oxen. In other words, He thoroughly cleansed the temple and declared, *"For it is written, My House shall be a house of prayer but you have made it a den of thieves."* Matthew 21:12-13. Jesus actually entered the temple to rid it from the contamination the leaders had permitted in the Holy Place. That is why He declared afterwards what the temple is to have been used for, a House of Prayer.

Jesus loves the sinner but will not compromise to see the sinner "saved." Whilst on earth, He challenged the Pharisees, Sadducees and the Scribes over their hypocrisy. Why then is the church now practicing political correctness?

We are not to accommodate sin and continue as if nothing is wrong. There is something seriously wrong when all manner of sins are accommodated instead of proper counseling to help people change. The Word of God, preached with power, has the ability and the power to deliver, heal and save. If this is not happening in our churches today, then, beloved, I am afraid the church is in serious trouble.

The devil has hijacked the reins of the church universal and demons are calling the shots from behind the scenes. We have permitted abominable things like some kind of dances, all kinds of inappropriate dress, entertainment instead of ministration and people blatantly living in sin. Some are permitted to lead the services or the praise and worship unto the Most High God. Why? Where is the fear of the Lord? We need a deep cleansing in the church of Jesus Christ now.

The scary thing is that we do not have time. All the signs in the world point to the fact that the coming of the Lord is near. As a matter of fact, it is nearer than we think. It is time to prepare to meet our Maker, whether we die or live to see the Lord coming through the clouds.

Dearly beloved of Christ, you have a role to play in your Father's business. You have a charge to keep and a God to glorify in the house of God and also outside the church. It is not only the Pastor's job.

Remember, you were bought with a price, the precious blood of Jesus Christ of Nazareth and, for this reason he has given you an assignment and He will demand full accountability, Matthew. 25:19 *"After a long time the lord of those servants comes, and reckons with them."* This was after He had given them talents individually. One was given five and another two, and the third one was given one; these were given according to their several abilities. He never told them what to do with the talents but, as I said earlier, nobody tells a child when to crawl or walk,

Instinctively the first two knew exactly what to do, that is work with it. The third person, unfortunately, like so many Christians of today, did nothing with his talent. The lord called him an unprofitable servant and he was severely punished. I recommend you read the entire parable of the talents to understand the Lord's heart and how he hates idleness in His vineyard.

Jesus even cursed the fig tree that did not bear fruit. He has wired us to be fruitful and if we are not bearing fruit, then know that there are consequences that will be meted out.

You cannot tell the Lord that nobody has told you to do something for Him. How long have you been a Christian? As it is with a child, learning to crawl, stand and walk is in-built by the Creator, so is it for anyone who is truly born again. Remember, in the story of the talents, the master knew their capabilities and gave to them accordingly. God knows your capabilities. He knows this because He created you and knows exactly what your capabilities are. He expects you to use what you got and no more.

Nobody needs tell you to do things in the house of the Lord. Nobody needs tell you to win souls for the Lord because there is this thing about the new birth; you want people around you to know that you are a new creation. The excitement in telling others about the Messiah is visible for all to see. You cannot wait to go to church meetings, as for lateness, it is not for you at all.

Remember what the Bible refers to as our "first love". It is time to go back to our first love and fall in love with Jesus all over again.

# CHAPTER 42

# Do You Know Jesus?

Dear friend and reader, I want to take some time to ask you, "Do you know who Jesus Is?"

Some of us went to church upon invitation by friends and when we arrived, we liked what we saw and experienced. Maybe the praise and worship attracted you, or it was the preaching that got your attention? It could have been other things like how friendly the people were towards you that made you to stay. These are all good reasons but there is something more important than these are. This is what I want you to think of, and answer truthfully and sincerely.

Did the minister make an altar call? By this I mean, did anyone lead you to accept Jesus Christ as your Lord and Saviour? Did anyone lead you to pray the 'sinner's' prayer, confessing your sins in repentance?

I know that many in the church only know about Jesus Christ but they do not know Him. How did this happen? Like me, many came to the church because of their problems and were prayed for without being led to the problem solver, Jesus Christ. Hearing the testimony of others, they hoped the Lord would answer them as well. Lo and behold, this happened; so they stayed. Not seeking to worship or serve the Lord, the church became a place of refuge. How can you serve Him of whom you have no knowledge?

There is nothing particularly wrong with this, but there are now many church-goers who just fill the pews. They have no knowledge at all of the Truth. They do not know the Lord intimately and so are not really committed to serving our God. I am not condemning anyone, but I am pointing out the difference so you will understand and make a choice whether you are in or out. It will be very sad, indeed, if the Lord should come today, only for you to learn that you are not actually a Christian having been in church for a long time.

We can blame it on the ministers, pastors, elders and everyone else but the bottom line is you are responsible for your own salvation. There is a day and a time that God Almighty makes sure everyone has the opportunity to hear the Gospel. This is recorded in Heaven so there will be no excuse. The Bible says in Isaiah 55:6, *"Seek the Lord while He may be found, call you upon Him while He is near."*

The onus is on the individual to seek God for themself. Nobody can do that for you. It is an individual decision. I recommend you choose Jesus you will not regret it.

The difference between the churchgoer and the true born-again believer is having the Holy Ghost within you. On conversion, the Holy Spirit comes in to you and over you. You, and others, will notice the *new* you. You will notice the change on the inside that will reflect on the outside and others will definitely notice and comment on it.

All experiences are not the same, but you will be drawn by an irresistible desire to be in church among the brethren, and to know the Word of God. Have you experienced anything different from the old you since you have been in church?

Jesus made a statement in John 3:3 *"Verily, verily I say unto you except a man be born again, he cannot see the Kingdom of God."* You have to understand the concept of being born again in order to make that life-changing decision. What if there is no-one around to lead you to Christ? It is the sincere heart-cry of any human being that can lead them to the Lord. This is often the case with people of other religions that have nothing to do with the Bible, or atheists who do not believe in God at all. It is often their heart-cry in situations that draw them to the Lord. Their conversion is the most drastic.

If you have not cried out to Jesus to save you and have not accepted Him alone as your Lord and Saviour, then I beg you to do it now, either on your own or go to your Pastor or any of the elders.

You can pray a simple prayer of repentance and ask the Lord Jesus to come into your heart as your Lord and Saviour. The Bible declares in Romans 10:9-10 (after hearing what the Scripture says concerning why you need to be saved), *"That if you shall confess with your mouth the Lord Jesus, and shall believe in your heart that God has raised Him from the dead, you shall be saved. [10]with the heart man believes unto righteousness; and with the mouth confession is made unto salvation."* If today, you do this with me, you secure yourself a place in the Kingdom of God. You are born again!

I want you to stop everything and repeat this prayer after me:

Lord Jesus,

I come to you today acknowledging I am a sinner.

I ask you to forgive me my sins and wash me in your precious blood.

Cleanse me from all my sins.

I accept you as my Lord and Saviour.

Come into my heart today and live in me.

Write my name in the Lamb's Book of Life.

I thank you Lord Jesus for saving me.

Fill me with your Holy Spirit.

From now on, help me to live for you.

Amen!

Hallelujah! You are born again and I welcome you in the name of the Lord Jesus into the Kingdom of our God. Know that the angels in heaven are rejoicing over you. Welcome to the Kingdom of our Lord!

If you are new believer, I recommend and pray that the Lord will lead you to a Bible-believing church so you will be taught and nurtured to grow in the knowledge of God and how to live the Christian life. You need to study the Word of God, the Bible, so you can learn about Kingdom living and also how to work the works of the Lord. If you are already in a church, and the church teaches the Bible and the emphasis is on the Lord Jesus and the Holy Spirit, then stay to study, grow and know Him for yourself and not from what you hear from others. May the Holy Spirit guide you through this journey and prosper you, in Jesus name.

Now to my question, who is Jesus? Do you know Jesus? And why do you have to know Him? How do you know that you know Him?

In Primary school, we were taught many songs and hymns about Jesus, and I loved singing about Him. We were also taught many Bible stories. In my own child-like way, I loved this Jesus whom I did not know. Then in Middle school, we were made to attend church. Failure to do so would result in severe punishment. This was because it was a Presbyterian School. I loved my school's white church uniform and the march from the schoolyard, through the streets in the town center, to the church cathedral every Sunday. I participated in almost all the yearly Children's day programs when a select few, picked to represent their class, would recite their chosen Bible verses. I was confirmed and started taking Communion.

In secondary school, I lost every desire to sing my favourite hymns or to attend church as I used to. At this point, I did not know Jesus but I was taught about Him in our Religious Studies and I loved listening to all the fascinating stories about Him. I was saved only in my late twenties. Before then, I did not know the Lord, but He knew me and He knows you too.

At the appointed time, He came for me. Your time has come too. I responded to the call, will you?

One of my favorite marching songs, going to church was:

Hark 'tis the Shepherd voice I hear;
Out in the desert dark and drear.
Calling the sheep who've gone astray,
Far from the Shepherd's fold away.

Bring them in, bring them in;
Bring them in from the fields of sin.
Bring them in, bring them in,
Bring the wandering ones to Jesus.

This song became my personal anthem when I became born again and it motivated me to win souls for the Lord. Dear friend, what is your story? We all have our moments when the Lord begins to knock on the door of our hearts, but it is our personal decision and choice to let Him in or not.

Who is this Jesus that I am talking about? The Bible says He is the Son of God who came to die in our place. Romans 6:23, *"The wages of sin is death but the gift of God is eternal life through Christ Jesus our Lord"*. Romans 3:23, *"For, all have sinned and come short of the glory of God."*

We were all born in sin as a result of the fall of Adam in the Garden of Eden. For this reason, man lost his fellowship with God, and that is why Jesus came to reconcile us unto God and to restore man to his original position appointed by God to have dominion over every created thing on the earth. Jesus became the Lamb of God that was used to settle the debt for our souls and His precious blood atoned for all our sins.

The Bible clearly states that Jesus is the only way to the one and only true, living God. He is the Creator of all things according to the Bible. Genesis 1 talks about how God created all things and Revelation 4:11 says, *"Thou art worthy, O Lord, to receive glory and honor and power: for thou hast created all things and for thy pleasure they are and were created."*

No deity of any religion has been able to make any claim of being the creator but God Almighty. No one has been able to declare that He died to save mankind but Jesus Christ. That settles it for me. Jesus is the Son of the living God who loved his own creation, man, so much that He gave His only begotten Son (Jesus) that whosoever believes in Him should not perish but have eternal life. (John 3:16)

Beloved Jesus is real. He can only reveal Himself to those who desire to know Him and it does not matter what you have done, where you are coming from or your religious background. All you have to do is ask Him to make Himself known to you.

Saul of Tarsus, who became the Apostle Paul, was a religious fanatic and a Jew who did not believe that Jesus was the Son of God. The name Jesus could not be mentioned around a typical Jew, and Paul persecuted the Christians in His days. However, when the Lord confronted him on his way to persecute the Christians in Damascus, he called Him, Lord.

Acts 9:3-7 *"And as he journeyed, he came near Damascus: and suddenly there shined round about him a light from heaven: and he fell to the earth, and heard a voice saying unto him, Saul, Saul, why persecute you me? ⁵And he said, who are you Lord? And the Lord said, I am Jesus whom you persecute: is it hard for you to kick against the pricks? And he (Saul) trembling and astonished said, Lord, what will you have me to do? And the Lord said unto him, arise and go into the city, and it shall be told you what you must do. ⁷and the men which journeyed with him stood speechless, hearing a voice, but seeing no man."*

How did Paul identify the speaker as the Lord? How could the men traveling with him hear the voice speaking but could not see Him? He is real, folks! There is a spirit in man that knows the voice of his Maker and Lord. Remember, He breathed His breath (spirit) into the formed clay and man became a living soul.

In the Garden of Eden, how was Adam communicating with God? The spirit of God in Adam made it possible for him to speak the same language and by the same spirit; Saul of Tarsus identified the voice of the Lord and went on, even in the face of death, to proclaim the Gospel Lord Jesus Christ.

The Spirit of God is in every human being to identify His voice when He calls. That is why some atheists, satanists and people of other faiths who have an encounter with Him, drop everything to follow Him like the disciples of old. If today, you surrender your life to Jesus, you will know Him.

Believe the Lord and believe me, if you ask Him sincerely to come into your life today, you will experience His very person. He is Love!

That was the passion that drove Him to die the horrible, painful and humiliating death for you and for me. My friend, it was LOVE! Jesus loves us so much that He laid down His life for us so we may come to the Father and enjoy the relationship that was originally intended for us.

*"O taste and see that the Lord is good."* Psalm 34:8a; not only on earth, but also to spend eternity with Him in heaven. Surely, there is life after death, there is heaven and there is hell. The choice of where you and I spend eternity is for us to make. *Hebrews 9:27 says "it is appointed unto man once to die and after that judgement."*

I ask again, my dear friend and reader, are you born again? The Bible says, *"The Spirit of God Himself bears witness with our spirit that we are the children of God."* Romans 8:16. The greatest miracle of all times is not physical but the internal transformation of a human being, which becomes manifest on the outside. This change cannot be hidden; it is plainly visible for all who know you to see.

I use myself as an example. Anyone who knew me before and after my encounter with the Lord Jesus will testify to the drastic change in me. I knew it too. It was instant, and sudden. Everything about me changed, including the clubbing; in my day it was called disco. I was living in the fast lane of life. I thought that lifestyle was the ultimate source of my joy and happiness, but the Lord took hold of me and changed all that and replaced them with His joy unspeakable.

I cannot explain the joy and the peace that was flowing inside of me but I loved it and could not wait to share it with my friends and colleagues. I won some for the Lord who are still in the faith, praise God!

I also saw a drastic transformation in a colleague who was "arrested" by the Holy Ghost during a crusade to which he had been invited by his wife. In his own words he was very reluctant to go but he went anyway. The first day, he said, as the man of God was preaching the message of salvation, he felt this severe headache and he left the place in anger. He was so angry when his wife asked him if he was coming on the second night that he snapped and asked his wife if the prophet is the one who pays the rent.
"No", said his wife.
"Is he the one who puts food on the table?"
She replied again, "No."
"Is he the one who pays the bills in the house?"
Again, "No."
Then he told her never again to ask him to come with her to the crusade.

The woman then left with their children. To her surprise, who walked in to sit next to her but her husband. When the man of God said there was a young man there the Lord had been calling but he has resisted Him until now, and would he please come forward, two men went forward but were told they were not the ones. At this point my friend and colleague with his head bowed looked at his wife and motioned her to ask if he was the one? His wife said yes, and he shook his head several times to say, no.

At this point the man of God came down, walked towards him and took him by the hand and led him onto the platform. The rest is history. His transformation was so drastic even his gambling, drinking, weed smoking and womanizing friendships stopped. Some of his former friends tried to test the waters to see if it was a one-day wonder, but they were disappointed. The women with whom he used to cheat backed off except for one who felt she could reverse things. She continued to seduce him but he never gave in.

God quickly endowed him with the prophetic gift and he was seeing into the spiritual realms as though he had been around for a long time. This man eventually became an ordained Pastor.

Why am I telling you these two stories? He later on told me he used to mock some of the Christians in our office with the exception of me and another woman. I asked him why, and he explained that there was some aura around the two of us and the truth that we both passionately lived for and defended, stopped him from coming anywhere near us. The rest of them, in his own words, were like paperweight for him.

Dear friend and reader, let your light shine before all men and the Light will shine more and more on you. Soon all men will know that He is, indeed, the Light that came from heaven. What is your story since you believed? Have friends and family testified to you about the changes in you? Can you, yourself, see the changes in you?

A colleague told me he was born again and began to go to church but was still battling with alcoholism. This is not to say he was not born again; as in some cases, some things change gradually and for others you may have to go through deliverance. What was troubling my spirit was he was a secret believer in a free world. So I challenged him and asked, "Have you been able to witness to the ones you drink with since you still hang around them?"

He said to me, "I am a private person and I like to keep my conversion private." Immediately the "Paul" in me jumped out and I told him, "Then, my friend, you are not born again because no one becomes born again and keeps quiet in the free world where no one will persecute you for your faith." I went on to tell him that although he had been invited to church by someone who believed, it would take the Lord Jesus Christ to redeem him and set him free from his addiction. He only went and was prayed for and then decided to go to church because he liked the Pastor and the people. There is a difference between that and having an encounter with the Lord. Oh, it was not long before he was back to his old ways, saying it was not for him.

Jesus said no man lights a candle and hides it under the bed because the purpose of the light will be defeated. It was meant to give light to you and others. A truly born-again Christian talks openly, freely and passionately about their conversion and the Lord Jesus. They have this strong desire to know Him and serve Him willingly. Are you passionate about the Lord Jesus Christ of Nazareth? If you are born again, are you growing? In your own eyes, would you say you are growing spiritually and maturing in things of the Lord?

The Bible says, *"But as many as received Him to them gave He power to become the sons of God, even to them that believe on His name."* John 1:12.

This is only the beginning of the process so it is wrong to remain there as Romans 8:14 says, *"as many as are led by the Spirit of God, they are the sons of God."* When you become born again, you are given power by God to become His son or daughter. It is just like adoption; the moment a child is adopted there is a change in his or her life. He or she is no longer known as A, B or C, but takes on a new identity. He is given a new name and the couple that adopted him, make provision for him in their will, which means he is engrafted into the family. This becomes a reality only after all the legal procedures have been completed. It is the same with our relationship with God the moment we accept Jesus Christ as our Lord and personal Saviour. It marks the beginning of the spiritually legal process.

The adopted child who flees the home of his new parents soon after he was brought home, and stays away for a long time only to appear after their death, cannot claim any inheritance. Likewise, there is nothing like *once saved forever saved*, you have to remain, to grow and to serve Him in whichever way He directs you. You have to grow to know His voice, His likes and dislike through His Word in order to please Him, then you will become a son or a daughter.

So now my question is, are you a son or daughter, or are you still in stage one after ten years in the Lord?

Does your church believe in discipleship and mentoring? If yes, then make sure to participate in every program set to make you grow in the things of the Lord. You have to make every effort to participate for your own benefit. Your Pastor's responsibility is to provide the tools for your growth and it is your responsibility to do all you can to take hold of the truth provided and be equipped for your growth and empowerment for service.

If there is no such thing in your church, and there is no home cell group either, then I recommend you look for a church that provides you with teachings. A child who is not properly nourished will definitely grow up with deficiencies that can seriously affect his or her health. So it is in the spiritual life. Seek to grow and be of good use to the Lord.

You have to develop your own appetite for the knowledge of the Truth. Hunger and thirst for Him. Desire Him and seek Him through prayer, fasting and in the Word. Draw out your own fasting plans and do not wait for the church to declare a fast before you fast. No, you set your own time and allow the Holy Spirit to guide you in all that you do. The Holy Spirit is ever ready to help anyone who desires to know Him and He will be there for you. The seeking heart will always find Him because He will make Himself known to you.

Do you serve in a department in your church? Find where your interest and passion lie and join that department, whether it is the music, prayer ushering or any other department. Have a word with the leader of that group and, I am sure, you will be more than welcome to join. This is your service to God and not unto man and it will also help you to enjoy the Lord as well. This is our reasonable service to the Lord. It is our living sacrifice unto the Lord, which is nothing compared to what He had to sacrifice for you and me.

# CHAPTER 43

# Soul Winning

This is simply telling others about your faith in Christ: your testimony since you believed in Him and gave your life to Him.

Have you ever witnessed to someone about Christ? Have you ever won a soul to the Lord? The Great Commission is for everybody to fulfill. The woman at the well went into the city to announce her encounter with the Messiah causing almost the entire city to come and see Jesus. John 4:28-38 *"The woman left her water pot, and went her way into the city, and said to the men, [29]Come, see a man, which told me all things that I ever did: is this not the Christ?.... [38]I sent you to reap that whereon you bestowed no labor: other men labored, and you are entered into their labours. [39]and many of the Samaritans of that city believed on Him for the saying of the woman, which testified, He told me all that I ever did... [41]And many more believed because of His own words. [42]and said unto the woman, now we believe, not because of thy saying: for we have heard Him for ourselves, and know that this is indeed the Christ, the Saviour of the world."*

This is a Biblical example of soul-winning. This is the fundamental duty of every believer. The Bible says, if you do this you are a wise man. Daniel 12:1c, *"...and at that time thy people shall be delivered, every one that shall be found written in the book [2]And many of them that sleep in the dust of the earth shall awake, some to everlasting life, and some to shame and everlasting contempt.*

*[3]and they that be wise shall shine as the brightness of the firmament; and they that turn many to righteousness as the stars for ever and ever."*

Dear reader and friend, now is the time to rise up and win souls for the Lord. What if you are in church and you are not born again? You cannot give what you do not have. So, first of all, you have to receive the Lord Jesus Christ as your Lord and personal Saviour and invite the Holy Spirit to come and live in you and help you to do what you have been destined to do for the Lord. It is the work of the Holy Spirit to empower God's people to be and to do all that God wants us to be and to do for Him.

And you ask, "Who is the Holy Spirit?" He is God Almighty. He is the Breath of God; He is everything that God is because He is God. He is the God who is so near to you that all you need to do is call upon Him in every area of your life, and He will come and do what you have requested of Him according to His will. Do you need healing, deliverance; salvation or do you need to know Jesus more? The Holy Spirit will help you. Jesus said in John 14:16, *"And I will pray the Father, and He shall give you another Comforter, that He may abide with you forever. [17]Even the Spirit of truth; whom the world cannot receive, because it sees him not, for He dwells with you, and shall be in you. [18]I will not leave you comfortless: I will come to you."*

He is the voice in every believer's ear, convicting us of sin and pointing us to the righteous path. He is our Teacher and Helper, our entire Christian walk hinges on Him. All you have to do is call upon Him and He will be there for you.

I pray that we will allow the Spirit of the Most High to lead His church and, as we allow Him to purge His church, the church will be a power-house drawing everyone in for salvation, deliverance and healing. The church as it stands right now is sick but The Lord will heal us and restore us if we return to Him in repentance. Hosea 6:1-3, *"Come, and let us return unto the Lord: for He has torn, and He will heal us; He has smitten and He will bind us up. [2]After two days will He revive us; in the third day He will raise us up, and we shall live in His sight. [3]then shall we know if we follow on to know the Lord: His going forth is prepared as the morning; and He shall come unto us as the rain, as the latter rain and the former rain unto the earth."*

We are expecting the greatest outpouring of the Holy Spirit on the earth, before the coming of the Lord but we need to get our houses in order. Jesus cleansed the temple in order for the temple to serve its original purpose as the house of prayer. Brethren, let us return to the Lord and let Him heal us and restore us. The day of preparation for His coming for His bride is now. Let the church be prepared and ready for Him.

Let us put aside the programs for now and let the cleaning of the house of the Lord begin. When He restores us, signs and wonders will follow in the churches drawing in souls, and when they come, our mandate will be fully executed by the Holy Spirit.

Dear reader, time is running out on us and we do not seem to know that we have entered the home straight. You ask what I mean by that. It means our Lord is coming and His coming is nearer than we anticipate. Remember, Jesus said it would be like the days of Noah, when men were enjoying themselves even though Noah was busy building the ark and was warning about the impending flood. I am sure the people saw the signs of God's wrath looming on the horizon but no-one paid heed until the day overtook them. Do not let the devil deceive you like he did to those in Noah's days. Arise and seek God.

On the 17<sup>th</sup> of December 2011, the Lord shared this with me after I had sought His guidance for some time. He said to me, *"I am about to bring a shaking that will cause the continents to quake with fear: a shaking that will cause the continents to be opened for my gospel, a shaking that will cause the nations to seek my Son, Jesus Christ, the Messiah, a shaking that will cause the nations to run into my sanctuaries to seek my help, a shaking that history has never known before.*

*Yes, warn my people to stand strong, for even some of my churches will fall. Yes, many of the well-known churches will fall; therefore, warn my people wherever I send you to preach. Preach this uncompromisingly for great fear is coming upon the earth and men will want to hide from their own shadows in sheer terror.*

*Arise, arise, for the days ahead are evil. I am going to shake the foundation of every organisation (Jeremiah 8:3) and men will lose the desire to live. Let my people know that I am coming soon. Prepare the way for me. Win souls for me. Make disciples for me. Turn the hearts of the unlearned and the simple to me. Teach and preach the gospel with all simplicity and clarity. Fear not for I will sustain my own and, yes, I will keep my own from falling."*

*"How do I declare this; it sounds very fearful Lord?"* I said.

*He said, "Is it your Word? It is my Word, yours is to declare it. Last year and the years past I used natural disasters to warn man. They took heed for a while and they went back to their evil ways again. This time I will be relentless. I will use the natural elements to warn mankind, many shall be swept away but those who are left standing will have a choice to seek me or still walk in the hardness*

of their hearts."
"Why the Nations?", I asked.

He answered, *"The voice of Christianity is being drowned whilst they allow and support the Islamic religion to grow and to take over nations. They persecute my Missionaries, they kill my Pastors, and they kill my messengers. They promote abominations, defiling my sanctuaries; marrying homosexuals. Now they want to force my church to perform that which is abominable to me? I will swiftly punish every nation that is propagating this.*

*Many are questioning my existence because of the progression of evil in the earth, saying, "If there is a God why is He allowing this and that to happen?" But I will reveal myself to the world in the elements of the world, even in the skies. I will show signs and wonders. Through my servants and my handmaidens will I perform signs and wonders. As many as will stretch their faith for the miraculous I will use them to bring in the last harvest before my appearing.*

*The churches that are called by my name are going to see an explosion of souls filling up the pews because men are going to seek the truth. I will cause them to come to the churches that are called by my name. I will provide money for my churches to promote my Kingdom. Muslims shall be converted in their numbers, devil worshippers will turn to Christ, even atheists, because of the things I am about to do in the years to come.*

*Watch out and be prepared. The kingdoms of the world will be shaken, even strongholds. Every organisation that promotes evil and devil worshipping will be shaken. The secret things they have been doing for the longest time shall be exposed by defectors into*

*Christianity."*

You may read this and think, if this was said in the year 2011 why has it not come to pass. The Bible says in 2 Peter 3:7-10, *"But the heavens and the earth, which now, by the same word are kept in store, reserved unto fire against the day of judgement and the perdition of ungodly men. [8]But, beloved be not ignorant of this one thing, that one day is with the Lord as a thousand years, and a thousand years as one day. [9]The Lord is not slack concerning His promise, as some men count slackness, but is longsuffering to us ward, not willing that any should perish, but that all should come to repentance. [10]But the day of the Lord will come as a thief in the night, in which the heavens shall pass away with great noise, and the elements shall melt with fervent heat, the earth also and the works that are therein shall be burned up."*

Let us not be deceived as it was in the days of Noah. He is coming and He is coming very soon. By the way, what if He does not come in my lifetime? Oh, my dearly beloved, what do I have to lose if He does not come in my days? At least I lived a prepared life and I am guaranteed a place in heaven. What about you that neglect to prepare and that day overtakes you? I recommend you be like the five wise virgins who prepared themselves and when the announcement was made that the bridegroom was coming, they were ready to go with him.

A man of God once preached at a funeral service and told how the people asked him, "Man of God, what if we die and there is no heaven or hell?"

He replied, "Yours is to believe and live the life of a believer, and if you die and there is no heaven or hell, you have lost nothing, but if there is, then you have heaven to gain and hell to avoid."

If you live a life without Christ, then you have heaven to lose and hell to go to for all eternity. Think about this, dearly beloved. Do not deceive yourself into thinking that going to church alone will qualify you to go to heaven. Jesus was clear about this when He said it is only those who do the will of the Father that will enter into the Kingdom of Heaven.

I used to use an illustration in my preaching until the Lord corrected me. I used to say, I have booked my reservation in heaven and I am looking forward to the day I will be welcomed by the angel of the Lord and prepare my napkin to dine with the Lord. One day, as I was praying, the Holy Spirit said to me, "Gina, do you know that the reservation is for everybody? But, as it is in the natural, some people are invited to a celebration such as a wedding, and will even acknowledge and confirm the invitation, but will not show up leaving their allocated seats empty on the day. They have accepted the invitation, they have confirmed it and yet did not show up. Was their reservation booked? Yes. Did they turn up? No.

So it is, that even though God has made reservations for all, still not all of us will show up. Let us live as if there is no tomorrow. Let the weak pray for strength; let the backslider return unto the Lord for He is a merciful God. Time is running out; we are living on borrowed time. The Bible says in Hebrews 9:27, *"It is appointed unto man once to die and after that Judgement."*

Brothers and sisters, have you considered this Scripture and what it means to anyone who dies without accepting the Lord Jesus Christ as his or her personal Saviour or accepted Him and yet lived not in His ways? If you have not made a conscious decision to surrender your life to the Lord, please do so now. Cry out to Him and He will graciously receive you.

Pray this prayer aloud:

> Lord Jesus, I come to you today and confess that I am the sinner for whom you died
> Today, I believe you shed your blood for me.
> Lord, forgive me my sins and wash me in your precious blood.
> I accept you, Lord Jesus, as my Lord and personal Saviour.
> Lord, write my name in the Lamb's Book of Life.
> Fill me with your Holy Spirit.
> I declare that I am born again.
> Amen.

Praise the Lord! From this point on, believe that you are a child of God and the Holy Spirit will make Himself relevant to you if you wholeheartedly confessed the Lord Jesus as your Saviour.

Let the church, as it stands. Be cleansed and be filled with pure unadulterated Word of God, pure Holy worship and not merely singing of songs, as it appears to be the case now. Let there be choir ministration and no fleshly performance. Let us bring back the fire of God into the house of the Lord so that people will come and be saved, healed and delivered.

Let our prayer be: Make the church your church again, Lord, and make it your Holy habitation. Let there be a clear distinction between churches called by your name and those who have chosen to be 'seeker-friendly' and 'man-pleasing', where everything goes, and void of the Presence of the Most High God.

Let us by the grace of God, prepare a people for the Lord's coming, for He is coming for a glorious church without blemish or spot.

# CONCLUSION

In conclusion, I want to recommend we go back to preaching and teaching and executing the full gospel of Jesus Christ. He preached salvation to the lost, He taught, He delivered the oppressed and the demon possessed and He healed the physically sick. Please do not let us omit anything; it is all or nothing. Let us make His praise glorious by honouring His Word that the world may know Him through His Son Jesus Christ.

It is my prayer that many will be greatly blessed by this book and the Lord will use it to change the way in which we perceived certain things of God. Everything under the sun is subject to change, so let the Holy Spirit lead us into His truth as presented in this book. I encourage you to seek to know the Lord for who He is and also seek to please Him.

All this confusion about the Word of God is to do with the orchestrations of the devil to bring division among us so we lose focus on our assignment. Is our God not greater than our differences and is He not able to correct us when we err? Correction is part of the work of the Holy Spirit and so let us trust Him to do His work in us. He is more than able to do just that and even more. Let us not be hasty in sharing our differences of what we think but prayerfully seek the Lord concerning His own Word.

Nobody but the Holy Spirit who is the author of the Word, has the definitive interpretation to His Word.

If you disagree with your brother or sister as the case may be, pray for him or her, that the Lord will let him or her see the truth and humbly make corrections. The sad thing about us Christians is that we are so quick to attack each other publicly not knowing that we are not hurting the person in question, but the Lord and His Kingdom. We want to win souls for Him and yet our attitude towards one another repels the people we want to save. Jesus made it clear in His word that a kingdom divided against itself will not stand so please, as the days draw closer and closer, let us unite with one vision; to win the lost before that terrible day catches us unawares.

The winning of the lost is far more important than any differences of opinion. Let us forget about our self for once and put our differences aside and focus on winning the lost for Christ.

How often do we see or hear of other religions lambasting each other openly on social media as we, Christians do? Some even refuse to condemn the atrocious deeds of their fellow worshippers. This particular group pay twenty percent tithes and only few outside their faith know this. If you confront or ask any of them, they refuse to discuss it and yet they have the audacity to talk about Christians giving their ten percent. Do you know what? I do not blame them because we, the Christians, have made this a controversial topic being debated in the public.

Topics such as speaking in tongues and healing have been debated for decades. I am pleading with all of us by the mercies of God, let us stop this divisiveness and focus on the reason why Jesus came and died for all mankind. Then, we can tell the world and emphasise their need to be saved. We have family members who are not yet saved and they are watching us fighting over doctrines. Some are led to say to forget these Christians, because they are themselves confused about their own beliefs. This is a travesty! That old devil is a liar!

The Apostle Paul said in Romans 16:17, *"Now I beseech you brethren, mark them who cause divisions and offences contrary to the doctrine which you have learned and avoid them. [18a]for they that are such serve not the Lord Jesus Christ, but their own belly; and by good words and fair speeches deceive the hearts of the simple."*

Paul's message is clear and straightforward. He is saying, <u>avoid</u> them. One of my bosses at work called me into his office and said to me, "Do you know I have done research into the Bible and have seen some contradictions in it so I have decided to be a Buddhist rather than a Christian".
I said to him, "Well if that's your choice then what can I say? But I want to point out to you the fact that you cannot research the Bible with your carnal mind. The Bible tells me to trust in the Lord with all my heart and lean not to my own understanding but in all my ways, I should acknowledge Him and He shall direct my path." (Proverbs 3:5-6).
I explained that for you to really understand what the Bible is

saying, you have to be born again and have the Holy Ghost inside of you to help you understand the Word of God.

When I said that he quickly told me to leave his office, which I did.

The next day he called me again into his office and asked me to write all the relevant Scriptures for him. I said, "Boss, the Bible is huge and the contents are vast, so what kind of Scriptures are you looking for; salvation, healing, or deliverance?"

Once again, he asked me to leave and as I headed towards the door, he called me back and said, "Hey, this does not mean I have decided to be a Christian." I just smiled and left.

The questioning went on for weeks. Finally the Holy Spirit arrested him and the rest is history. He was seen sporting the biggest Bible, openly going to the fellowship at work and many were amazed at the transformation of this man that most of the work force used to call the prince of darkness. Argument and debate would not have won this man but the simplicity in witnessing did.

Let us put our differences aside and win the lost for Christ. The disciples who later became Apostles never strove over doctrines; they all went where the Spirit led them. When Paul confronted Peter, it was not over doctrine but about the way he (Peter) conducted himself in the absence or presence of the fellow Jews. Their problems were not about doctrine but rather individual behavior, which is understandable because we differ from each other in character. This affects our behaviour and this can be problematic to others to bear.

If we were to meet by chance and you found my behaviour intolerable, you have the choice to avoid me, if possible, but not to attack me. Not even on how I preach or teach as God has made us all different.  I believe if there has ever been a time when we need unity in the Body of Christ, it is now!

Let us do it, it is possible. Let us make the passion of our Lord ours. Jesus only attacked the Pharisees, the Sadducees and the Scribes because their doctrine of tradition was hurting the Kingdom of God. He told them, *"Woe unto you, you're not entering and you're preventing others from entering the Kingdom of God."* Matthew 23:13

My prayer is that this book will help someone understand the concept of deliverance in the Kingdom of God and be set free once and for all in order to enjoy the journey. We are all sojourners just passing through this planet and, someday we will all depart from the earth to spend eternity with Jesus Christ our Lord. That is if our name is found in the Lamb's Book of Life.

God Almighty, help us all to make it, in Jesus name.

www.ingramcontent.com/pod-product-compliance
Lightning Source LLC
Chambersburg PA
CBHW051539030726
47592CB00001B/45